RUNNING
TO BEAT HELL

RUNNING TO BEAT HELL

A BIOGRAPHY OF A.M. (SANDY) NICHOLSON

by BETTY L. DYCK

Canadian Plains Research Center
University of Regina
1988

Canadian Cataloguing in Publication Data

Dyck, Betty.

Running to beat hell

1st ed. —

Bibliography: p.
Includes index.

ISBN 0-88977-051-4

1. Nicholson, A.M. (Alexander Malcolm), 1900-
2. Co-operative Commonwealth Federation — Biography.
3. Politicians — Saskatchewan — Biography. I. University of
Regina. Canadian Plains Research Center. II. Title.

FC3525.1.N52D92 1987   971.24'03'0924   C87-098142-0
F1072.N52D92 1987

Book jacket design by Amanda K. Maslany

Printed in Canada by Hignell Printing Limited, Winnipeg

Dedication

To the little known politicians of all parties who have carefully, and with dedication and personal sacrifice, tried to have the government in power "enact legislation to provide that the wealth and work of Canada shall be distributed more fairly and equitably."

A.M. Nicholson,
Hansard, August 1, 1940

Contents

Illustrations

Photograph Credits

All photographs, unless otherwise credited, are from the Nicholson Family Archives.

Foreword

Any biography of A.M. (Sandy) Nicholson must of necessity be a compromise, for the subject is broad and multifaceted. For the biographer, two questions must have arisen. Should she tell the interesting story of a life which is still going on? Or should she write a history of social change in Canada, and tell of its origins? In *Running to Beat Hell: A Biography of A.M. (Sandy) Nicholson,* biographer Betty L. Dyck has achieved the ideal by drawing together the facts of this remarkable man's life, at the same time showing the many ways in which his contributions in the field of social welfare have benefitted the Canadian people.

It has been a feature of my life to live abroad for spells of three to five years or more, then to return to Canada for short intervals. Under these circumstances, I have been able to observe the great changes that have been wrought in Canadian society, although many of them have gone unnoticed by Canadians themselves. These changes have been brought about gradually, with little social disruption and totally without violence. It is a wonderful fact that Canadian social development takes place by *evolution,* not by *revolution,* with its attendant destructive phase.

Canadians in the late 1980s should ask themselves how these improvements came about. Who were the idealistic reformers who sought to improve the quality of the lives of fellow citizens?

All social change begins with an individual's dream, sometimes the result of reading powerfully significant literature, sometimes the result of observing some incident, on other occasions, the result of discussion with like-minded persons. But dreams die unless they are put into action by means including education, publicity, and legislation. The social changes that have come about in Canada, particularly those that have occurred since the Depression of the 1930s and World War II, have been very great indeed, and all have taken place through evolution.

Sandy and others like him, who thought themselves rebels when they were younger, have implemented their dreams. What better people to carry out evolutionary changes than these individuals with their socio-religious convictions? How better to implement socio-religious convictions than by religious study combined with political action? Sandy's life story shows that he had the courage of his convictions, as well as the determination and know-ledge to transform his dreams into reality.

Sandy's dreams were realised in many ways. It was through his actions that the pioneers of Hudson Bay Junction received better health care, education, welfare and rural housing assistance. His skills as a political organizer went far towards enabling the Co-operative Commonwealth Federation (CCF) to form a government in Saskatchewan, and to enact far-reaching legislation in the 1940s which has benefitted the old, the infirm, farmers, labourers, and the poor. He was instrumental in the development of the port of Churchill in 1953 and, in that same year, his actions resulted in the development of a vocational training programme for the mentally handicapped. In 1958 came the development of the South Saskatchewan river. The realisation of Sandy's two greatest dreams came in 1960 and 1961. In the earlier year, Saskatchewan's CCF government enacted legislation which made possible the establishment of prepaid medial services in the province; the next year saw Sandy's pleas for improved housing for the elderly answered.

Sandy's departure from active political life enabled him to affect the lives of other disadvantaged persons, among them the disabled who found new happiness in the Cheshire Homes projects he brought to fruition through his fundraising efforts. Early in 1988, Sandy's vitality was unimpaired, his enthusiasm undiminished, his compassion for those less fortunate than himself undiluted, his idealism and integrity unblemished.

As the old gospel hymn says, "Every rung goes higher, higher . . ." Who placed the rungs there? The rungs on the ladder of social development in Canada were placed there by people who, individually and in groups, implemented their dreams for a better Canada. Lest we forget these pioneers, we must have some record of who they were and what they achieved. In many of these developments, Sandy was a leader — a leader ever since public school track meets. His leadership has been given with typical modesty; the social programmes he initiated are his monument. This biography will serve as the record.

R.B. McClure
Toronto, 1988

Acknowledgements

Although this book was commissioned by A.M. (Sandy) Nicholson, he did not interfere at any time, or put restrictions on me, neither did he attempt to direct the line taken. His conscientious assistance in locating photographs, sources, and setting up interviews during the two and one-half years of research simplified my task. His daughter, Ruth Dibbs, accepted the onerous editing of the initial drafts and her scholarly comments helped to make the final version more readable.

Our Canadian interlibrary loan network allowed me to read back issues of *The Commonwealth* without leaving Winnipeg. The Saskatchewan Archives Board forwarded the reels of microfilm to the Winnipeg Centennial Library. Personnel at all repositories I visited were helpful in locating material. I wish to acknowledge the assistance given by: the National Archives of Canada, Ottawa; the United Church of Canada Archives, University of Winnipeg; the Saskatchewan Legislative Library; the Saskatchewan Archives Board in both Regina and Saskatoon; the Manitoba Legislative Library; and the Archives of Ontario. I would especially like to thank Roger E. Nickerson of the Archives of Ontario, Douglas Bocking, now retired, formerly of the Saskatchewan Archives Board in Saskatoon, and Merle McLeod and Raymonde Doyle of the Manitoba Legislative Library.

Guidance from Professor Gerald Friesen, Department of History, University of Manitoba, is gratefully acknowledged. Some of his suggestions have been incorporated into the final work.

Members of the Penhandlers writers' group listened patiently to some chapters and criticized them, adding outsiders' opinions which helped to clarify the context. My heartfelt appreciation goes out to the many friends and colleagues of the Nicholsons who took time to write and share their reminiscences with me. I would like to acknowledge the support of my family, in particular my husband John, who retired from the teaching profession about the time I began the final draft, and made life easier by tackling some of the household duties and allowing me uninterrupted hours to write and type the manuscript. Finally, I wish to thank my editor, Gillian Wadsworth Minifie, for her patience and perseverance throughout the stages of preparing the manuscript for publication.

Betty L. Dyck
March 1988

Chapter 1

Beginnings in Bruce County, 1900-1914

N ICHOLSON INDIVIDUAL CHAMPION OF THE MEET
ran the headline in the 15 October 1925 edition of
The Sheaf.[1] A.M. (Sandy) Nicholson cut one-fifth of a
second off the 220-yard race, beating records set three
years earlier. A little more effort and he would have broken
his previous year's mark in the hammer and shot put;
instead, he equalled it. By the end of that cold autumn day
at the University of Saskatchewan's annual field meet in
Saskatoon, the final point count showed that Nicholson was
easily the individual champion. He had collected five firsts
and one third for a grand total of twenty-nine points.[2]

Writing about Nicholson more than forty years later,
veteran Saskatoon newsman Pat O'Dwyer commented,
"The first time I met Sandy Nicholson he was running to
beat Hell on a varsity track; and it seems to me he has
been running to beat Hell, damnation, and man's
inhumanity to man ever since."[3]

Sandy was born 25 November 1900 on Lot 8,
Concession 2, Kinloss Township, Bruce County in Ontario,
and christened Alexander Malcolm, although he was
usually known by his nickname, Sandy, throughout his
long life. His athletic stamina came from a sturdy Scottish
clan called *Nicolson*. His grandfather, Norman Nicholson,[4]

1

emigrated from the Isle of Skye in 1851. Sandy discovered the spelling discrepancy when visiting Skye in 1926 where he found Donald Nicolson, a retired schoolteacher at The Anchorage, Kyleakin, Kyle (just across from Skye), who closely resembled his father. When Sandy returned to Canada, he learned his father's first schoolteacher had insisted the proper Canadian spelling included an *h* and so it became *Nicholson.*

Sandy Nicholson often paid tribute to his pioneer ancestors during his tenure in the House of Commons, where he sat as Co-operative Commonwealth Federation (CCF) member for Mackenzie constituency, Saskatchewan. On one occasion he told members of Parliament, "I was born in a little town in Ontario where they still have a flour mill. Originally the people of this community made their own clothing on the farms. Every farm had a spinning wheel. Many of the farmers made their own shoes [and] all their farming implements."[5] His grandparents, when they were both about thirty years old, had sailed from Scotland on a seven-week voyage to Canada with a group of other young people, all of them looking to the new land for a better life.[6] Included in the group were three couples who were close friends — the Martin McInneses and the two Mackenzie brothers and their wives.

In the 1850s Sandy Nicholson's grandfather, Norman, toughened his muscles hewing out a homestead in the "Queen's Bush" of Ontario's virgin Bruce County. This bush was the large portion of unsettled lands lying north of the Huron District.[7] The Nicholsons' first child, Margaret, born 14 May 1852, recalled hearing that her parents, accompanied by Mr. and Mrs. Martin McInnes and the Mackenzie families, had journeyed by boat through Lake Erie, Lake St. Clair, the connecting rivers, and thence into Lake Huron. They landed at Port Albert,[8] about halfway between Kincardine and Goderich, on the beach "amid the breakers as they rolled and broke in foam on the sandy shore, for pier or wharf existed not."[9] They unloaded their possessions on the shores of Huron County, where all the land had been apportioned.

The first settlement in Bruce County occurred in 1847, ranking Nicholson's grandparents among the initial wave of settlers. The men had selected two hundred-acre bush farms in the backwoods of Bruce County, some twenty miles inland from Port Albert. Norman Nicholson and Martin McInnes chose Lots 7 and 8 on the Second Concession in Kinloss Township. The Mackenzie brothers took adjacent Lots 67 to 70 on the First Concession.[10]

Sandy Nicholson's Aunt Margaret, who lived to the age of ninety, delighted in repeating the family's history. She recalled that Mrs. Martin McInnes, favourite midwife available to the concession settlers, had helped deliver her brothers Malcolm and John, as well as Sandy's father, Alexander, who was born 14 November 1856. Another girl, Mary Ann, later rounded out the Nicholson clan.

Sandy's grandmother died in childbirth at the delivery of her sixth child in 1861, when she was only thirty-seven years old. Complications set in during the delivery and the doctor fetched from Goderich by a neighbour took so long to ride through the roadless bush, that he arrived too late to help the woman. In 1940, when he addressed the House of Commons regarding the lack of medical care in his constituency, Nicholson drew on his family history to make his point. He told members of Parliament, "Pioneers in my constituency are not complaining about difficulties [but] about being forced to live in 1940 under similar conditions to those which prevailed in 1860. When my grandmother died in the bush, the nearest doctor was twenty miles away."[11] When the local doctor had left Hudson Bay Junction, Saskatchewan, in the early 1930s, because he could not eke out a living in that depressed area, ". . . there was not a doctor within seventy miles . . ." for several years.[12]

Sandy's grandparents and their neighbours had claimed ownership to the land only as squatters, and they were anxious to secure the deeds. A land agent had been appointed in the district and eventually the government opened an office. Norman Nicholson and Martin McInnes, along with about two thousand other settlers, walked to

Southampton to make good their claims. This meant having their names entered as purchasers, making a first payment, and obtaining a licence of occupation.

The big land sale on 27 September 1854 was an important event in Bruce County history. Sandy often repeated Norman Robertson's rendition of the story:

> The limited accommodation of the village could not begin to house the throng. Hundreds slept in sheds, others under the first stories of buildings which stood on posts and many had to find resting-places among the cedar and juniper bushes near the beach. The sole baker in the village worked night and day. He kept his shop door closed to keep the unmanageable crowd out, but as soon as baking was completed, loaves were handed out through a window to his hungry customers, whose struggles to secure some of the baking were so great he had no time to make change. A "York shilling" (or quarter) was paid gladly by those of the mob who were fortunate enough to get to the window before the supply of loaves, hot and steaming from the oven was exhausted.[13]

As for actually securing the deeds, an extract from agent McNabb's papers tells this story:

> The Crown lands Agent stood at the window of his office and the money was handed up to him. So quickly did the bank bills roll in that he did not have time to count them, but threw them into a large clothes basket, and when the basket was full put a cloth over it. In two days, upwards of $50,000 in cash was thus taken in and $8,000 in drafts. The strain on the agent was so great after some days that he was completely prostrated and Doctor Haynes would not allow him to do any more business for a week or so . . .[14]

When Norman Nicholson returned from his one hundred-mile walk to and from Southampton, he carried only a receipt for Lot 11, Concession 3 in Kinloss Township — poor land nobody else wanted.[15] The premature closure of the land office left him still a squatter on the land he had begun to clear. A local historian wrote, "The hundred acres sold for 7s 6d ($1.50) an acre and were paid in ten installments with interest. Before getting a patent for the land, settlers had to comply with a number of conditions such as clearing at least two acres in each one hundred annually for the first five years, and building a dwelling at least 16 feet by 18 feet."[16]

In January 1855 the land agent came to Kinloss and all settlers received a receipt for the lot on which they lived. An agricultural survey taken in 1861 showed that Norman Nicholson had cleared only twelve acres and had about six acres in crop. His machinery was valued at a total of twenty-five dollars. By this time the Norman Nicholsons lived in the house where Sandy would be born — a roomy, two-storey building situated in the middle of their land.

Being born in a pioneer house in 1900 provided a proud heritage for Sandy, but he chastised the federal government for allowing less desirable conditions to prevail in the 1940s in his Mackenzie constituency in northeastern Saskatchewan. Long before he moved to Saskatchewan, he had become acquainted with the problems of settlers who lived far from large centres. Childhood tales and his own experiences as a youngster in Bruce County had made deep impressions on him. He decided early that there should be a more equitable distribution of social services throughout Canada. That idea would be strengthened during the Depression as he tramped across his Saskatchewan mission field in the district surrounding Hudson Bay Junction, assessing the needs of destitute settlers and arranging assistance for them, much of it coming from the more affluent eastern Ontario churches.

Sandy witnessed these settlers, forced to abandon once prosperous farms in southern Saskatchewan, ". . . coming north in covered wagons carrying all their worldly possessions. And there wasn't any relief available there at the time. This was unorganized territory and conditions were very, very difficult." It may have been on some of these long trips when he became convinced that neither the governments formed by the Liberal nor Conservative parties could meet the basic needs of these people, and that there must be some other way — possibly another party more attuned to the interests of the working classes and the poor — to fill the gap. Quite unconsciously, he had formed his basic political tenet by assessing political parties in terms of their interaction with the total social system. It would be a number of years before this idea propelled him into the political arena. Sandy first let his name stand for nomination at a 1933 convention of the Farmer-Labour Group [forerunner of the CCF] in Tisdale, Saskatchewan. There, he drew the parallel of preaching the gospel with being a socialist. The social gospel premise said Christianity was a social religion "concerned with the quality of human relations on this earth."[17]

Sandy Nicholson's maternal grandparents, "Big Sandy" MacDonald and Mary Stewart, met for the first time when they were carrying wheat to Goderich. Both had been born in Prince Edward Island and had arrived in Bruce County about the same time as the Nicholsons. Before the turn of the century, Kinloss pioneers had to make long journeys to obtain ordinary necessities. The absence of water power strong enough to drive a grist mill was an added drawback and early concession settlers walked to Goderich to have their wheat ground.[18]

"Big Sandy" and Mary walked the same road to Goderich on 29 April 1857 when they were married in the Presbyterian church.[19] They raised a family of nine, with Sandy's mother Isabelle Ann being the third oldest. Sandy's parents met at the South Kinloss Presbyterian Church where both the MacDonald and Nicholson families worshipped. His mother died as the result of a brain hemorrhage when he was three, leaving Alexander Nicholson with three children: Norma, aged five, Sandy, and Mary Anna, thirteen months. Jane Phillips was hired as housekeeper, and she remained in the family for about six years, leaving the children with many happy memories of her care. She might have married Alexander Nicholson, had he not believed that it would be better for his children if he did not remarry; his own experiences with a stepmother had been unpleasant. Sandy thought that his father "did everything one could reasonably be expected to do" in bringing up his family, but after Jane left to marry a local farmer, a number of housekeepers followed.

In 1873 the Toronto, Grey and Bruce Railway threaded its way from Toronto to Palmerston, Lucknow being the third to last station on the Kincardine branch, preceded by Wingham and followed by Ripley.[20] This railway access to markets helped to improve the district's economy. Alexander Nicholson spent several winters loading square timber, bound for a company in the United Kingdom, onto freight trains. The British firm offered Nicholson a permanent job, but he decided that clearing his land and farming took priority. By 1903 many of the district's farmers had become cattle drovers, and Alexander Nicholson and his brother Malcolm formed a partnership in that business. They learned that buying cattle in spring, pasturing them on the grass, and then selling them in autumn, provided a better living than growing grain. Every Saturday, except during the Christmas and New Year season, cattle would be brought to Lucknow and shipped by freight train to the Toronto stockyards.

As a boy on the farm, Sandy often helped his father cut hay in summer. When rain threatened or the horses were feeding, his father would nap, a habit that Sandy adopted and he thereafter had the good fortune to be able to sleep well in quiet moments, restoring his energy. He spent many hours in his father's company, and he recalled another early lesson. As a lad of about eight years, he cared for a neighbour's milk cow for a few weeks. Upon returning to retrieve the cow, the farmer insisted on paying the boy for his work. When Sandy dutifully turned over the ten dollars to his father, his father told him, "We mustn't do that with neighbours. This is the sort of service any person should do. So you run as quickly as you can and tell them we were very glad to look after the cow and under no circumstances will have the money." This experience would develop into a Nicholson tenet. He went through later life helping all kinds of people and reiterating, "no charge, no charge."

In his youth, Sandy's homelife centred around the strict religious beliefs of his family's church. The original South Kinloss Presbyterian Church, built in 1856, the year of his father's birth, stood in a district settled mostly by immigrants from northern Scotland, Nova Scotia and Prince Edward Island, nearly all of whom were Gaelic-speaking Presbyterians. Although most settlers had small quarters, families living close to the church always found room for visitors. From the 1930s onward, after Sandy married, accommodating travellers became a natural and integral part of Sandy and Marian Nicholson's household. At their first home in Hudson Bay Junction, Saskatchewan, where trains converged, the Toronto couch on the front porch was seldom empty as people enjoyed the Nicholsons' hospitality overnight or between trains.

In 1906, when young Sandy Nicholson started to attend the South Kinloss Presbyterian Church, a new church building had been erected. Although there was neither organ music nor hymn-singing in that church until 1930, his Uncle Johnny MacDonald acted as precentor, leading the congregation in singing psalms and paraphrases. Sandy remembered his uncle's role in the church from those long-ago days: "He used a tuning fork but he also had a good ear for music." The Alexander Nicholsons did only a minimum amount of work on Sundays, although that included a quick cleaning of the barn. He recalled walking to Sunday School with the superintendent, Jimmy Henderson, one day during harvest, and to make conversation he asked about the crop. Replied Henderson, "There are six days in the week for farm conversation, and this is the Sabbath Day. You shouldn't be asking questions like that!" A boy of eight had limited topics to discuss, so they walked on in silence.

Visitors arrived frequently at Alexander Nicholson's farm house, travelling by horse and buggy. Sandy's cousin, Sally McDougall, who often spent the weekends there, recalled, "We grew up together going to the same public and high schools. We all had quite a religious upbringing in those days — to church and Sunday School every Sunday; to young people's meeting on Monday night; to prayer meeting Wednesday and choir practice on Friday."[21] Cousin Sally also remembered that Sandy could be mischievous. Walking home one evening after choir practice, he suggested that Sally and he throw some stones at the manse window to scare the minister and his wife. They hurled the stones, then sprinted away into the dusk.

From the time Sandy could carry a lantern, he stayed up and accompanied guests to the barn to help harness the horses when they left. Sometimes he would overhear interesting conversations, one of them regarding the financing of a new church building. The Reverend F.A. MacLennan, minister for twenty-five years, had a brother-in-law who had made a fortune and had given money to local Kincardine organizations. Plans for a new South Kinloss church had been drawn up in 1910 by a local architect and the minister reported that he had discussed with his brother-in-law the possibility of a bequest to support the cost of the new building.[22]

The minister's relative replied, "You have some people in the congregation who can afford to give. Have at least two families give five hundred dollars and others can give less. There's no use thinking of a church unless you can get some of the congregation to invest money in it."

Sandy was surprised when his father and his Uncle Malcolm (who carefully portioned out his money) agreed to invest five hundred dollars. But eavesdropping on this occasion provided him with an approach to fund raising he later adapted to collecting money for the CCF — one that appealed to people who were careful with their money ordinarily, but who were willing to give to a cause once they became convinced of its validity.

Alexander Nicholson possessed a strong sense of community. He set a record in the district by serving for forty years, 1890-1930, as chairman of the board of management of South Kinloss Presbyterian Church.[23] In 1911 when his son was not yet eleven years old, he headed the construction committee. As Sandy recalled, "The brick for the church had to be shipped in by CNR [Canadian

National Railway] rail. My father saw to it that the brick would be available for unloading on Saturdays. He organized several men with teams and wagons to form 'bees' to haul brick from the station to the church site. Everyone took lunch and the men brought feed for the horses. One of the farmers was a good ball player. When he and I were unloading alone, I would throw two bricks and he would catch them. This saved walking! I'm sure I handled more brick than any other person in the building of South Kinloss Church that summer."

Alexander Nicholson also served as board chairman of Kinloss school district, with John MacLeod and Alex Gollan as the other two trustees. Young Peter MacLeod and Sandy Nicholson were the same age. Classmates arranged a fight between the sons of the two trustees when they began grade one. As soon as young Nicholson's nose started bleeding from the punching, he decided he did not want to be the best fighter in school, so he ran away — and remained a runner.

Kinloss School stood one and one-quarter miles from the village of Lucknow, and served settlers on the First and Second Concessions. The School had a large enrollment under the guidance of one teacher, although few teachers stayed long. "We had quite a number of teachers," Sandy remembered. "With a big class came discipline problems. One of my early teachers, a woman, determined to have order. The students challenged, and it wasn't very long until every boy in school wanted to demonstrate she couldn't make him cry by strapping. She left at Christmas."

A male teacher, who had recently retired in the neighbouring township of Ashfield, came to Kinloss for one term. Surprisingly, he experienced no trouble. However, he smoked heavily and the boys felt justified in emulating him. When he caught them smoking he delivered a stern lecture, "This is really a very dirty, filthy habit and it's costly. Anybody who has an interest in running shouldn't smoke. If you wait until you are twenty or older you will never be sorry."

Sandy, who believed at the time that the lecture was

being delivered for his benefit, remembered years later, "I had been smoking — all the boys did and one or two even bought a packet of tobacco in town. We found in spring that cedar bark made pretty good cigarettes. We rolled our own with newspaper, any sort of paper." Following the lecture, he stopped smoking. He admitted to being an average student who might have done better had he applied himself like his sisters, Norma and Anna, but he preferred to be involved in extracurricular activities. Because he was a fast runner, he often acted as a messenger before telephones were installed. He developed a keen interest in athletics because family members participated actively. His grandfather, "Big Sandy" MacDonald, and his uncle, Malcolm Nicholson, both took part in local tug-o-war competitions, and his father excelled in shot put.

In his last year at public school, Sandy's teacher, Hugh MacMillan, influenced him profoundly.[24] By 1914 MacMillan had decided to become a minister, but he had taken a course and had earned a third class teaching certificate. As World War I had created a teacher shortage, he had agreed to teach a term at Kinloss after Christmas.

In 1914, when MacMillan came to the Kinloss School, Sandy's younger sister, Anna, was in junior fourth.[25] "Hugh was convinced there was no reason why she shouldn't try her entrance [examination for high school entry], and he promoted her to senior fourth," Sandy recalled. "She and I tried our entrance [examinations] and passed, with Anna ranking the highest of all Lucknow students. It was Hugh who would be chiefly responsible for my later deciding to study for the ministry. I had no notion then or for years. But Hugh was going to be a minister and mentioned his hopes many times."

At recess MacMillan taught the students sportsmanship and how to be good winners and losers. "Considering the brief time he was there, it was remarkable that one person would be such an influence," Sandy commented. Fresh from his teacher's course, and with hopes set on the ministry, MacMillan probably adhered strictly to the board of education manual which stated:

> Let no opportunity escape, but use tact and judgement
> in taking advantage of it so that good and not bad
> results shall follow. Remember the law of harvest: We
> reap more than we sow. We sow a thought, we reap
> an action; we sow an action, we reap a habit; we sow
> a habit, we reap a character; we sow a character, we
> reap a destiny.[26]

Sandy's destiny was evolving. He and his sisters had
been encouraged by their father to go to Lucknow to write
the entrance exams for high school entry. One child who
grew up at the same time as the Nicholson children later
told Sandy in an interview that a teacher had encouraged
him to try the entrance exams. When the teacher
approached the boy's father, he had responded "No, no,
no. He's already got a better education than I have. An
education takes them away from the community. I need
him on the farm." Alexander Nicholson, who had only a
few years' education, fortunately had a more enlightened
view, and he wanted his children to be well educated, so
life would be easier for them.

Chapter 2

Becoming a Man, 1914-1921

S andy Nicholson competed in track events as a student at Lucknow Continuation School and later at Wingham High School, and he won most of them each year. He was also involved in other extracurricular activities and these sometimes provided an outlet for his promotional abilities. In his last year at Lucknow he became president of the school literary society. As well, Harold and Stanley Burns, Harold Freeman and he were in demand locally as a male quartet with the leader, Harold Burns, playing the piano. The group decided to attempt to rent a piano for the year, and Sandy suggested placing an advertisement for the instrument in the *Lucknow Sentinel*. To the surprise and delight of the group, a piano appeared in the principal's room in time for Christmas concert practices. Sandy recalled, "I was Master of Ceremonies at the [concert]. A local member of the Legislative Assembly, J.G. Anderson, attended the affair and kindly said the concert compared with Toronto productions, and he predicted I would have a political career some day."

Sandy developed his sense of social justice early. When two brothers were requested to leave Lucknow Continuation School because their family resided in a neighbouring district, Sandy supported them in their bid for re-entry. Explaining how this initial contact led to a lifetime friendship, Graham MacNay wrote: "I first met Sandy when I went to secondary school. He was a couple of years ahead of me and a leader in student activities. The school was filled to capacity and in order to get admitted, my father had to become a ratepayer, so he purchased a small house in the village . . . My older brother and I moved into the house and did our own housekeeping. Sandy, being the extrovert and humanitarian that he [was], felt the injustice of our plight."[1]

Sandy's older sister, Norma, had graduated from Wingham High School and was keeping house for her father while Sandy was in high school, but at weekends brother and sister would travel to local dances by horse and buggy. Anna, his younger sister, who had determined to be a doctor and possibly a medical missionary, dedicated herself to less frivolous activities.

By the time Sandy turned fifteen in 1915 he had grown to a solid six feet. Most eligible young men in the district had joined the armed forces; some had been killed or wounded. After Sandy visited Vimy in 1953, he remarked, "I was only thirteen when the war broke out. I remember that among the first boys who left from our home town in Ontario was one of my boyhood heroes — one of the best ballplayers I had ever seen at that time of my life. Although I was a country boy he called me by name. I never forgot that. What I had forgotten was that my young friend was only twenty-two when he lost his life in France. I found his name on the Vimy Memorial."[2]

The parents of some soldiers asked Sandy, "Why aren't you in uniform?" Although a few friends had enlisted while still underage, Alexander Nicholson refused to consent to his son's enlistment until the boy was eighteen, so young Sandy had to be content to remain at home.

In 1916, because there was an acute shortage of farm labour, the Ontario Department of Education initiated a programme, Soldiers of the Soil, whereby high school students in grades ten and eleven could leave at Easter and be excused from writing exams if they worked on a farm.

Sandy's father was not a grain producer, so the boy thought it unfair to remain at home, and instead he found work at twenty dollars a month on Dan MacKinnon's grain farm, one and one-half miles away. MacKinnon also had a one hundred-acre field further on in Huron Township. After milking the cows each morning, Nicholson and MacKinnon would drive the horses to the field, complete a day's work, and then return for the evening milking. Sandy dutifully gave his wages to his father, although he wished to buy a bicycle.

In that summer of 1916, Sandy's uncle, Malcolm, suffered from a hernia which the two Lucknow doctors were unable to replace. They telephoned a Wingham surgeon to inform him that they would be bringing a patient for surgery in the morning. Diagnosing the seriousness of the problem, however, the Wingham surgeon believed that a delay might be fatal, and he recommended that the patient not be moved. Instead, he would operate on the patient in his own home, if a nurse could be found to assist him.

A local nurse, Marian Macdiarmid, had just finished a case; road conditions were good, so the surgeon would be able to arrive by midnight. He asked to have the nurse standing by and a boiler of water ready. Marian Macdiarmid lived a few miles away and had gone to bed already, but she was ready when Sandy arrived to fetch her in the horse and buggy. Another neighbour, "Black" Dan MacDonald, always came when needed, and, although he also had been asleep, he agreed to help when Sandy awakened him by pounding on his door, asking "Would you come and keep an eye on the fire? There's going to be an operation at our home at midnight." Besides the two Lucknow doctors, a Dr. Calder of Wingham, a woman anaesthetist, assisted the surgeon. Sandy came to believe that the presence of Dr. Calder that night greatly influenced his sister Anna in her decision to become a doctor.

A day or two after the successful operation, a carload of choice cattle was ready to go from the Nicholson farm to market in Toronto. Alexander Nicholson had been to the Toronto stockyards recently with cattle for which he had received a top price of six cents a pound. He had asked whether the stock dealer would promise to pay the same price for the next load. The buyer replied he would give him the best price being offered, "take it or leave it when you come next time." Alexander Nicholson always travelled with his cattle, as he believed it important to care for them during their journey. Despite this, he hesitated to leave Malcolm alone so soon after his operation. However, Sandy asked if he might travel to Toronto with the cattle. After careful consideration father and uncle agreed a visit to Toronto and its stockyards might be a good experience for the fifteen-year-old lad, who could stay with the family near the stockyards where his father boarded regularly.

At the stockyards, young Nicholson searched for the agent with whom his father usually dealt. He believed his bargaining powers would persuade the agent to pay the previous price. Instead, the agent offered him 5.9 cents a pound. Sandy explained, "My father was here two weeks ago with cattle of equal value and you paid him six cents. I'll be in trouble if I go home with anything less than that."

The agent responded that the market was off, and it was 5.9 cents or nothing! Nicholson spoke to the commission agent who informed him if the cattle were not sold that day there would be a fee for keeping them until the next day, and he believed Alexander Nicholson would agree that his son had done his best in settling for the agent's price. Subdued, Sandy accepted the offer. When his father met him at the Lucknow station, he immediately apologized for accepting a lower price, adding he felt the agent took advantage of him because of his age.

"Don't worry," replied Alexander Nicholson, "it merely supports my view that the owner should be there to decide, and that's a good experience for you, too." Sandy would remember this power of presence following his defeat in the 1949 general election, realizing that he had sacrificed his own constituency by being absent in other parts of Canada, campaigning on behalf of other nominees.

While he was waiting to enlist, Sandy taught at Holyrood School, about five miles from Lucknow, from January until

Easter 1918. During his tenure there the Nicholsons learned that the Mackenzie brothers were about to sell their 150-acre farm in Kinloss. Alexander Nicholson asked Sandy whether he would be interested in becoming a farmer if the Nicholson family purchased the Mackenzie farm.

"Since we owned the 150 acres just west and 100 acres north and 50 acres on Lot 11, Third Concession, I thought it a fine idea. After delivering me to school by horse and buggy, he called at the Mackenzie farm only to discover they had just sold to Bill Henderson, also a drover. We did not explore buying any other farm." Not until 1945, when Sandy became a member of one of the first co-operative farms established in Saskatchewan, would he have the opportunity to use his accumulated knowledge of farming.

World War I ended with the signing of the Armistice on 11 November 1918 — two weeks before Sandy's eighteenth birthday. Now he had to rechart his course. A teacher shortage still existed despite the end of the war. The Goderich school inspector, who was familiar with his teaching abilities, arranged to hire him for Varna School, about thirty-five miles south of Lucknow, from Christmas 1918 until Easter 1919. Sandy travelled back and forth again by CNR train. After Easter he taught at Hillsgreen — another school in the Varna area — until midsummer. He always managed to be home on weekends, although the train schedule necessitated an early Monday morning departure which delivered him to Brucefield station. From the station, he jogged the four miles to the school, arriving sharp at nine o'clock.

During his weekend travelling, Sandy had an hour's stop-over in Wingham on his way home, and this enabled him to visit his Uncle Malcolm, who had been transferred to Wingham hospital. Eventually, the doctors notified the Nicholson family that they could to no more for him and Malcolm Nicholson wished to go home. He died on the homestead at sixty-five years of age on 10 August 1919. While he lived, the family had deferred to his thriftiness, but shortly after Malcolm's death, Alexander Nicholson, now sixty-three, purchased his first car, which his son taught him to drive. By this time, the older Nicholson had become a partner of W.R. Durnin, another drover in the Lucknow district. Durnin owned a car and preferred to use it for business, leaving the Nicholson car for family use.

Still having made no definite decision regarding his future career, Sandy decided to attend Wingham High School where he took his senior matriculation, although his sister Anna had entered the six-year medical course at the University of Toronto by this time. Sandy was able to use his father's car for the fourteen-mile trip to Wingham, and word quickly circulated around the district that he would be driving to and from Wingham five days a week. It was not long before he had passengers in the car. Mrs. Dave Thompson wondered if he would take her and her little deaf son, Bobby, along, as a Wingham chiropractor felt he could help the child hear if he could treat him daily. Unfortunately, the expensive treatment did not seem to help, so Nicholson soon lost these two passengers. Later, however, Bobby went to the Belleville School for the Deaf, where he learned to be a good hockey player; he eventually became a printer. In 1967, when Nicholson became executive director of the Saskatchewan Association for Retarded Children,[3] he recalled this first encounter with a learning disabled person. At Whitechurch, about halfway between Lucknow and Wingham, he also picked up Angus McKay and a girl — "no charge." Angus McKay was to become a Presbyterian missionary in India, and a member of Sandy's "world family." Fifty years later, the McKays would entertain Sandy and his wife, Marian, when they visited India.

Snow blocked the Bruce County roads about the middle of November in 1919, and Sandy was forced to travel by train again. This meant a two-mile walk to the station from his home to catch the six o'clock train Monday morning, and the walk home on Friday evening at ten o'clock from the Lucknow station. He spent the week in a Wingham boarding house, where he shared a room with another rural student, Joe Stephan, a Roman Catholic of French origin. The two young men became good friends and

Sandy's circle widened. In addition, his early experiences with train timetables and the personal contact he had with railway conductors later helped him establish invaluable relationships with railway personnel during his pastoral duties in northeastern Saskatchewan. There, a combination of train travel and hiking afforded the only access between isolated points.

Sandy persevered with his studies and by the end of the 1920 school year he had attained high marks. His sister, Anna, wanted him to enter medical school so they might eventually work together, but Tom MacMillan, the Liberal member of Parliament for South Huron, for whom Alexander Nicholson had bought feeder cattle, thought Sandy more suited to law, with a view to a career in politics. Teaching at three schools had given Sandy an interest in education, but he had not yet made any firm decisions about his future by the summer of 1920. Mr. and Mrs. John Mackenzie, the old family friends who now lived near Moose Jaw, were on a trip to Lucknow, and they praised Saskatchewan. They suggested to young Nicholson that the idea of working in the west should not be ruled out. Wages of six dollars a day and an assured job appealed to him and he accepted the offer of work on the Mackenzie farm. He had no forewarning of what awaited him.

In the community where he had grown up, church teaching decreed that if one had to choose between working on Sunday and losing one's job, one should forego the job. His task the first Sunday on the Mackenzie farm outside Moose Jaw was to haul water and clear out the boilers of the large steam engine used for threshing. He tactfully questioned the Mackenzie brothers about the ethics of doing this on the Sabbath and found that "they were very congenial, but this job had to be done today." He did it. When he returned to the dormitory and found that the two dozen men belonging to the threshing team were playing poker, he was shocked. Upon inquiry he learned there was no church nearby. It was about this time that Sandy remembered Hugh MacMillan and the numerous times he had mentioned his hopes for entering the ministry. Sandy had joined the Presbyterian church without questioning its teachings, but never before had he consciously considered a vocation as a minister. He decided that if he could secure a teaching job and remain in the West for a year, he would have time to make a mature decision as to his future. In 1920, after working on the land until freeze-up, he found a school which would accept the offer of his services.

Harold Burns, his piano-playing friend from Lucknow, had travelled west the previous year and was teaching at Davidson, Saskatchewan, midway between Saskatoon and Regina. He informed Sandy that the Maple Valley School, about twenty miles away, required a teacher and he told him to go there immediately. When the new Maple Valley School had been built, a portion of the old building had been converted into living quarters for the teacher, and there Sandy kept house for himself. The area was populated by Orangemen as well as a large Catholic contingent, so Sandy decided to keep his ideas about entering the Protestant ministry to himself.

At the end of the school year, he arranged a community picnic which drew a large crowd. Fired by the event's success, he wondered if he should take teacher's training and return to Maple Valley for another year. Instead, he decided to enroll in a summer school class at the University of Saskatchewan in Saskatoon with the idea of entering theology eventually. That summer he lived in the university residence and waited on tables to supplement his income. He decided to take arts classes before discussing theology with the head of the Presbyterian college on campus. First, however, he returned to his family in Lucknow at the end of summer school. "By the time I arrived home the family thought I should study at the University of Toronto, even if I later returned to Saskatchewan."

Sandy entered the University of Toronto in the autumn of 1921. He thought that his western experiences had matured him considerably, but later in the House of Commons he admitted, "Although I have been to university myself, all who have been there readily recognize that you can get a university degree and still be very ignorant about a great many things."[4]

Fortunately, Sandy was not without friends in Toronto. His former teacher, Hugh MacMillan, was finishing his year at Knox College, and Hugh and his brother Clarence were living in the Knox College residence where they arranged for Sandy to receive room and board. Sandy's sister, Anna, lived nearby in a residence for female medical students. On campus, the Nicholson brother and sister represented an exception to the common attitude taken by rural families regarding post-secondary education. In 1921 it was most unusual for a farm lad (let alone a lass) to go to university. Sandy remarked later that he and Anna were the first in their clan to attend university. Nonetheless, he succumbed to the strongly developed element of fun in his nature, and participated actively in Toronto and university social delights. Years later, he would wryly regret wasting the year and failing his studies. In the autumn of 1922, he decided to enter the Presbyterian College in Saskatoon and to proceed with attaining both arts and theology degrees.

Chapter 3

University Days and the Student Christian Movement, 1922-1925

I n 1922 St. Andrew's College at Saskatoon was the theological college of the Presbyterian church in Canada for Saskatchewan. The church General Assembly of 1912 approved of the college's establishment at Saskatoon in affiliation with the University of Saskatchewan. A cover of *Saskatchewan History* later featured a photograph of the first building located at 290 Albert Avenue, with the caption: "on the day classes began 1 October 1914."[1] Sandy started his studies here in the building students referred to as "the barn."

His principal, Edmund Henry Oliver, had come to the west in 1910 to teach history and economics, but he also held a degree in theology. In 1913 Oliver became the founder and first principal of the Presbyterian theological college and professor of church history and New Testament. Sandy discovered early in Oliver's classroom that they had a common goal regarding the establishment of churches in farming communities to "stand as a guarantor of their moral and spiritual life."[2]

During the period when Sandy attended the University of Saskatchewan, he took a class in education taught by the university president, Walter Murray. Murray's ability to address each student personally impressed Sandy, and he undertook to develop this trait of remembering names. Earlier in 1919, the Reverend Dr. D.S. Dix was appointed to the chair of systematic theology.[3] As principal of St. Andrew's in 1930 Dr. Dix would open Sandy's new church at Hudson Bay Junction. Another professor, William Ramsay, who lectured in the classics, proved to be an excellent teacher and friend. Ramsay was to become principal of Regina College, but the two men later renewed their acquaintanceship in Edinburgh, Scotland, where Sandy continued with postgraduate work.

Sandy's initial contact with Professor Frank Underhill also happened in Saskatoon. Underhill had a great interest in the Student Christian Movement (SCM) and frequently entertained students in his office to discuss religion and social consciousness. Dr. Walter P. Thompson, dean of arts, and later university president, proved to be a popular speaker at SCM meetings. He and Sandy would become associated in the 1960s when Thompson acted as chairman of the committee appointed by the Saskatchewan government to recommend procedures for introducing medicare.

At university Sandy took an active role in the SCM. The movement, which became an important influence in Sandy's life, was described as:

> a fellowship of students based on the conviction that in Jesus Christ are found the supreme revelation of God and the means to the full realization of life. The Movement seeks through study, prayer, service and other means to understand and follow Jesus Christ and to unite in its fellowship all students in the colleges of Canada who share the above conviction, together with all students who are willing to test the truth of the conviction upon which the Movement is founded.[4]

At the first Canadian national student conference, held in Guelph, Ontario, 29 December 1920 to 2 January 1921, it was decided to form the Student Christian Movement of

Canada; a national conference would be convened in Toronto during the Christmas break of 1922. Meanwhile, elected officers visited all the Canadian universities to set up organizations.

The SCM has been described as a "student-controlled movement, governed by a National Council, meeting yearly, made up of accredited student delegates from each affiliated local university movement."[5] Before 1920, student Christian work centred in the college programmes of the Young Men's Christian Association (YMCA) and the Young Women's Christian Association (YWCA), and in the Student Volunteer Movement (for missions). The SCM evolved from these three streams of student activity to address the discontent of World War I veterans, the new emphasis on coeducation, and a modern approach to Christian missions.

In the autumn of 1922, Sandy attended the SCM meeting called at the University of Saskatchewan. As Escott Reid said of the SCM at the University of Toronto in 1923 in his book, *On Duty*, it "included most of the leading radical students of Protestant Christian upbringing."[6] The liberal attitudes did not extend to equality of the sexes, which did not concern Sandy at the time although sexual equality was to become a plank in his future platforms. He remembered separate meetings were held for male and female students, and "happened to be elected president of one and Marian Massey the president of the other." Marian was working on a Bachelor of Arts degree (majoring in mathematics and home economics) at the university. Their friendship grew into more than mutual interests in the SCM and they became engaged when she graduated in 1924.

The SCM began with a restricted budget and the provinces started collecting money to subsidize travelling expenses for conference delegates. University of Saskatchewan groups held a joint meeting to discuss fund raising. They decided that the women students would have a bazaar, while the male students would canvass some of the business and professional friends of the university, who were also active in local churches. Sandy's talents as a fund-raiser soon became apparent, although he claimed modestly that he had learned the techniques for success as a young eavesdropper.

There was no difficulty in finding students who were willing to attend the Toronto conference. Marian and Sandy were two of the delegates from Saskatchewan. As Sandy recalled, "Since the universities of Alberta and Saskatchewan were on the main lines of the CNR we decided all western students would travel by train on 'tourist' cars equipped with a stove, fridge and other facilities so food could be cooked; and upper and lower berths available. A number of students from Ontario left the west earlier and spent Christmas at home, as I did, before attending the conference at the University of Toronto."

The Christmas vacation proved to be an ideal time for the conference, and Toronto had been chosen rather than Winnipeg, Canada's geographical centre, because the most concentrated student population was in eastern Canada. On 27 December 1922, Sandy and Marian were among the seven hundred delegates and about five hundred others who filled Convocation Hall for the opening meeting of the first national conference of Canadian students organized by the SCM. This conference was, in its size, its widely representative nature, and the type of its programme, something new in Canadian history. Sandy recalled that students' minds turned readily from the thought of themselves as Canadians to a realization of themselves as world citizens, "deepened by the presence of co-workers from sixteen other countries: Africa, Barbadoes [sic], Czecho-Slovakia, Denmark, Germany, Great Britain, Holland, Hungary, India, Japan, Korea, Poland, Servia, Trinidad and the United States [plus] two Chinese scholars Dr. Y.Y. Tsu and Professor William Hung who presented a very clear and vivid picture of present day China."[7]

Summarizing the conference later, Professor George M. Wrong stated:

> The first shock came when one realized that the conference was not technically Christian or even religious, but was open on an equal footing to all opinions and creeds. This attitude of mind seemed

unique, especially in Canada, remote from countries where adherents of half a dozen different religions come into daily contact. The freedom justified itself. While the Conference revealed fundamental differences, it revealed also a fundamental unity based on the sense of human brotherhood.[8]

At the meeting of the SCM legislative assembly, Sandy heard speakers who included Lord Byng, governor-general of Canada, who spoke on character; the Honourable E.C. Drury, premier of Ontario, expanding on the rural situation in Canada; and Senator N.A. Belcourt of Ottawa, discussing the Anglo-Saxon French-Canadian question. Sandy listened as Byng defined character as "the accumulation of your impulses modified by reason" and encouraged the students to "help those with whom you are connected. Do not act the part of a horse-fly which settles on the animal, sucks its blood and drives it wild; but get into the saddle and gently but firmly endeavour to guide it."[9]

Dr. E.H. Oliver delivered a stirring address on "The New Canadian Situation," expressing distress over the treatment of newly arrived immigrants, saying they "have been largely shunted off to the parts of the country where the work was the greatest, where the land needed clearing." He foretold what Sandy would encounter in northeastern Saskatchewan in the 1930s — for new Canadians "no land has been too covered with bush; no distance too great for market; no stones too heavy to lift; they have fared on potatoes; they have brushed their own land; they have hauled their own grain to distant markets through zero weather . . . [and] they hate war." When Sandy befriended Charlie Quan of Somme, Saskatchewan, in the 1930s, he particularly remembered the following words of Dr. Oliver: "You don't need to give up the best in your past to become a good Canadian. Whatsoever things are good and whatsoever things are beautiful ought to be welcomed from whatsoever source. They are to bring their genius, bring their spiritual qualities, and devote them on the common altar of our Canadian life."[10]

Speaking about the place of religion in national life — a

controversy often addressed by Sandy once he entered the political field — Dr. Richard Roberts asked, "Are we going to build a strong state or a living society; a powerful nation, rich in gold and resources, or a great living co-operative commonwealth?"[11] Forming a co-operative commonwealth federation would come later, but Sandy heard the phrase here for the first time, and the concept stayed with him. He learned more, too, about Canada's international responsibility from the Honourable Newton W. Rowell, Canadian representative at the League of Nations, who stated that "our international obligations grow out of our existence as a Nation in a community of Nations, and are inseparably associated with it." Rowell mentioned the Christian attitude, calling it "the fundamental unity of our humanity, and the essential brotherhood of all nations of men," and stating further that people "should seek to make war impossible by providing some other method of settling disputes among nations."[12]

Sandy listened attentively, knowing that at the University of Saskatchewan "there were quite a number of veterans who were concerned that there didn't seem to be any organization on the scene in Canada actively trying to get public opinion aroused to make it impossible to have a war every generation." Now, he believed the SCM could fill that void and he took the messages back to his campus. Sandy and other delegates felt the best contributions at the conference "were made by people of religions and races other than our own." One student wrote that "the day is coming very soon when we shall cease to send 'missionaries' anywhere, but rather we shall exchange people with universal ideas who are willing to co-operate with others in building the Kingdom of God."[13]

From the students who spoke, Sandy heard messages which he remembered for future occasions. Hans Tiesler, from Berlin, who had come to the conference with some misgivings, feeling the war was still too fresh in some memories, said, "I do not come as a German to English and Canadian people; but . . . I speak as a human to humans . . . Let us remember this in all time to come and so work towards the realization of the spirit of Christ."[14]

This and other SCM conferences provided valuable learning experiences for Sandy. When he graduated, he took the concepts with him into the world, along with a network of lifelong friends. His daughter Ruth said, "The SCM was a recruiting ground for politically oriented young people — not necessarily just for the CCF. My father had an amazing number of contacts in the business, church and government worlds that all seemed to lead back to the SCM. For example, the mother of Hal Jackman (former Conservative member of Parliament for Toronto-Rosedale) has been a long-time friend of my parents and was a contact from SCM days. Her father was the Judge Rowell of the Rowell-Sirois report." For Sandy, the narrow confines of provincialism, of denominationalism, of nationalism, had been broken and he gained a broader outlook on the world and its problems. In retrospect, he said, "It is hard to understand that by the time I was twenty-two I had not questioned the religious beliefs brought from Scotland so many years ago."

Along with his SCM involvement at university, Sandy took an active part in athletic activities. He enjoyed team sports and began playing Rugby football, soccer and basketball. Numerous accounts in *The Sheaf* link Sandy with Bob Paton and Fred Musk in a "three musketeer" friendship. Reporting an interfaculty basketball final in March 1923, the college paper stated that the theology college Presbucks

> stepped out on the gymnasium floor and waded into the famous Meds, emerging with the odd bloody nose and sore side, but consoled with the long end of a 23 to 17 score. This win gives them the championship of the league, an honour held by their opponents for the last two years . . . Armitage [of the Meds] had his hands full keeping an eye on little Musk, who even at that, netted six of the 10 baskets made by the Presbucks, and Brown and McRoberts [Meds] were kept submissive by Paton and Nicholson.[15]

When sports director Joe Griffiths saw how well Sandy

performed in track and field, he encouraged him to concentrate on individual competition for fear he might be injured on the Rugby field. Although it would be later when the name Nicholson became synonymous with track events victories, by the autumn of 1922 Sandy had begun breaking records. Chronicling the events of the interfaculty field meet, *The Sheaf* gave Sandy credit for beating the former record distance in the shot put, coming third in the hammer throw, and being the individual leader in points for his faculty.[16] Competing in the 1923 track and field meet, held at the campus stadium, Sandy "of the Presbyterians, gave [the individual champion, Werthenback of Arts] a great run for the championship and was only two points behind . . . [and he] increased the distance on both the shot put and discus throw."[17]

The autumn of 1923 brought a new building to the University of Saskatchewan campus. The combined college residence and school of St. Andrew's College stood at the gateway of the university:

> The building included lecture rooms, library, residence for about 90 students and dining room. It also provided accommodation for young men who came to the city to attend collegiate institutes, normal school and university, for whom the church would provide the atmosphere of a home with sympathetic supervision and a measure of instruction in the Bible.[18]

Abraham, "The Patriarch," reported the move from the "old barn" to the new college and residence on campus in 1923 in the column "Presbyterian Gleanings" in *The Sheaf*:

> Boom! Bang! Rip-sa-sill!
> Things are humming with us still,
> We may be slow — but you can bet
> The "Old Barn" spirit is with us yet.
>
> Our brand New Barn is 'andsome, swell,
> 'Tis filled with boys and lassies as well
> As fine a bunch as ever did yell,
> Fire and brimstone, well! well! well!
>
> . . . We have at last made our official appearance as a college, on the campus, and we feel . . . it therefore

> behooves us to make our presence known . . . We
> feel that there will be a decided mutual benefit from
> "church and state" fraternizing so intimately
> together . . . As a college we must congratulate our
> representatives on the inter-faculty team: —
> Nicholson, D. MacLaren, W. Graham and L. Schnell,
> and our representative "Sandy", of the inter-varsity
> track team.[19]

Besides the local athletic events, the western universities competed each autumn for the Cairns Cup, "symbolic of the championship in the Western Canada track and field contests."[20] Even though Saskatchewan hosted the 1923 track meet, being on home territory did not help them break the fortunes of Manitoba athletes, and for the fourth time the Brown and Gold carried off premier honours. The Saskatchewan team finished second, and Alberta third. Sandy made a good showing in the hammer throw but could not beat McLean, the weight man from Manitoba. An important first meeting took place here between Sandy and one of the Manitoba field judges, King Gordon, son of the Reverend C.W. Gordon. Social gospeller C.W. Gordon, under the pen name of Ralph Connor "popularized social issues in a series of best-selling novels and became one of the nation's most successful mediators in industrial disputes."[21] Growing up in a household where the cause of the common man was championed, King Gordon followed his father's footsteps into the ministry. In 1923 he had returned from Oxford and was at college in Winnipeg, training to be a Presbyterian minister. Sandy learned that he also had a keen interest in the SCM and planned to attend the next conference.

A week later, in October, the University of Saskatchewan Rugby team travelled to Manitoba for the inauguration of the intercollegiate series, with Sandy as right inside on the Saskatchewan line-up. Coach "Doc" Nagel and Professor Hardy accompanied the team as faculty representatives and Rugby managers. *The Sheaf* reported that because of almost perfect weather

> both teams resorted to an open style of game, with

the result that the ball was in the air a good deal of the time, and many exciting exchanges back and forth kept the interest of the fans from lagging . . . Saskatchewan's line men were on the job all the time and showed how a line could hold when called upon to give a solid front, while the wing men were actively at work blocking and tackling.[22]

The play was so close that a fumble or a misplay in the last quarter might have turned the tables, but Manitoba held the edge and won.

Sandy's involvements in sports gave him good lessons in both winning and losing, which would benefit him in the political arena. By the autumn of 1924, Sandy began shattering records:

In the hammer throw he heaved the weight 96 feet six inches breaking the record of Bill McLeod . . . topped his old record in the discus with a heave of 101 feet 7 inches [by 2 feet 4 inches], and the poor shot likewise suffered — when it landed a distance of 34 feet 11 inches out on the prairie.[23]

Even with Sandy's excellent showing, St. Andrew's College came fourth. Sandy continued to participate in team sports, and he particularly liked basketball, where his height and speed were valuable assets. In the spring of 1925, the Presbucks won the interfaculty basketball championship where "Nicholson and Musk were the backbone of the team, scoring most of the baskets," with Bob Paton playing a fine game of defense.[24]

In the autumn of 1925, Sandy trained under the watchful eye of his coach, Joe Griffiths, who wrote in the college paper, "Perhaps some of you freshmen have noticed about a hundred and ninety pounds of energy about the campus the last few days. Well, that is one Sandy Nicholson, who on weekdays slings the weights such as the hammer, shot and discus; and believe us he sure flings them far, far, away."[25]

At the university track meet, Sandy earned the title of individual champion. A week later, the University of Manitoba again won the intervarsity track meet, with

Alberta coming second and Saskatchewan third. Sandy
must have given his all at the university meet a week
earlier for his only claim here was third place in the discus.
The issue of *The Sheaf* which had reported the results of
the track meets carried another item announcing Sandy's
election as president of the Western Canada Inter-Collegiate
Athletic Union (WCIAU) at a meeting held in Winnipeg
during the intervarsity competition. The article stated:

> Sandy Nicholson the leader of our U.A.D. will for the
> next year direct with his executive the destinies of
> Inter-Collegiate sport. The responsibility could rest in
> no better hands, and we congratulate Sandy on his
> appointment.[26]

As well as his physical and administrative athletic
activities and his SCM involvement, Sandy studied diligently
and found time for helping others. When addressing a
Kiwanis Club in Saskatoon in 1960, he recounted an
experience he had had with a blind person, which left its
imprint on him:

> When I was a student at the university here friends in
> the city phoned one day to inquire if I would mind
> taking a blind pianist, who was giving a recital in the
> city, over to see the university and come around to
> their place for supper afterwards. Those of you who
> have lived in residence will recall that a person will do
> nearly anything to have a home cooked meal. I
> thought it rather a strange request to take a blind
> person to the university. However, we visited the gym,
> convocation hall and I told about the sunken gardens
> and something about the beautiful stone buildings
> and explained the lecture theatre in the chemistry
> building and we dropped in to see the President, who
> was, as you might expect, most gracious. I have never
> forgotten the description of our tour as related at the
> supper table by the blind pianist . . . I could not
> have given as interesting a description of the
> institution as the guest did after a two-hour tour when
> he depended on his impressions from his guide.

While at university, Sandy spent most of his summers on
the mission fields. The church General Assembly accounts

of 1920 indicate that the regular salary for such activity at the time was thirteen dollars a week. In 1922 Sandy's first field mission was at Maple Creek in the southwestern corner of Saskatchewan, where he had a three-point charge: Hay Creek, Michener, and Murraydale. He boarded with the Beveridge family where a good saddle horse was available to him, but he had to buy his own saddle. In *Memoirs of a Mountain Man*, Andy Russell mentioned that a common expression was "as tough on a horse as a preacher . . . for these young fellows went like pony-express riders to make their appointments. It took a good horse to stand up to it, and the best of them looked jaded by fall."[27] Sandy held three services on Sundays, conducted funerals, and arranged social evenings.

Jack Beveridge reminisced in a letter:

> On your first 'tour of duty' in the spring of 1922, I had the honour of escorting you on saddlehorse, starting at our ranch on Piapot Creek, three and one-half miles southeast to Michener school on the north slope of the Cypress Hills. From Michener, about ten miles south and west over the hills to Murraydale school on the Bench, for the afternoon service. From Murraydale we rode north, northwest downhill to Hay Creek school on Hay Creek about ten miles, from Hay Creek six miles east to the ranch. Probably we had dinner and supper at Carsons and Fauquiers — we didn't go hungry.[28]

Sandy returned to this charge the next spring — one of fifty-eight students in southern Saskatchewan under appointment by the Home Mission Board.[29] The Saskatchewan Wheat Pool was being organized then and Sandy agreed to canvass for memberships. In his spare time he instructed the Beveridge boys in shot put, discus and hammer, using borrowed equipment from the university.

In 1924 the church sent Sandy to Asquith, about twenty miles west of Saskatoon, where he served an additional three charges — McTavish, Polar Crescent, and Douglas Plains. He preached in Asquith every Sunday and alternated with the three rural charges. His mode of travel varied —

on foot, horseback, and in Mr. Hasting's white horse and buggy which was driven by various members of the congregation. Sometimes he substituted in district schools.[30] Sandy returned the following year and several men remembered him vividly, almost sixty years later, as an enthusiastic teacher in track and field as well as in spiritual instruction. Others recalled his happy nature, his friendship, interest and devotion to the Asquith community.

During the summers of his university years, Sandy also attended the SCM conferences. At the first student conference in Toronto, it was decided that the following summer at Carlyle Lake, Saskatchewan, there would be a summer conference for students in Manitoba, Saskatchewan and Alberta. Sandy and Marian attended. Hugh MacMillan had not left for Formosa yet and he arranged to be at Carlyle Lake for this conference. Davidson Ketchum, who had been a prisoner of war in Germany, spoke eloquently on the SCM objective that there should be no more war and he asked the students to become involved in building a Christian society. He encouraged Sandy to attend the autumn SCM conference at Elgin House, in the Muskoka district of Ontario.

Each year before the opening of university, the branches of the SCM across Canada sent delegates to this annual conference to discuss plans for the year. The owner of Elgin House, a Mr. Love, took religion seriously. He did not permit any drinking or smoking on the premises, and he made his lodge available at the end of the tourist season to the SCM at a reasonable rate. Travel to the secluded lodge was by train, then by boat. Among the delegates in 1923 were Sandy, his sister Anna, and Hugh MacMillan. Sandy said,

> They planned these conferences with a view to generating a good deal of interest. J.S. Woodsworth, a Labour MP for Winnipeg, was on the programme. He was interested in the fact that I was a student for the ministry. I was anxious to know how he happened to give up his work as a minister. Woodsworth replied he was in jail during the Winnipeg strike and forced to

resign his work with the Methodist church of Canada because of his opposition to war.

At Elgin House he used one of the devices he had used during the period when he did educational work after leaving the church. He brought with him a golf bag that had fishing rods cut into yard sticks to hold up a large screen, about 12 feet square. The fishing rod pieces were held together by aluminum bands. The message that provoked most interest with the students was a spider's web with a spider in the centre. Woodsworth claimed the people on the frontiers, the fishermen, the forestry people and the farmers out on the fringes of this square[,] did a lot of hard work and got very little for it. However, in the centre, this spider was able to collect the cream of everything. Woodsworth was quite anxious that some of the students should look forward to a political career. There were too many wealthy people elected to represent ordinary people . . . only two Labour MPs at the time. He assumed most of the students there would think in terms of joining the Liberal or Conservative parties but he said, 'I have come to the conclusion that the two old parties have demonstrated they really have a great deal in common and there isn't any difference when one is in and the other is out.' So Woodsworth made quite an impression on me.

Woodsworth's pacificism was a major influence which led Sandy to become critical of war.

Woodsworth believed also that all Canadian students had a duty to identify with some political party and to support it actively, and that if they could not agree with then current party policies, they should start a new party. In due course Sandy did help to start a new political party. Once he became involved with the CCF he learned that Stanley Knowles also had met Woodsworth for the first time at an SCM conference.

In 1929 Knowles, acting as a student delegate from Brandon College, where he had completed his second year of studies, attended the western SCM conference at Jasper where he listened to Woodsworth's chart presentations. Before the establishment of political clubs on campuses, the SCM attracted young people interested in equating their religious beliefs with practical purposes. Woodsworth's social gospel message challenged both Sandy and Knowles during the Depression to think about the ways in which social reforms might be accomplished through pertinent legislation, although several years passed before either of the two young men sought election.

Throughout Sandy's university years, while he attended SCM conferences and worked on the mission fields during summer holidays, Marian Massey taught in rural schools. Many such schools were unable to attract teachers except in summer when university students became available. Sandy later recalled an incident when Marian was teaching at the Port Arthur School near Nora, Saskatchewan, about halfway between Wadena and Tisdale. The CNR between Nipawin and Wadena was nearing completion, with stations and sidings selected, but in September the only way to reach the school was by driving cross-country. Marian's birthday fell on Labour Day and Sandy arranged to call for her on Friday and to take her home to Wadena for the weekend.

When the mailman from Wadena delivered to post offices in the surrounding rural area, a few passengers would take advantage of the seats fashioned from egg crates on the back of his half-ton Model T Ford. Marian had made a sketch of the route from Kelvington to the school when she travelled with the mailman and Sandy used this map when he drove the borrowed Massey car from Wadena, then to Kelvington, and on to the school. On the way he remembered opening and closing the twenty-eight gates necessary to keep livestock from wandering.

By choosing a teaching career, Marian was continuing a family tradition established in 1855 when her grandmother, Ann Eliza McClatchie-Massey, studied to be a teacher at Huntingdon Academy and taught in her home district of Huntingdon County, Lower Canada. Grandfather Levi Massey taught also and Marian's father, Norman Levi

Massey, graduated as a gold medalist at Victoria College in 1877, travelling west to Moose Jaw in 1908 to teach high school, then moving to Wadena in 1919 — the centre for his school inspectorship until his retirement in 1928. In the 1920s, school board regulations decreed that married women could not teach, so Marian and Sandy agreed it would be wise to postpone their marriage until he graduated. Their engagement lasted four years while she continued to teach and he completed his theological studies.

Chapter 4

University, Marriage, and Postgraduate Studies, 1926-1930

C olleagues continued to associate Sandy with athletic competitions, although he never surpassed the standing in sports he held in 1925. Interfaculty sport at the university experienced its greatest seasons in 1925 and 1926, flourishing in all departments, "turning out strong teams which produced the keenest of competition. Sixty men competed in the track meet." Twenty-two basketball teams battled for supremacy in three separate divisions, "most of the teams so evenly matched that several games had to go into overtime, and many a game was won by a single basket."[1]

The Sheaf recorded all aspects of sports. In the autumn of 1926, following the interfaculty track meet, an article on the respected physical trainer Joe Griffiths showed him "walking around with that satisfied appearance."[2] Records had been smashed, broken and bent. Chilly breezes whispering through the stadium failed to hinder com-petitors — "in fact it drove them to exert themselves to greater efforts in trying to keep warm." Orville Gratias captured the individual championship, his score augmented by hurling the discus two feet one inch further than Sandy's previous record. Sandy managed to come first in shot put. In the "B" basketball league the Presbucks trounced the Pillpounders. The theologians had "all the earmarks of a snappy team, with a couple of sharpshooters such as Bob Paton and Sandy Nicholson, who accumulated 22 points for their team."[3] The following year, when Sandy competed for the last time in the interfaculty track meet, he threw a first in discus and a second in shot put.

The University of Saskatchewan could not seem to break the jinx at the intercollegiate track meets, and Manitoba won for the seventh consecutive year in October 1926 on the Saskatchewan campus. This time, King Gordon competed as a member of the Manitoba team. Alberta came second and Saskatchewan third, with Sandy taking thirds in shot put and hammer. Competition for the possession of the Cairns Cup took place in Edmonton in 1927. Saskatchewan came third again, "severely handicapped by lack of training,"[4] but special mention went to Sandy Nicholson, Mac Young and Orville Gratias "for the splendid showing they made." Gratias finished first in the hammer and a third in javelin, while Sandy garnered his points by a second in the shot put and hammer, and a third in discus. In the races, Mac Young collected second place in the century in a blanket finish that had onlookers gasping, a third in the 220-yard sprint and a third in the 440-yard race.

Sometimes the university newspaper amused its readers with tongue-in-cheek journalism. A 1926 spring edition reported:

> Some of the theologs are already planning where and how they will spend the summer — Bob Paton, Sandy Nicholson, Fred Musk . . . are being accompanied by an Agro, Bunny [Bunce]. This is significant, as they are travelling as valets to the "auld kine". They have already procured mouth organs, tonsil grease, ukuleles and harps (jews) to soothe the cattle. They are using the University of Saskatchewan song book.[5]

At the 1925 SCM conference at Elgin House, plans had been made to participate in the international SCM meeting in Denmark in the summer of 1926. Canada could send three students, one each from the west, Ontario and the east. Selections were: Harry Avison of McGill University in Montreal; Mary Rowell of the University of Toronto; and Sandy from the University of Saskatchewan. All would be required to make some financial contribution to costs. When Sandy attended SCM conferences at Elgin House, he usually visited his father at Lucknow. This year, his father had accompanied his livestock to the United Kingdom. "Since he had been over with his own cattle and students had been signed on to help care for them, and were able to return on the cattle boat — no charge — I wondered if it would be possible for me to get over the next year," Sandy recalled. "He was able to clear this for me, and I in turn arranged that Bunce, Paton and Musk could come."

The four young men travelled from Saskatoon to Quebec by stock train. They boarded the SS *Canadian Victor* at Quebec City and headed for Cardiff, Wales. Later, in the House of Commons, in one of many bids for better use of the port of Churchill for shipping prairie grains, Sandy said about this experience, "We left Quebec City in June. We rode at anchor for some three days in the Newfoundland area. There were ice hazards nearby, we were in dense fog. It has never been suggested that the St. Lawrence route should be discontinued because of those hazards."[6] Besides the ice floes and fog, the students attended a burial at sea when a crew member died. Bob Paton, who had already been ordained, conducted the service.

Sandy's friend Fred Musk was to remain in Scotland where he completed his postgraduate studies in Edinburgh. Bunny Bunce was returning to England to marry his fiancée. He had graduated in spring, receiving the Governor-General's medal for the outstanding graduate of 1926. His father was a wealthy textile manufacturer in Manchester, England. When Bunce developed asthma, the family's doctor suggested that the Alberta climate would alleviate the condition, and that the young man should visit the province with a view to becoming a rancher. As Sandy recalled:

His father arranged with the CPR [Canadian Pacific

Railway] to pay sixty dollars a month to some responsible person in Alberta to teach his son how to become a rancher. Bunce was just there a month when he realized the only teaching he was getting was doing the same work that half a dozen hired men were being paid to do.

An Anglican minister in the community recommended the agricultural college in Saskatoon, where Sandy met Bunce at SCM meetings. Some interesting discussions took place at that time regarding the establishment of the ideal society, and, among other topics, co-operative farming claimed the attention of the young men.

While he was in Great Britain in 1926, before attending the SCM conference, Sandy found an opportunity to visit the Isle of Skye. "On the Sunday I had gone up in the boat and stayed at the hotel near the port," he said. He found one elderly woman who remembered his grandfather as "Fair Norman" some seventy-five years earlier. One of the Portree school teachers invited Sandy to attend Sunday worship with her, at a church known as the "wee free" Presbyterian church. The minister announced that the flagship of the *Revenge* lay in harbour, "but we're God-fearing people and we can't understand why the authorities in London permit this on the Sabbath Day and I hope none from this congregation will go aboard the boat on the Sabbath." That settled, Sandy headed out to search for relatives, with the teacher as his guide. They received a good reception at the first place because the people had relatives in North America and they were interested in sharing stories. But, Sandy recalled, "At the second place we were in trouble. I knew enough Gaelic to understand I'd blundered." Although the teacher explained that Sandy had come a long way to find his ancestors, and he was planning to be a minister himself, the people stood firm. "There are six days for visiting." they said. "We pity the poor people he'll be preaching to if he hasn't more respect for the Sabbath. But you're a teacher and your example should be better than that." The teacher decided it would be wise to curtail the calls. Before leaving Scotland, Sandy learned that Edinburgh would be an ideal location for postgraduate work.

At the annual SCM conference in Swanwick, England,[7] about fifteen delegates arranged to go to the European Student Relief Conference in Yugoslavia, before attending the SCM Conference in Denmark. The European Student Relief Conference was organized after World War I by the YMCAs in Great Britain and the United States, and it later became known as the International Student Service. Conditions were serious on the continent, especially in Germany and Austria. Those who lived in the cities, in particular, were starving. The YMCA and the SCM, along with similar organizations around the world, believed students in countries which won the war should help those in the defeated countries. Meeting together might help reduce prejudices. Thus began annual conferences held at various locations in Europe where those giving and those receiving came together, with Yugoslavia the site for 1926.

Sandy and his friends availed themselves of reduced student rates while travelling in Europe. They encountered difficulties in understanding foreign rules, and in Berlin Sandy nearly spent a weekend in jail. When the group arrived with all their baggage in city railway stations, it had become a habit for somebody to jump out of the coach window and take the baggage through there instead of carrying it out through the train door. Sandy leapt out in the Berlin station, a policeman nabbed him for breaking local laws, and informed him he would have to appear in court next day. Fortunately one young woman in the group spoke fluent German and came to his rescue. She explained that Sandy was a Canadian who did not know he had violated a German law. She continued diplomatically, "You'll do a great service for international goodwill if you accept whatever the fine is and we'll pay today — and this will never happen again." The policeman accepted the fine.

Sandy absorbed more than a knowledge of local laws. Arguing for better relations with other countries during his tenure in Parliament, he recalled this trip:

Young people were greatly concerned about fitting

into a society that seemed to have so few openings. The European countries particularly found in a few short years that a serious employment problem had developed. Most of the young people were concerned about getting into business or the various professions. I recall when the suggestion was made of going into politics and trying to do something about the complex international problems that prevailed, they dismissed very lightly the thought of entering the political field. Politics was a business for the aged but not for the young.[8]

That trip across Europe in 1926 made evident to Sandy that students should be involved in attempts to create a better society. A number of experiences made it clear to him that at some point in his life he would be promoting international relationships. He learned about labour conditions in industrial Germany, and made a firsthand study of co-operatives in Denmark, where the Social Democrats had formed the government in 1924.[9]

Opportunities on this trip to meet and talk to foreign students, despite language barriers, made a lasting impression on Sandy. Years later, during the debate in Parliament concerning Canada's delegation to the 1945 San Francisco Conference, he commented on the importance of improved international relationships. Citing the Yugoslavian conference, he said, "At first there were strained relationships between the students of different countries, but after we had been there for a few days, we found that we had a great deal in common and if we were willing to give and take, sufficient agreement could be reached to make real progress in our discussions."

European governments offered reduced train fares to students to encourage them to travel, and Sandy and his group had taken advantage of this inexpensive transportation. "In all the university cities we were met by groups of students who took us to their hostels where it was possible to have room and lodging at prices students could afford to pay . . . We were able to visit centres of learning in those cities during the limited time at our disposal, and we came away with a better understanding and appreciation of these important centres."[10]

The second national SCM conference in Canada was held from 27 December 1926 to 3 January 1927, in the Assembly Hall of Macdonald College, Ste. Anne de Bellevue, Quebec.[11] Whether international or national, the fun of travelling to conferences remained an integral part of SCM involvement. On Friday evening, 24 December, representatives of the University of Saskatchewan boarded their special tourist car on the eastbound CNR.[12] "The five delegates from Alberta University completed the exuberant party and we were away with a Montreal ho!"

Sandy rejoined the party when it arrived in Winnipeg on Christmas morning. Marian was teaching at Melfort, Saskatchewan, and was unable to get away for the conference, so Sandy visited her and her family briefly at the Massey home in Wadena, then left for Winnipeg. He spent Christmas at the home of Professor R.C. Wallace whom he had met in summer at Carlyle Lake. The Winnipeg chapter of SCM arranged "that the Western delegates to the national conference would be entertained by the members of the local unit of SCM during their stay in Winnipeg."[13] The train pulled out of Winnipeg on Christmas evening. In their private tourist car the SCM delegation enjoyed a jolly Christmas party which included a tree and a carol service. Everyone received a present under the tree — "some of the soap resembled the CNR variety, but nobody could but receive it happily from the hands of our jolly 'Sandy' Claus," reported *The Sheaf*, adding that Sandy had kissed everyone, including the porter. On Monday, 27 December, the western car was joined to the special conference train in Toronto and as the train pulled out the station rang with a variety of school yells. At Kingston, the Queen's University delegation came aboard, then the train pulled into Ste. Anne de Bellevue in the late afternoon.[14]

Here, on the western end of Montreal Island, about twenty-five miles from the heart of Montreal, a company of students from every Canadian university and several colleges gathered in a six-day session, together with representatives from England, the United States, Australia, China and India. Free periods throughout the days were devoted to skating, hockey, hikes, basketball and skiing. One of Canada's most prominent churchmen, Dr. Richard Roberts, addressed the students the first evening, challenging them to action, advocating that too much discussion might make problems seem more complex.

One afternoon the conference group took a special train into Montreal and toured the city, a trip culminating in an enjoyable dinner-dance in the McGill Union Building, the University Men's Club. The New Year's Eve programme included carols and stunts, with the Saskatchewan and Manitoba groups teaming up to produce the three-act melodrama *Bluebeard*. The conference took on a serious note next morning when two foreign students from Columbia University addressed the conference. A Mr. Ho, a Chinese student, gave a brief account of the spread of Christianity in China. A Mr. Rockett, an Indian student who was a Hindu from Calcutta, provided an insight into the workings of the Hindu mind by explaining the tenets of his faith. Sandy felt that there had been determination throughout the conference to arrive at conclusions which would aid students in preparing for active life once they graduated. Personal experiences, knowledge, and new friends gained at SCM conferences considerably broadened Sandy's own horizons.

At the autumn 1927 SCM conference, Sandy met Bruce Copeland, once a missionary in China, who had returned to take a theology degree at McGill University. Copeland planned to be married in 1928 and to spend a year in Edinburgh, as postgraduate training was not obtainable within Canada until the 1930s and many students went to Great Britain. Marian had agreed with Sandy that Edinburgh would be the best place to study. Until he graduated, she spent one term at Lintlaw, Saskatchewan, and then taught at Melfort High School from 1925 to 1928.

A number of Presbyterian churches in Scotland were anxious to hire Canadians as assistant ministers while they earned their degrees. Bill Maxwell, one of Sandy's former friends from Bruce County, was the assistant minister at St. Stephen's Parish Church in Edinburgh, while he was finishing his doctoral studies. Maxwell recommended that Sandy succeed him, and the suggestion received agreement. Following his graduation and ordination in spring, Sandy and Marian were married in the Wadena United Church on 15 August 1928. Norma Nicholson, Sandy's sister from Lucknow, represented his family and participated in the wedding party as a bridesmaid. The *Wadena News* stated:

> The happy couple left on the evening train for a brief honeymoon in Ontario, after which they sail in September on the "SS Antonia" for Edinburgh, where the groom will continue his studies and also act as Assistant Minister at St. Stephen's Church.[15]

The newly-weds enjoyed the leisurely travel of the day, and Marian became initiated into Sandy's organized world and privy to his growing family of national and world friends. In Winnipeg they stayed at the Fort Garry Hotel, where Sandy had prearranged a "reunion of the Carlyle crowd for afternoon tea in the Maple Room."[16] Their train took them to Duluth where they boarded the *Hamonic*, docking in Ontario at Fort William, Port Arthur, Sault Ste. Marie, Sarnia, thence through the St. Clair River to Detroit in the United States, and across to Windsor, Ontario, where they disembarked. They visited Sandy's relatives in Lucknow first, arriving by train at Wingham where Anna and "Papa Nicholson" met them and drove them the twelve miles to Lucknow. Marian wrote in her diary:

> Attended the Presbyterian Church on the hill, a mile from town, where Sandy used to attend. Except for the absence of a piano or organ, the service was quite similar to our own. Anna and Norma sang in the choir. Only psalms and paraphrases were sung. The minister, Rev. McLeod, 75 years old, gave a splendid address, even though he won't tolerate anything modern — even to doxologies.

The following Sunday the local United Church minister

invited Sandy to speak at Sunday School and to lead a Bible class.

Following a whirlwind visit with Marian's relatives in southern Ontario, Sandy and Marian sailed from Montreal harbour on 14 September aboard the Cunard liner SS *Antonia*. As previously planned, they met Bruce and Margaret Copeland on board and spent pleasant hours together during the six-day Atlantic crossing — quite a contrast to the conditions Sandy's grandparents had endured in the 1850s on their seven-week voyage to Canada. Sandy and Marian left the SS *Antonia* in the North Channel of the Irish Sea, boarded a tender to land at Greenock, Scotland, and travelled by train to Edinburgh.

The Nicholsons checked into the Clarendon Hotel, then they found and rented two rooms — bedroom and living room with kitchen privileges — on Howe Street for their eighteen-month visit. Sandy ordered his first clerical suits, one black, the other grey. Next, they purchased two second-hand bicycles to enable them to tour the country-side. On one excursion they bicycled far enough to stay away from their lodgings overnight. Marian recorded, "There were no temperance hotels so we went to the Inn to a big room under the eaves, but the smell of beer reached us even here. We flung open the windows and then came down and put our wheels in a vacant room at the rear."

Another day they visited the historic town of Stirling and Stirling Castle, birthplace of Scottish Kings, travelling by train from Edinburgh and then by horse-drawn coach, which "wound ever higher on a private road, the towering hills purple with heather. Sandy had a great sport jumping off and getting some heather — then clambering up again." The four-in-hand "reverted to a three-in-hand as one of the horses had the 'staggers'. Loch Lomond proved much more beautiful than Loch Katrine."

Sandy first acted in his official capacity as assistant minister at St. Stephen's on 7 October 1928. A month later Marian wrote in her diary, "Sandy this day accepted by the Presbytery of Edinburgh with standing as a fully ordained minister. His case was the first from the United Church, so we were glad to see it was fully recognized by the Church of Scotland."[17] This church had policies governing the recognition of ordained ministers from other denominations which dated back to 1866. Because the United Church of Canada was relatively new,[18] definite guidelines had not been formulated, but the General Assembly of the Church of Scotland "recommended that fraternal relations be maintained" with the United Church of Canada and "in the event of application being made for admission by ministers in it, each case should be considered on its merits in accordance with the standards of the Church of Scotland" regarding applications from other churches.[19]

While in Edinburgh, Sandy attended university classes in the mornings. Marian audited some too, and when she was the only woman in the class the professors politely began with "Gentlemen and Mrs. Nicholson." Afternoons found Sandy tending his flock. St. Stephen's had a congregation of about twenty-four hundred members and the assistant minister was expected to visit as many as possible. The congregation had been divided into twenty-four districts, with names and locations of members outlined and provision for recording visits. In addition, Sandy organized young people's work on Sunday and other evenings.

Five afternoons a week he gave high priority to visiting district residents. Sandy's passion for social involvement, a primary characteristic of Canadian Protestantism at the time, was early evoked in Edinburgh. He learned "that Auld Reekie had other lesser known facts than the historic castle"[20] — the slums and the poverty made a lasting imprint on the student minister. Here lived men who had given their best in World War I and ten years later, unable to find jobs, were barely existing on the inadequate dole. Many did not attend church, their excuse being that they did not have proper clothing.

"The Lord doesn't care what you wear," Sandy said.

"Well," they answered, "Lord So-and-So does. He turns up his nose."

The Nicholsons soon learned first-hand about the class

Sandy Nicholson and his sisters Norma and Anna were born in this house, built by their grandparents, Norman and Ann Nicholson, on Lot 8, Concession 2, Kinloss, Bruce County, Ontario.

The seven-bedroom house occupied by Alexander and Isabelle Nicholson and their family in the spring of 1903. Isabelle died here on 17 May 1903 at age forty-two.

Norma, Alexander Malcolm, and Mary Anna Nicholson in 1911.

Sandy Nicholson (right) and his friend Harry Jewitt earned two dollars a day cutting brush along the road between Bruce and Huron in November 1918.

The South Kinloss Presbyterian Church picnic in 1920 was held at Point Clark, Ontario, and attended by (left to right) Sandy Nicholson, Irene MacIntosh, Rena Fraser, and Martin McInnes.

Marian Massey in 1922.

Sandy Nicholson, aged twenty-two, in 1922.
(Saskatchewan Archives Board 5-B1750)

Sandy Nicholson (seated front row, far right) was a Saskatchewan delegate to the Student Christian Movement National Council Meeting at Elgin House, Muskoka, Ontario, in September 1924.

*In the summer of 1926, Sandy Nicholson and his friend Fred Musk worked their way to a Student Christian Movement conference in England aboard the cattleboat SS **Canadian Victor.***

E.H. Oliver (left) and D.S. Dix both played influential roles in Sandy Nicholson's life long after he graduated from St. Andrew's College, Saskatoon, in 1928. (Saskatchewan Archives Board S-B2087)

Sandy Nicholson at the time of his graduation in 1928. (Saskatchewan Archives Board S-B2087)

Marian Massey became Sandy Nicholson's bride on 15 August 1928 at Wadena, Saskatchewan.

Sandy Nicholson, John Lamont, and Anna Nicholson Wright visited Donald Nicolson at Kyle of Lochalsh, Scotland, in July 1929.

Sandy Nicholson, wearing clerical garb, is seen with the congregation of the Hudson Bay Junction United Church in front of the local theatre, the congregation's meeting place before the church was built.

Drama flourished in Hudson Bay Junction in the 1930s, and Marian Nicholson often directed actors in such plays as "A Poor Married Man." (Kay MacKinnon)

This family benefitted from the fresh milk of the Missionary Cow, seen to the left of the picture, with Sandy Nicholson beside her.

system. They had bicycled to Stirling one Sunday to attend service at one of the ancient churches. Sandy recalled, "We'd gone the thirty-five miles but we weren't dressed in our best clothes. We noticed it was communion Sunday. In the Scottish Presbyterian churches they have white cloths covering the seats for communion services. We were being taken up to the gallery but we thought we'd like to go in on the main floor."

The usher asked, "Are you members of the church?"

Sandy replied, "We're from Canada and we aren't dressed for church."

"Oh well, if you're from Canada, yes."

Thus, the Nicholsons understood what it was like to want to go to church when most people wore their best clothing, and one arrived in ordinary workaday clothes.

The entry in Marian's diary on St. Andrew's Day illustrated how some of the wealthy lived. A Miss Robertson had invited the Nicholsons to tea, "and a most bountiful feast it was — ten plates containing different scones and cakes. Her rooms were furnished with antiques." Other friends invited them to the annual St. Andrew's dinner in the North British Hotel. Sandy sported a new dinner jacket. The women were in evening dresses and the majority of men were wearing the kilt. Pipers led the guests to the dining room, where bunches of heather tied with tartan ribbon were place favours. The menu featured haggis. Marian's diary entry continued, "A piper led the way in, the waiters following holding the haggis high on platters, and behind other waiters with bottles raising them up and down alternately. This we discovered later was the 'nips' referred to on the menu. The haggis was much like highly seasoned hash to us and was served with mashed potatoes. After dinner there were speeches, and messages from other St. Andrew's Societies all over the world — including Winnipeg, Manitoba."

To celebrate their first Christmas as a couple, they invited a few friends for roast chicken, mince pie and plum pudding. In the evening, Marian wrote, "Sandy took me to see the famous French actress Alice Delysia in 'Her Past' at the Lyceum. We had lovely seats, a box of candy and everything so it was a lovely evening . . . We sat in front of the fire when we returned for a nice talk and decided this our first Christmas in our own home had been a most ideal and happy one (thanks to all the nice little happy thoughts and actions of my good husband)."

New Year's Eve, Scottish style, was described in Marian's diary, after the Nicholsons had gone to the Tron Church to witness the celebrations: "The square round the Old Tron Kirk was getting well filled. We walked down High Street having to take to the road most of the time. Hawkers were selling horns, hats, rattlers, and many were the worse for liquor. As midnight approached, the crowd jammed round the church and when the clock chimed the bottles were passed then broken on the pavement and even against the church . . . The sad thing was to see so many children about and small boys trying to copy their fathers." When the crowd loosened, the Nicholsons escaped and made their way to "first foot" Mrs. Paton.[21] She gave them a warm welcome and brought out the lemonade and cakes. Marian wrote, "We in turn gave her some sweets for it is bad luck to come in empty handed." After this they decided to go across the city to "first foot" the Copelands, arriving back home around three o'clock in the morning where they "decided a quieter welcome to the New Year was more in keeping."

Early next day Sandy and Marian went to Caledonia Station to join the crowd heading for the SCM conference in Liverpool. They were billeted in the same hostel, but not together, as Sandy had been placed with the men in another wing of the building. Many of the meetings were held in the Cathedral, a comparatively new structure, begun in 1904 and consecrated in 1924, which remains one of the largest ecclesiastical structures in the world. The Nicholsons were treated as foreign delegates and entertained at many teas and luncheons.

In the new year, Marian's diary described the important event of May in Edinburgh — the Church Assemblies, where the four chief Presbyterian churches meet together.

On the first day a civic holiday was declared, and "this year the Duke and Duchess of York were the royal representatives to the Church of Scotland . . . 1929 was marked too because of the last separate assemblies of the United Free Church and Church of Scotland before their union in October." Previously, the United Free Church had shunned union, demanding freedom from state control. To sever state connections, the Church of Scotland framed declaration articles in "matters spiritual" and presented them to Parliament in the form of a bill which was passed in 1921. This action was followed by the act of 1925 which dealt finally with the issue, and led to the union of the two churches in 1929, achieving a Church of Scotland united, national and free. A minority remained separate and continued under the name United Free Church. Thanks to a friend, Marian had a ticket to the assembly when the motion for union was brought in and debated. Sandy wore his clerical garb when he was presented to the Duke, managing a stiff bow when his name was called.

On the morning of 2 October, the Nicholsons watched as "the moderator and chief men of each church marched from their respective halls and met at the corner of Bank and High Streets, bowed, shook hands and proceeded together to St. Giles" for a morning prayer service. The actual Deed of Union was signed in a hall on Annandale Street accommodating more than twelve thousand people.

Besides church-related activities, Marian and Sandy absorbed as much culture as time permitted, taking season tickets for the international celebrity concerts. This year, Mme. Jeritza, a soprano, and Wolfi, the famous boy violinist, were the first artists. The Nicholsons carried this enjoyment of music and drama to Saskatchewan where they directed and participated in local productions.

By the late autumn of 1929 Sandy had fulfilled the doctorate requirements, except for his dissertation. He and Marian planned to stay abroad until after Christmas, but they received a cable informing them that his father had undergone surgery at the Toronto General Hospital. A friend, Dr. Jack Hannah, another Canadian completing postgraduate studies in Edinburgh, advised them to return immediately because Alexander Nicholson was seventy-two years old and complications might arise at this advanced age. They booked passage on the first available ship, arriving in Toronto early in February. Knowing his son was coming home, Alexander Nicholson held on long enough to see him and died a week later, on 13 February 1930. When the estate was settled, Sandy found he had inherited some money, and he considered returning to Scotland.

At this point, however, Dr. John L. Nicol, superintendent of missions for the Saskatchewan Conference of the United Church, contacted Sandy and asked to meet him in Toronto. Dr. Nicol had a map of Manitoba and Saskatchewan showing an area in northeastern Saskatchewan, about 150 miles in diameter, not far from the Manitoba boundary. At the centre of this area lay a town named Hudson Bay Junction. Dr. Nicol explained that the Roman Catholics and the Anglicans had established churches in the town, and that many United Church members in the area were anxious to have a minister there. Sandy was convinced he should accept the posting to Hudson Bay Junction because Dr. Nicol "made such an interesting story about the railway being completed to Churchill so there would be an open port; and the new line going into Flin Flon and to Sherritt Gordon; and a new railway line was being built across from Hudson Bay Junction to Sturgis and another extension from Reserve Junction to Crooked River around to Arborfield." The Board of Home Missions guaranteed Sandy a minimum salary of $150 a month, and a further living allowance of $400 a year to compensate for the absence of a manse. Filled with a sense of mission and adventure, Sandy and Marian set out for Saskatchewan. But not with the blessings of their respective families and friends, who thought Sandy's talents were better suited to a large Toronto congregation.

Chapter 5

Mission Field,
1930-1933

Two factors which contributed to making northeastern Saskatchewan an important home mission territory for the United Church of Canada in 1930 were the great railway expansion and the severe drought which prevailed in the southern part of the province. The wealth of the land resources in the north — forest, fish, furs and minerals — became better known and the two great railways vied with one another in building lines into the north. An estimated twenty thousand new settlers trekked north in the first two years, with the rural population being two to one non-Anglo-Saxon, a large percentage being Hungarian, Ukrainian and Finnish.[1]

In May 1930, when the Nicholsons arrived in Hudson Bay Junction, they found an attractive and promising railway centre with a population of about four hundred. Twenty years earlier, when the Hudson Bay route was begun, real estate agents capitalized on the fact that all traffic to the north would pass through this junction, and buildings were erected and lots sold at enormous prices. In the meantime, work ceased on the "Bay" route until discovery of the rich mineral deposits further to the north. Hudson Bay Junction then became the promised divisional point and the CNR built a branch line to Regina, with the result that all rail traffic to Churchill coming from Winnipeg, Regina, Moose Jaw or Prince Albert, converged there.

To the north of the village lay the Pasquia Forest Reserve, with the range of hills of the same name. Situated forty miles south, the Porcupine Reserve included another hilly range. These surrounding hills, towering above the trees and silhouetted against blue sky, added to the scenic beauty of the area. Numerous sawmills operated on the reserve, which yielded cuttings of splendid spruce. The Etomami district, about ten miles south, had been settled by returning soldiers. Once the land was cleared, excellent soil lay underneath. A few years earlier it would not have been thought possible to grow wheat successfully at this latitude. So the area had three important industries — railroading, lumbering and farming — with mining a future possibility.

When the Nicholsons' train pulled into the Hudson Bay Junction station around three in the morning, they were surprised to learn the stores and restaurants stayed open around the clock to serve train crews and passengers. Eventually, the local merchants found it was unprofitable to keep the stores open all night, so the four restaurants agreed to rotate. Hudson Bay Junction was still a village with an overseer and two councillors.[2] Sandy remembered that the village soon experienced tremendous expansion with the railway being built to Churchill. Although railway workers were not keen on coming from other large railway centres, the Depression resulted in many layoffs and seniority made it possible for people to hold work at Hudson Bay Junction, with lots of "bumping" and a big turnover in the CNR labour force.

Dr. Nicol had supplied the Nicholsons with a contact — a railroader who worked nights. The train conductor suggested that they stay at the village hotel until morning, and street lights helped them find their way to it. The Dominion Electric Company had opened its plant the previous November and supplied twenty-four-hour service. Fred Stansfield, the company's one employee in Hudson

Bay Junction, lived in the power plant and was on call seven days a week. Sandy recalled, "We checked into the hotel where Marian discovered the sheets had not been changed. People going north or west could sleep till their train came in. Marian hesitated about going to bed, but I had lived in the north country long enough to know this wasn't unusual, and not to make any fuss." Next day they learned many people in the village were excited about their arrival. Mary Johnston, a cousin of Marian's mother, had married a railroader and was living there. Although they had never met, Mrs. Johnston expected the Nicholsons for lunch. Some old acquaintances lived in Hudson Bay Junction also, among them the druggist, Don Hood, who had attended university with Sandy; both men had lived in the St. Andrew's residence. There was also Stewart Hawke who owned the lumber yard — Marian had boarded with his parents while she was teaching at Melfort.

Reminiscing about this era, J.T. Bradford, CNR station agent at Stenen, between Hudson Bay Junction and Canora, said that the Hudson Bay Junction rail centre mostly handled freight trains which were hauling mineral shipments from the north, although there were also lumber and log trains which originated in the area. The route to Churchill opened officially a year after the Nicholsons arrived. Rolling stock on this line was used to haul grain to the port of Churchill during the shipping season. As a member of the local Board of Trade, Sandy promoted the use of this new route, and spoke in its favour in the House of Commons later whenever the opportunity arose. Mixed trains originated in mining areas such as Flin Flon, Sherridon, Optic Lake, and Osborne Lake.

Marian's relatives, Edythe and Grenville Smith-Windsor, visited the Nicholsons in 1932, travelling home on one of these mixed trains, which included a passenger coach, a baggage coach, and a caboose in a string of boxcars. Edythe wrote, "It was a great adventure for us to visit northeastern Saskatchewan's new frontier. We had never seen evergreens and birches in forests . . . In Hudson Bay Junction, Sandy borrowed a car and we drove on the trails around the settlement. I had my first ferry ride across the Red Deer River on one such trip. Hudson Bay Junction was a young people's town, a railway town, a night town. Activities were geared to arrival and departures of trains."[3]

Sandy held his first church service 4 May 1930, and it was attended by seven people, including the minister. "We met in the theatre at 3:00 PM so we might not conflict with the Anglican evening service, but an afternoon baseball game proved more of a drawing card," Sandy recalled. "After trying afternoon services for a month, competing with ball games, we changed the hour of worship to evening as the Anglican minister agreed there would not be any serious conflict."

Sandy and Marian decided to use some of their inheritance to build a house suitable for a church manse in Hudson Bay Junction. When Dr. Nicol, the United Church superintendent of missions, arrived on 9 July 1930, he approved of the adjoining lots selected for the house and the proposed church. Herbert Walton, an experienced carpenter who led a crew which had just finished the Anglican rectory, agreed to build the Nicholsons' house. They selected a bungalow-style, with a full basement. The village stood on a sandy ridge and people put down sand points, striking potable water at a four or five-foot depth. The village did not have sewers then, but, as Sandy said, "We did have a furnace, a fireplace, oak floors throughout, and a good well."

Most settlers in the area could not boast of such grandeur, and when Sandy saw the squalor in which many lived he made it a priority to improve their living conditions. Indeed, after his election to the House of Commons, he spent a major portion of his time as CCF spokesman for better housing. He once told the story of three veterans in his constituency: "They were carpenters who just could not get a job in Regina at any wage, so they journeyed to the Hudson Bay Junction district where I lived, under a scheme financed partly by the city, partly by the provincial, and partly by the federal authorities . . . Under the housing programme the governments of the day provided a payment of $6.70 for six windows. The next item is $3.80 for stovepipes, tar paper and hinges. The next item is $33.75 for lumber. The ceiling that was permitted in those days was $50 per unit, and you can see what a careful manager this settler was because his total expenses came to $49.75 . . . All logs were free for the cutting. They were on a plot of land of 160 acres with trees so thick you could not possibly drive through them with your oxen." As Sandy pointed out, these settlers thought "if they had 160 acres of free land, all the fuel they needed, some berries and maybe some wild game in the winter, if they would not be in heaven [at least] they would be better off than they would be on relief in Regina."[4]

On 6 August 1930, Walton completed construction of the Nicholsons' comfortable home in time for a visit from Marian's family. Norman Massey had retired from his position as a school inspector and had decided to return to Ontario. Walton had staked out the area where the church was to be built while he had been working on the house, and he tendered to build it. Workmen's Compensation had been initiated that year, and Sandy took out the first local compensation contract before work began on his house. The church board did likewise. Constructing the church became a community affair. A local architect designed it, some members excavated the basement, and railway carpenters helped, along with others in the congregation who had some building experience. The Bulow Lumber Company had a huge pile of excellent spruce lumber for which there was little demand during the Depression. The church was built in record time and it was ready for its official opening in September. Meanwhile, Sandy continued to conduct services in the local theatre. The few sawmills still operating paid low wages, and many were unemployed. CNR employees who had retained jobs were willing to contribute to the new church, however, and by 23 August the Ladies Aid had raised one hundred dollars towards building costs.

St. Stephen's United Church was dedicated on 21 September 1930, with the Reverend Dr. D.S. Dix of

Saskatoon officiating. The Nicholsons' guestbook records two other signatures on that date: W.A. Macdonell of Prince Albert who "officiated at Sandy's induction" and the Reverend Geoffrey Glover of Melfort who "assisted Mac..." The Reverend W.A. (Mac) Macdonell was principal of Nesbett School Home at Prince Albert, and convener of home missions for Presbytery.[5] Glover had been the United Church minister in Melfort while Marian taught there, and he was a graduate of St. Andrew's College. At the morning service the ministers administered the sacrament of baptism to twenty children. Twenty-seven members signed the charter roll at the evening service where they celebrated the Lord's Supper.

The pulpit Bible, presented by St. Stephen's Presbyterian Church of Edinburgh to its "Canadian daughter" was read from for the first time. A Heintzman Company employee from Toronto presented the organ, with the Reverend D.G. Rideout of Toronto adding the choir hymn books, and the ladies of the congregation donating the pulpit. The church received two more gifts at the first Easter service in the new year — a walnut communion set from Norma Massey, and a silver plate for sacramental bread from the Reverend Dr. D.S. Dix. At this Easter service, Sandy said he was proud of the "Sunday School which has had an average attendance of forty-two. The first time we met no one could tell me the name of the first book in the Bible, and when we tried to sing 'Dare to be a Daniel' no one could tell me anything about Daniel. Last week five of the scholars repeated correctly all the names of the books of the Bible."

The United Church Year Book of 1931 listed the Reverend A.M. Nicholson in the Prince Albert Presbytery, minister in the pastoral charge of Hudson Bay Junction with other preaching places — Doncrest, Erwood, Etomami, Meek's Siding and Reserve Siding.[6] His nearest United Church ministerial neighbour to the northeast was Stephens of The Pas, to the east there was Reid of Swan River, to the south, Kirkpatrick of Preeceville, and to the west Gingrich of Star City. These four neighbours were almost equidistant from Hudson Bay Junction. When he visited Sandy in 1932, the Reverend J.L. Nicol wrote: "If Sandy took a notion to visit any one of his ministerial neighbours, before he would get home again, he would be obliged to travel a distance equal to that from Dan to Beersheba, which, if my old Sunday School teacher taught me correctly, is a distance of about 150 miles."[7] To cover his circuit Sandy had to travel in all directions. No roads existed to accommodate cars in or out of Hudson Bay Junction for years, except in winter, so he never owned a car during his ministry. As in his school days, Sandy took to the trains, thankful for the conductors' "no charge." Trainmen all knew Sandy and understood his charitable work. If an emergency developed, and Sandy's presence was required while there were no trains scheduled CNR officials would ask him to sign a release, and the section foreman would take him on his track motor car (jigger).

On his missionary circuit, Sandy encountered many suffering from the difficulties of the Depression — settlers who had come north in covered wagons carrying all their worldly possessions. No relief agencies had been set up in the unorganized territory. At that time the local member in the provincial Legislature, Walter Buckle, was minister of agriculture. Then, on 28 July 1930, R.B. Bennett became prime minister of the Conservative federal government and appointed Bob Weir, the local member of Parliament, federal minister of agriculture. Sandy remembered one of the points J.S. Woodsworth had stressed at SCM conferences: "You know you should write to your MP, you can do that postage free. He is your hired man. Don't hesitate to write to your MP if you have any problems." So Sandy wrote to both the provincial and federal members about the need for relief. The federal government appointed a relief officer, but before this happened, the United Church became involved.

Sandy's ministry at Hudson Bay Junction coincided with the appointment of Dr. E.H. Oliver as the first western moderator of the United Church. Oliver became the fourth moderator on 17 September 1930.[8] In the new year the

Reverend R.B. Cochrane, secretary of the home missions board, and Dr. C. Endicott accompanied Oliver on his tour of the drought-stricken Saskatchewan areas. A United Church *Record and Missionary Review* issue of November 1931 painted this desolate picture:

> Nothing but sand, wide-reaching sand, powdered and shifting relentlessly, wind-shipped, sun-scorched, cutting as a razor any tender roots that dared to try to grow . . . Here and there as spectres of a ruined town rose the gaunt mockery of grain elevators to remind men of unfulfilled hopes and labors lost.

In January 1931 Oliver convened a meeting in Regina which "led to the establishment of the National Emergency Relief Committee by August. The original intent of the committee was to try to provide clothing for the destitute in western areas but this goal was quickly expanded to provide food as well."[9] The Reverend Mr. Cochrane became chairman of the committee. Both levels of government soon became involved and in September the federal government agreed to pay the freight on the first twenty rail cars of relief sent to western Canada. In time, the two major railways began transporting all relief supplied "no charge."[10] The encouraging feature of the situation was the readiness of other districts in the province to come to the rescue — Yorkton, Canora, Wynyard, Theodore. A voluntary rural relief committee worked energetically to secure help.[11]

Later, to honour Dr. Oliver, who had devoted his life to the prairies "even though he had received throughout his career offers to take powerful and prestigious positions in Eastern Canada,"[12] the alumni of St. Andrew's College presented him with his portrait, painted by J.W.L. Forster of Toronto.[13] It was hung in the college on 19 September 1933, at a ceremony presided over by the Reverend A.M. Nicholson, president of the alumni association, who was responsible for procuring the portrait.

The relief officer appointed by the federal government in the autumn of 1931 had the authority to issue vouchers for groceries at the rate of five dollars a month per man and wife, plus one dollar per child, to a maximum of ten dollars a month. He could not give vouchers for clothing, but he knew St. Stephen's United Church received clothing from the east. Sandy remembered working closely with the relief officer. "It wasn't long until I was doing a land office business in distributing used clothing. You'd have some fine men's suits, almost new, and lots of ladies' dresses, coats and high-heeled shoes, but barely any children's clothing." The community set up a volunteer relief committee with the Anglican clergyman, the Reverend Mr. Ashmore, as president and Sandy as secretary. The CNR section foreman delivered to outlying areas. Eventually, the Red Cross became involved and used the local committee in a consultative capacity.

Years later, Sandy gave a graphic description of the people he had come to represent, and for whom he hoped to help achieve a better standard of living. He cited the case of a veteran who came to his constituency under the northern settlers' reestablishment plan "under what was known as the $300 scheme. The provincial government, the federal government and the city of Regina each contributed $100, and with this amount the family was supposed to become self-supporting. [Besides the $50 for house building] . . . they were allowed $100 to purchase farm stock and implements and an allowance of $10 a month for foodstuffs."[14]

Sandy was not merely a man of many words, but also one who acted on his convictions. Mrs. Hawke, wife of the lumberyard owner, wrote: "Sandy Nicholson, as our first United Church parson with his young wife . . . to better appreciate the position of these unfortunate people during those dreadful depression days . . . voluntarily lived on a relief allowance for one month. Their diet ran heavily to potatoes and porridge. To remedy these conditions he sought a larger sphere of influence" and entered politics.[15] The daughter of Bill Morgan, the ferry operator on the Red Deer River in the 1930s, remembered stories about Sandy returning home from visits to outlying areas in his stocking feet more than once. He had encountered a homesteader who needed boots, and had left his for the man. The social gospel, towards which Sandy gravitated, required a concrete response to human needs.

The only source of revenue for many local people was the cutting and selling of cordwood. The Nicholsons burned wood exclusively in their house furnace and also at the church, buying their supply from the settlers. Sandy also had contacts in the wood business in Regina and Saskatoon. Although such companies sold coal chiefly, there was always a demand for some wood and they paid one dollar a cord. (A cord of wood is a pile of sticks four feet in length, piled four feet high and eight feet long.) It took seventeen cords to fill a boxcar. Sandy negotiated contracts of carloads for settlers with special needs, such as those who required money for medical costs. Before a homesteader could cut and sell wood from his unimproved lot, the government required him to purchase a two-dollar permit. Then he had to make a further payment of twenty-five cents for each cord cut and sold. It took a man nearly a day to cut a cord and another full day to haul a load to market and then to transfer it to a boxcar, or use it for barter. Storekeepers in most small communities had hundreds of cords of wood for which they had given groceries, and they had difficulty selling it. Porcupine Plain, for example, became known as the "cordwood city of the north."

As a work with wages programme, the provincial government decided to start clearing land for a road from Hudson Bay Junction north to the Manitoba boundary. Those in charge called on the rural relief committees to recommend settlers in order to give everyone a fair share of the jobs available. Sandy said, "We had ten people for every job. The wages were low and applied on the welfare people received. In some cases these men would come forty miles from their homesteads for two weeks' work, leaving the women and children at home fending for themselves."

Not long after the Nicholsons moved into their new home, Albert Webb, an unemployed CNR engineer who was also proprietor of a store at Doncrest, near Weekes, came to inquire the cost of a marriage ceremony. Webb knew of a couple who wished to be married — a young immigrant, and his fiancée who had arrived recently from Yugoslavia and could not speak English. Sandy informed him, "No charge." "It was an unusual marriage" Sandy recalled later. "Jim Machala and the girl were engaged in the old country and they expected to be married, but the little girl was born after Jim left for Canada. So on 24 October 1930, we had a wedding and a christening — the first in our house."

Webb's parents, Mr. and Mrs. H.K. Webb, who had recently come to homestead in the Doncrest area, lived in a large log building suitable for services. They, along with others, wanted United Church services. Thus began Sandy's stint as the "walking parson." He took the train to Kakwa (later called Bertwell), and from there he used quite a good trail through the bush — ten to twelve miles to Webb's. By this time, a request to have services at Porcupine Plain had come — a further distance of twenty-four miles. So it was decided that Sandy would be at Doncrest on Monday, that he would break the trip some place on Tuesday, and have a service in Porcupine Plain on Wednesday, returning to Hudson Bay Junction by train on Thursday.

In those Depression days, missionary work inevitably involved seeing to both spiritual and physical nourishment. The first time the relief officer went to the Doncrest area he invited Sandy to attend the meeting in Webb's store. Eighty people arrived. Sandy made a list of the children in the homes where clothing was needed and he gave the list to the relief committee in Hudson Bay Junction that worked with Marian from the Nicholsons' basement. Parcels were made up for the needy and were taken by Sandy on the train to Kakwa where he was met by H.K. Webb, who was driving a team of horses. Among the parcels was one for an immigrant family known to be in need, but who had not applied for assistance because neighbours felt it was scandalous that so many people received relief, and they became judge and jury, insinuating to immigrants they might be sent back to Europe if they asked for help. Canadian historian Carl Berger has explained this phenomenon: "The anti-foreign feeling that had been heightened during the war had by no means vanished in the later 1920s and 1930s."[16]

Sandy found upon delivering this clothing that all the settlers had was a stack of hay and a baby about the age of the Nicholsons' little girl, Ruth. He was profoundly moved by this scene for, as he recalled years later, "I never saw a child that looked less as though she would pull through, and her mother couldn't nurse her." Fortunately, John Joynt, Lucknow's Conservative MP who was a member of the United Church there, had heard about Sandy's appeals and sent a fifty-dollar cheque. Sandy suggested that the money be used to purchase a cow for the family. The family suspected some catch.

"No, no," Sandy said. "We'll call this the missionary cow. This will tide you over and sometime she will be passed on to somebody who is in greater need."

Dr. Oliver sent the superintendent of missions to take pictures which appeared in *The New Outlook* in December 1931. The head office of the United Church also prepared a picture story on slides and this show was used when appeals were being made for relief aid. Six months after delivering the cow, Sandy and Webb visited the family and found that the baby had blossomed into a beautiful child. The other children were obviously healthier, too.

"You have come for the cow," the family chorused. Sandy assured them that the gentleman who had supplied the cow would be happy she had made such a difference to their life, and the cow would remain with them.

On his missionary treks, Sandy stopped at Somme, one of the new stations on the CNR line between Reserve Junction and Crooked River, southeast of Hudson Bay Junction. The name Somme was chosen because of the large number of World War I veterans who had moved north when 160-acre sections became available for ten dollars each. Sandy avoided calling at mealtimes and often went hungry because most families had no food to spare.

He said, "I always had good meals at Webb's and usually carried a few chocolate bars in order to pass up the noon meals. I would make a lot of calls [in the morning] but walk between 11:00 AM and 1:00 PM. By the time I turned up people assumed I had eaten. Anyway it was never an embarrassing situation for them, but I always had an appetite when I reached Somme where Charlie Quan served a good meal for thirty-five cents."

Charlie Quan and his partners owned several restaurants in southern Saskatchewan. When commercial travellers told them that the new district had no café, Quan opened one. Sandy had called at the New Somme Café for the first time one day when he was walking from Doncrest to Porcupine Plain. "The building was like so many of the pioneer places, about sixteen feet by twenty feet with a few tables and chairs and a few groceries in the front, with kitchen and sleeping quarters at the rear," he recalled. When Quan learned that Sandy was conducting services once a month, "no charge," he offered to close his café for an hour and take his gas light to the community hall next door, as he did for other community affairs. After the services people often waited with questions for Sandy. Some wished to be married. Sandy explained there would be "no charge" because he could publish the bans, thus eliminating the necessity of a licence. Should someone give him an envelope containing money, he would pass it on to the bride, and he would whisper to the groom, "If you want to impress the bride, put more in!"

Quan suggested that Sandy sleep at his home. He took the upper bunk and gave Sandy the lower. "While they had neither springs nor mattresses they were not unlike other board beds of the era," Sandy remembered. The two men became friends; Sandy would be instrumental in assisting other members of the Quan family to emigrate to Canada in the 1950s. In 1913 Charlie Quan had sold a portion of his small farm in China in order to pay the five hundred-dollar head tax[17] and to buy a one-way ticket to Canada. Canadian immigration law at that time neither permitted him to become a Canadian citizen nor to bring his family to

Canada. While he worked in Somme, serving meals at thirty-five cents, making and selling ice cream, in addition to doing all his own baking, Quan made sufficient money to send to China for his elder son Ping to attend university, while his daughter trained to be a teacher. Ping graduated with an engineering degree. In August 1938, Quan spent a weekend with the Nicholsons at Hudson Bay Junction. He had sold the Somme Café and planned to return to China permanently, following a visit to Toronto, but, by the time he was ready to leave Toronto, World War II was in progress and this altered his plans. He stayed in Toronto for a while, then moved back to Saskatchewan. After Sandy became member of Parliament for Mackenzie, Quan requested permission for his son to take his master's degree in engineering at the University of Toronto. The war prevented this also. The head tax was formally repealed only in 1947 and Quan then became a Canadian citizen. Sandy simmered at the injustice of the restrictive immigration laws and addressed them when he sat in the House of Commons.

In May 1947 Sandy spoke to a bill on immigration, confining his remarks to the part of the bill affecting the appeal of the Chinese Immigration Act. Parliament was asked to alter the act but to keep those of Chinese origin in an inferior position. Sandy objected "to having legislation which says that we shall have one law for Asiatics, another for Scots, another for French, and another for people from another country . . . If Canada is going to subscribe seriously to the principles of the United Nations, then I say we cannot afford to have racial discrimination in our statutes, or to have orders-in-council which give effect to racial prejudice." He illustrated how diligently Charlie Quan had worked as "cashier, waiter, cook and dishwasher; he ran the entire establishment. One day his total sales amounted to only five cents for a package of chewing gum, and on another day two chocolate bars comprised his total sales."[18]

Charlie Quan's meagre sales in 1931 reflected the plight of prairie people during the Depression. Serious crop failures, the low price of farm products, and the lengthy welfare rolls also created major problems in financing the operation of schools. In rural districts school boards had no money other than the school grant, which amounted to one dollar a day, and teachers often received only the grant and their board for teaching. When Sandy conducted evening services at Frederick's Mill near Mistatim he noticed many children were in attendance. He inquired about their education and learned that they did not have a school in the area. He wrote to complain to the local member of the Saskatchewan Legislative Assembly. The Saskatchewan Department of Education acted to provide a local school building. In homestead areas such as Hudson Bay Junction, where it was impossible to sell school debentures, settlers could undertake to build schoolhouses from local materials with voluntary labour, and a two hundred-dollar grant towards expenses would be made available. The 1933 annual report of the Department of Education stated:

> This policy of assisting districts that show a willingness to cooperate and a desire to keep out of debt has far-reaching effects. A district that early learns the lesson of economy is not likely to present a problem at a later date through extravagant expenditure.[19]

When the Frederick's Mill School opened, Glen Hanna came as teacher. Another two hundred-dollar school, called Dunwell, was built in the district. Area mills could saw lumber for five dollars a thousand feet, but money was needed for windows and other furnishings, so the district men cut all the lumber for the flooring, roofing and for the desks with a whip saw. Glen Hanna went to Dunwell School when Frederick's Mill School closed. Next, Sandy initiated the Nixonville School, near Weekes.

During his missionary treks, Sandy often visited district schools. He visited Erwood at its first Christmas affair, bringing candies and nuts donated by eastern United Churches. The railway section foreman's children were the only ones who had seen nuts before, so they busily exchanged peanuts for walnut and hazel nuts, as the other children could break the peanuts with their fingers but did not know how to manage harder shells.

One teacher recalled of Sandy:

> He did not come garbed in clerical collar or cossack [cassock] gown but dressed in sensible bushman's attire and high boots for he traversed the country on foot. He walked miles through forest and swamps and visited and held prayer services in cabins wherever he stopped. When the day ended he was welcomed to spend the night to rest from his long travel, then in the morning breakfasted he would be on his trek to the next cabin. Thus one day he came upon the little Souchez School where I taught. We welcomed him and he was invited to speak to the children. He told them he had walked from Hudson Bay Junction, a distance of more than thirty miles and they listened to the adventures of his travels, followed by a Bible story. Though a sophisticated and educated young man, Sandy Nicholson never lost the common touch. He regularly visited the men in the lumber camps at Greenbush, Mile 20, Prairie River, Orley, Bamack, Mistatim and Crooked River and the lumberjacks welcomed him as a brother and were at ease in his presence. My father and brothers worked in the lumber mill in Prairie River and spoke highly of him and appreciated the visits he made at the mill.[20]

In developing a school system these homesteaders in northeastern Saskatchewan "grappled with problems such as the fluctuating school year, which in turn emanated from farm labour conditions, inclement weather, poor transportation facilities and epidemics."[21] In addition, problems including poor water supply, inadequate heating and lighting, lack of hygienic facilities and classroom equipment plagued them. Pupils often spoke a foreign language at home, studying and speaking English only during school hours. A young woman from Sandy's constituency, Nettie Forsiuk, wrote:

> We attended Evadale School which was a one-room building accommodating 89 students when we came

on the scene. In due course, it was partitioned into two rooms but High School was still available only by correspondence. Books, or reading matter of any kind, were difficult to come by and it was a constant struggle to get an education and to come up with sufficient funds for books . . . I dug seneca roots, picked berries to sell in town and if this didn't cover all the books, Mother allowed me to sell some of the vegetables from our garden . . . We hungered for information and read every scrap of newspaper that came into our home by way of wrapped groceries. It was indeed, a very enlightened programme which the CCF introduced when they supplied books to schools in outlying areas.[22]

This young woman went to Ottawa in 1943 after working her way through business college in Yorkton. She stuffed envelopes for the CCF and eventually, with some help from Sandy, found employment on Parliament Hill where her efficient secretarial skills elevated her to a responsible management position.

During his first two years at Hudson Bay Junction in the 1930s, Sandy encountered so much misery that he continually encouraged his United Church superiors to visit his area and see for themselves the plight of the poverty-stricken people. Dr. Nicol finally found an opportunity to visit in December 1932. His impressions appeared in an article in *The New Outlook*:

Mr. Nicholson met me on Friday night at Frederick's Mill, some 45 miles west of the Junction. It was nearing nine o'clock when we arrived at the schoolhouse where service was to be held. Notwithstanding the lateness of our arrival, we found the schoolhouse full of people, young and old. And what a cheery welcome awaited us! It was the time of Mr. Nicholson's monthly visit to the place and all were expectant. An outsider would be dull indeed if from the rollicking enthusiasm of the boys and girls and warm reception of the older people, he did not realize that Mr. Nicholson is the idol of the children, the trusted friend of the young, and the adviser and helper of the older ones upon whom fall the burdens of the day which are perplexing for all, but distressing and almost overwhelming for those who are out of work, and whose families have scarcely enough for the barest subsistence. But as the whole community, Anglo-Saxon and non-Anglo-Saxon, surrounded a common altar and sang the common tunes and listened to the familiar words from the Old Book, their worldly cares were, for a time at least, not uppermost . . .[23]

Dr. Nicol signed the Nicholson guestbook at Hudson Bay Junction on Sunday, 18 December 1932. He and Sandy left at 6:00 AM next morning on a mixed train to visit Doncrest township, thirty-five miles southwest. Dr. Nicol's article stated that here "a year ago, took place the community Christmas-tree at which Mr. Nicholson married a couple, baptized some children and made 125 boys and girls happy by the distribution of Christmas gifts sent to him from the Humboldt United Sunday School."[24]

H.K. Webb met the men at Bertwell station and took them by horse and sleigh to his home where "Mrs. Webb, whose hospitality is known far and wide, was ready" for them with a steaming hot turkey dinner before they left for Doncrest school, bearing more presents from Humboldt. Dr. Nicol continued:

When we arrived at the fine log schoolhouse . . . more than 200 crowded in and around the building. The great majority of them were from the one township . . . Many walked three [to five] miles in order not to miss it. But how disappointed were some. One little girl had no shoes, her father told us, and the mother could not come "Because she has no good feels today." Although there is no schoolteacher there yet, the children had been trained to say their "pieces" and dialogues and sing the choruses . . . Mr. Nicholson was chairman. [My heavy part in the programme] consisted for the most part of lifting the artists up on a box which did service as a platform upon which the little ones stood when they said their pieces.[25]

The excitement of the programme and the anticipation

of receiving the gifts gave great happiness to the children. For the adults, the entertainment aroused memories of past Christmases, and during the singing of some carols tears misted eyes and overflowed down cheeks. For most, this evening was only a lull. Tomorrow they would have to face the same stern conditions and problems. Next day, Dr. Nicol and Sandy travelled to Somme. On the way they stopped to see the "missionary cow." Dr. Nicol's account continued:

> At Somme we had an evening service of worship. Every person in the little village except one man who was sick, and his son, was in attendance. Here also Mr. Nicholson acted as Santa Claus for the children. On Wednesday we went to Porcupine Plain . . . [where] the public school is in operation with an enrolment of 60 . . . We held a service during the evening in the community hall. About 100 were in attendance. Seven children were baptized. [In the area] we had warm welcome at many homes but at none was the welcome more hearty than at the Frasers' . . . Although Mrs. Fraser is confined to her bed, no Highland welcome could have been more hearty, and the warm expression of appreciation of our visit was more than sufficient recompense for a trudge over [poor] trails.[26]

Back in the village, the toot of the slow-moving train signalled time to leave, and to return to Hudson Bay Junction. The men arrived late Thursday night to find Marian and Ruth just back from the east where they attended the funeral of Marian's father.[27]

Besides the bare existence they could eke out in the area, settlers also suffered from lack of health services. Sandy later described the situation in his constituency in the 1930s:

> The Hudson Bay Junction district was served by one medical doctor who cared for farmers, townsfolk and about 800 men working in the bush. But when the depression came, and the sawmill operators could not sell their lumber, many of the mills closed down. At the same time, large numbers of people in the drought

area came north, and brought with them little money . . . Dr. Collins, who practiced in [the village] at that time left and we were without a doctor for some considerable time. There was not a doctor within 70 miles when he left . . . [In 1935] when the Liberal government decided to do something about these people they made the provision for $50 a month to pay the doctor. The doctor had to agree that every person who was on relief would come to him and receive treatment. He was not prevented from making additional collections. But people who were getting $10 a month for relief and selling cordwood at $1 a cord were not likely to be able to pay much to a medical doctor.[28]

The Board of Trade asked Sandy to advertise in the Saskatoon *Star-Phoenix* for a doctor. The arrival of Dr. R.M. Cumberland headlined the local paper, *Junction Judge,* on 17 March 1932.[29] Dr. Cumberland had a difficult time supporting his wife and four children on the meagre salary, for few local residents could pay him, and the salaried railroaders preferred to travel by pass to doctors in Saskatoon or Winnipeg. The Nicholsons' first child, Marian Ruth, was born in City Hospital, Saskatoon, on 22 May 1931, when Hudson Bay Junction had no resident doctor. Their guestbook featured the signature of Dr. R.B. Cochrane of Toronto, with a note, "Baptized the babe — a great honour," on 19 July 1931.

Sandy and Marian's second child, Norman Nicholson, was born in Hudson Bay Junction on 15 June 1932, but the baby lived only four days. Dr. Oliver wrote a letter of condolence, saying, "May you both feel the Divine nearness in this trial."[30] A little later when a woman came to the Nicholsons' door selling pint sealers of strawberries at twenty-five cents each, Marian said, "You can't afford to be selling these."

The woman replied, "We're expecting our first baby and have no money. I've been to see the doctor and he can't come out to our place. I would have to come to town to the nursing home."

Marian invited her to come and talk to Sandy in his

study. The woman told of two previous generations of mothers who had died in childbirth, and she was understandably terrified. The relief officer had indicated it would cost thirty dollars to go to the nursing home, a sum beyond her means. Sandy wrote a letter and in due course the woman was accepted at Tisdale hospital. "But the relief officer in refusing to authorize the thirty dollars reminded her that her neighbours managed without coming to town."

In 1933 when Marian became pregnant again, the rheumatic fever she had suffered as a child recurred. Sandy wrote his sister Norma of the ordeal:

> This has been a very anxious Easter in our home. What we feared, but hoped against, happened on Saturday, when Marian had a miscarriage. With her heart condition, as a result of inflammatory rheumatism . . . it was very serious.

> The local doctor felt by the afternoon that there was very little hope. I had him phone Anna in the hopes that there might be something else, and she decided to come by plane. They made the trip in just a little over two hours. Marian took new hope when she heard Anna was coming and felt that if she could only last till Anna came she would come around. After Anna felt her pulse, I heard her remark to the Dr. that she was afraid she was nearly gone. However Marian kept fighting on, and by Sunday morning was a good deal better. Since then she has steadily improved, and unless complications set in, she should come around. We feel she owes her life to Anna.[31]

Anna Nicholson by then had a medical practice in Saskatoon. There was no road access to Hudson Bay Junction from the city and no scheduled train would get her there soon enough. A bush pilot in Saskatoon offered to fly her to the village, although no plane had ever landed before at the Junction. The pilot gave instructions for the local people to prepare a safe place to land. The *Star-Phoenix* reported:

> Chartering the M. & C. Aviation Company's cabin plane "Lady Wildfire", Dr. Nicholson winged her way north with Pilot Angus Campbell at the controls.[32]

Anna wrote to Norma:

> The landing was rather treacherous. So little cleared
> land, and so much bush, but they had fires lit on their
> field and he was a good pilot. Of course the whole
> town was out . . . The people were so kind, brought
> in all kinds of food, and a man every night to be a
> janitor, keep the fires and any odd jobs. They have
> given so much up there . . .[33]

Sandy could afford the two hundred dollars for the
airplane trip, although this sum was a year's income for
many at the time. He thought it seemed a pity that having
enough money to charter a plane should be the factor in
saving a life. Little did Sandy know at the time, but this
flight by Anna would eventually trigger a government air
ambulance service which would regularly make dramatic
flights into remoter settlements to rescue patients who were
then flown to city hospitals, "no charge." Sandy believed
his petitions to the Douglas government encouraged the
initiation of the Saskatchewan Air Ambulance Service. On
3 February 1946, the first mercy flight took off

> on the heels of an old-fashioned prairie blizzard
> which had blocked highways and roads in every
> direction. The Norseman aircraft with Pilot Keith
> Malcolm at the controls, demonstrated its usefulness in
> a fast trip to Liberty, Saskatchewan, about 50 air miles
> northwest of Regina. It landed in a stubble field, less
> than 100 yards from the patient's home, and brought
> her safely to Regina.[34]

Life was not all calamities in Hudson Bay Junction. Hugh
and Kay MacKinnon had arrived shortly after the
Nicholsons. Hugh was CNR locomotive foreman, and Kay
became the church organist. At the church's first sports day
Sandy won the five-dollar prize for the one hundred-yard
dash, beating a surprised Hugh MacKinnon, who had never
been defeated in this race before. Sandy "selected a five-
dollar silver pitcher in the Kowalenkow store instead of
cash to preserve his amateur status." The Nicholsons, the
MacKinnons, and five other families formed a group called
the Rinkey Dinks. Kay MacKinnon wrote: "Each week we

would have a gathering of some kind. Treasure hunts, kids' parties or just talk fests. Each family bought a book one year, when they had read it passed it along to another family, so we each had seven books to read. We would then discuss the contents, which gave us diverse reactions to the contents. We never lacked for activities — played tennis, the men played hockey and baseball. Sandy was always there to do his part."[35]

The first weekly edition of the *Junction Judge* appeared on 30 November 1931. Glancing through the first few editions shows that hockey was in full swing. "The Hudson Bay Junction All Stars were challenging all comers and a hair-raising broomball league took over where hockey left off."[36] Committees of the Board of Trade were busy trying to establish a Red Cross Outpost hospital there, and a notice said the highway from Hudson Bay Junction would be completed in the spring. Sandy remembered that radio became important as the Depression deepened, as it provided a diversion from the hopelessness besetting many people. One of Prime Minister R.B. Bennett's most unexpected creations in 1932 was the Canadian Radio Broadcasting Commission (CRBC) which came about largely as a result of efforts on the part of the Canadian Radio League, formed by Graham Spry and Alan Plaunt in 1930. The Radio League had pressed for a Canadian-owned national broadcasting system, which would free Canadians from the influence of the commercialized networks of the United States.[37] Sandy agreed with the premise. Much later, he and Graham Spry became political partners.

In Hudson Bay Junction, the Nicholsons spearheaded an assault on the lack of culture, bringing entertainment to northeastern Saskatchewan long before T.C. Douglas would state:

> I've always maintained that people of the prairies, by virtue of the fact that we haven't got many of the advantages of living in a city like New York or London, are hungry for what are commonly described as things of the mind and the spirit — good music, literature, drama, paintings and folksongs.[38]

Under Marian's direction, the Women's Association of St. Stephen's United Church decided that an annual play would provide not only cash for the church but also fun for the cast and entertainment for the community. Looking backward, the *Junction Judge* reported that because there was insufficient money to pay the Dominion Electric Company, the street lights were turned off for the week of 10 March 1932. After two weeks of darkness, the street lights were lit in time to illuminate the throngs on their way to St. Stephen's Church, "the setting for a splendid musical staged by local and visiting artists."[39] A month later *Bashful Mr. Bobbs,* a comedy, was presented at the Gaiety Theatre with the Reverend A.M. Nicholson starring in the cast.[40] In the third week of April, "Mrs. A.M. Nicholson picked the first pansies from her garden . . . Lard sold at 9¢ a pound, and the football season was underway, with the tennis courts in shape and the first games played the previous week."[41]

Still, the fun times could not erase the hardships Sandy encountered regularly on his circuit. He often left church literature at homes, and the father in a poor family drew his attention to the unrealistic stories in the Sunday School pamphlets. The man said, "No doubt you are saying to yourself, there is no excuse for people being dirty. We have read a great many stories about families being very, very poor but very, very clean. You can take it from me that poverty and cleanliness do not go hand in hand. Have you ever tried washing without soap? . . . Well, this morning I thought I would have a wash for a change and asked, 'Mary, where is the soap?' She said, 'We haven't had any soap in the house for ten days.'

"I do not use tobacco; I do not use liquor. When I get my relief allowance, if there is a five cent piece that has not been spent, I tell the storekeeper to put in another cake of soap or another spool of thread."[42] The enquiring mind of the young pastor began to question a form of society where some starve while others feast.[43] The social gospel premise regarding the quality of life on earth pushed Sandy into striving "to realize the Kingdom of God in the very fabric of society."[44]

Chapter 6

Kingdom of Heaven on Earth, 1933-1935

R eminiscing about the political struggles of the 1930s at a dinner party in the Parliamentary Restaurant in September 1983, Stanley Knowles said, "Sandy was a United Church minister and practiced a religious approach to social problems at first. His goal was, and still is, to improve living conditions for all people. He decided it was necessary to get into politics to do this. You see, we were all ministers — Woodsworth, Douglas, myself and Sandy. But we believed in a better life now — here on earth — not hereafter. Religion lost its appeal for him as it failed to improve social conditions for people generally. He decided the CCF struggle was the place where he could put his ideas for social reform into practice. He wanted to make life more factual and good in perspective."[1] Social gospellers all, each of the four men had found that "the sense of an immanent God working in the movements of revival and awakening was easily transferred to social movements."[2]

In 1932 when the Farmer-Labour party formed in Saskatchewan, its ideology appealed to Sandy. He recalled, "My father was a very enthusiastic Liberal. If I had been the CCF candidate running in Bruce County when he lived he would have found it difficult to decide to vote for me."

Unlike conservatively-minded Ontario, Saskatchewan had a long tradition of social democratic ideas and collective co-operation. The United Farmers of Canada (UFC), Saskatchewan section, decided at their 1931 annual convention to take political action, and within a few months activity began at the constituency level. In July 1932 the UFC and the Independent Labour party in the province united to form the Saskatchewan Farmer-Labour party. The leaders of this new party played a major role in launching the national CCF in Calgary one week later.[3] The Nicholsons became the first members of the Farmer-Labour group in Hudson Bay Junction in the autumn of 1932. To encourage others to join, Sandy bought additional cordwood from local people who expressed an interest in becoming party members, thus enabling them to earn the one-dollar membership fee.

At the same time the Reverend T.C. Douglas was experiencing similar effects of the Depression, and in 1934, when he was minister of the Weyburn Baptist Church in southern Saskatchewan, "he organized the unemployed and found the means to keep them clothed and fed. Realizing what he was doing was too little, he wrote to his old friend and idol, James S. Woodsworth" to seek his advice on how Douglas could do more to aid the poor.[4] Woodsworth encouraged Douglas to enter politics, and to run on the Farmer-Labour ticket for Weyburn. Douglas lost in the 1934 Saskatchewan provincial election but won the Weyburn constituency in the 1935 federal election, preceding Sandy to the House of Commons by five years. In that interval, Sandy closely associated himself with the CCF, mainly in campaigning and fund raising.

Sandy's political interests stemmed from a number of factors, among them the problems created by inadequate health care in northeastern Saskatchewan, and his personal experiences with the absence of medical facilities. As he remarked in the Saskatchewan Legislature many years later, "I am sure you will appreciate the problems of a clergyman who is called to officiate at funerals where everyone believed that, had there been medical and hospital care, death would not have come at that particular time."[5]

Following Anna's mercy flight to save Marian's life in the spring of 1933, Marian had remained bedridden from April until mid-August, and Sandy was unable to leave home for anything other than his ministerial duties. However, he began corresponding with King Gordon whom he had not seen since intercollegiate track meets during university days. In answer to a letter from Sandy, who at this time already seriously questioned his role as a minister, Gordon wrote:

> It is very good to hear of others among one's friends who are taking an active interest in the social problem from a Christian point of view . . . There is just a chance that the widespread discontent with things as they are may be directed into constructive channels, and so I, for one, have still a great deal of faith that the CCF will be able to accomplish much.[6]

At that time Gordon taught ethics at the United Theological College in Montreal and he was active in the League for Social Reconstruction (LSR). The Fellowship for a Christian Social order (FCSO) had not been organized yet although there was an active group of United Church ministers determined that the church should play a part in alleviating the social crisis that was having such a disastrous effect on the lives of thousands of Canadians.[7]

King Gordon's letter also referred to the conference on social and economic issues organized by the YMCA at its island in Lake of the Woods, near Kenora, Ontario, which Eugene Forsey, J.F. Parkinson and he were attending as speakers, en route to the CCF convention in Regina. They were taking with them a draft of the CCF manifesto, commissioned by Woodsworth, which with a few amendments became the Regina Manifesto.[8] Woodsworth received the draft before the convention opened, although he had first read it hurriedly when he had seen it at the Lake of the Woods Conference.[9] Marian's illness kept Sandy from attending the first formal convention of the CCF in Regina, 19-23 July 1933, but he soon became involved in the important Mackenzie federal constituency byelection that autumn, when the new CCF tested its strength.

Milton Campbell, a railway station agent, had been elected as Progressive member of Parliament in Mackenzie riding in 1921 and had been re-elected in 1925, 1926 and 1930. His resignation, when he was appointed to the tariff board at a salary of ten thousand dollars a year by Prime Minister R.B. Bennett, resulted in this byelection. As Sandy later commented, "When an MP resigned to take [a job with] one of these fabulous salaries there was bound to be a reaction." The CCF believed Mackenzie constituency would be a good place to begin putting forward its ideas and to gauge public opinion towards them. Although Sandy was not a voter in this byelection (Hudson Bay Junction would not be a part of Mackenzie constituency until after redistribution for the 1935 federal election), he followed the proceedings closely. "Woodsworth, Angus MacInnis and his wife Grace, who was Woodsworth's daughter, and everybody who was anybody in the CCF, were up to Mackenzie to make sure the CCF would win this first crucial election," Sandy remembered. "Who would be the CCF candidate?" While many local residents had been active in starting the party, it did not seem as if anybody in the constituency might be a winner. However, a candidate appeared in the form of Judge Lewis St. George Stubbs, a Manitoban who had declared that there was one law for the rich and one for the poor. When he could not be persuaded to relinquish this slogan he was requested to resign as a judge.[10] Stubbs's candidacy does not appear to have been his own decision. Apparently J.W. Dafoe, the famous editor of the Winnipeg *Free Press,* had the idea, and the *Free Press* publicized a story to the effect that Judge Stubbs had been invited to let his name stand for the CCF in the Mackenzie byelection. The story was headlined across the country. Nobody in Mackenzie ever admitted to having thought of this, or to being in touch with Stubbs, but neither did anybody stand against Stubbs at the nominating convention. Initially, it seemed he would be a sure winner; any judge who gave up a career because he favoured equitable sentences for both rich and poor offenders, made many friends amongst the common people.

In rural elections the weather always played an important role, and the autumn of 1933 proved no exception. Gertrude Telford of Pelly, Sandy's colleague and an avid CCF supporter, recalled an occasion when J.S. Woodsworth and Judge Stubbs were forced to spend three days at the Telford home during the campaign because rain made travel impossible. She told what a comic picture "Mr. Woodsworth with his white beard, bent over the dishpan washing dishes, and Judge Stubbs doing the drying" had made.[11] Many would have preferred Stubbs to be storm-stayed for the whole period. Friendliness turned into animosity during the campaign as Stubbs's poor judgement became apparent in the course of speeches when he told Mackenzie residents how fortunate they were not to be stuck with some farmer as their candidate.

At one point Mrs. Stenen, another active woman worker said, "The only way we can win this election is to have an accident and see that Judge Stubbs goes to the hospital for the duration of the campaign. If we get him in hospital we'll win, but if he keeps on talking we'll lose!"

Sandy chuckled, "He must have been quite a character. He later became an MLA in Manitoba, but he sure took the wrong tack in Mackenzie." Liberal candidate John Angus MacMillan beat Stubbs by 1,614 votes.[12]

The CCF was down but not out, realizing that success should not be expected at the first attempt. They chalked up the byelection to experience and began preparing for the Saskatchewan provincial election scheduled for 19 June 1934, at which the party continued under the Farmer-Labour title. The first nominating convention took place in the Tisdale provincial riding, which included Hudson Bay Junction, and represented something of a beachhead in CCF history for numerous people in northeastern Saskatchewan in the 1930s. Sandy had undergone a good deal of pressure to let his name stand for nomination, and Marian, by then greatly recovered from her ordeal, agreed that since an election was not slated for another year,

Sandy had better attend the convention and let his name stand. Marian's support was crucial, and Sandy knew that she had shared his belief in a better society for all from the beginning of their relationship. Knowing the importance of a candidate's outward appearance, Marian suggested to Sandy that he wear his clerical suit; she did not believe his usual garb worn on his missionary treks — breeches and high boots — would be appropriate for the occasion. Sandy was the only Hudson Bay Junction resident at the convention, but more than two hundred others from the district attended. Nine men allowed their names to stand for the nomination and candidates spoke throughout the day, dropping out one by one.

One Melfort man who met Sandy at the convention remembered overhearing him remark to a group outside the hall during a recess, "I couldn't preach the gospel of Jesus Christ and not be a socialist."

The man commented, "That is the kind of person we need in government, but much to my disgust Sandy lost. As it happened it turned out for the best; Sandy Nicholson became one of the best. I don't think the party ever produced any better."[13]

J.B. Ennis, who had covered the riding with horse and toboggan the previous winter, was winner of the nomination. When the Farmer-Labour party organized he took on this assignment, leaving his wife and sons to look after the family farm for weeks on end. Others who had stood for nomination included John H. Brockelbank, who would be elected in the next provincial election; Percy Wright, later a federal member for Melfort; and Oakland Woods Valleau who became member of the Legislative Assembly for Melfort and then a cabinet minister. Although Sandy lost the nomination, he remained active in the party and agreed to become an organizer in the area.

During the spring of 1934 when Sandy became a CCF organizer in the provincial ridings of Pelly, Kelvington, Wadena and Tisdale, one of his objectives was to identify future party candidates. Early experience had taught him that those who did the most talking at conventions often became candidates at nominating conventions. When it came to election day, however, the party might discover that the best candidate had not been selected. Another part of his job involved scheduling public meetings for important CCF personnel who visited the area. The Nicholsons' guestbook confirms 2 June 1934 as the date M.J. Coldwell arrived in Hudson Bay Junction by CNR jigger.

Major (a name, not a rank) James Coldwell, who rated as the most effective speaker in the province, had been chosen leader of the Farmer-Labour party in Saskatchewan for the 1934 provincial election. Born in England in 1888 and educated there, Coldwell came to Alberta as a teacher in 1910 before moving to Regina where he took up a post as a school principal. Coldwell had requested permission from the Regina School Board for a leave of absence during the campaign for the 1934 election, a period extending from the first of April or May to the end of June. The board would neither grant this nor accept his resignation. What next? In his memoirs, Coldwell noted:

> A former pupil of my Sedley school days, Willie Bunn, had a small plane — a little Monocoupe. He offered to fly me to points in the province for speaking engagements . . . for a minimum charge, covering gas and oil at 10¢ a mile from point to point, to include the return trip . . . By leaving school immediately it closed in the afternoon and having a car ready to take me to the airport we could take off before five, address a meeting, stay overnight and leave, if the distance was fairly long, by six a.m., have a car at the airport run me home for a wash, and get to school on time.[14]

The Farmer-Labour party officials had approached Sandy to set up an afternoon meeting in Hudson Bay Junction, as Coldwell was scheduled to speak at an evening meeting in Tisdale. Coldwell's airplane developed engine trouble and the pilot decided to land at Crooked River. Coldwell's memoirs continued, "We came down safely on a piece of rough ground. I telephoned Hudson Bay Junction.

Nicholson suggested we might be able to get permission to use the jigger."

The delay in arrival meant a four o'clock meeting, so Marian cancelled the planned lunch. Coldwell downed some ginger ale — he had an aversion to local water, and went off to the meeting, which Sandy chaired. It was at this meeting that Sandy made his first political appeal for funds to cover the cost of the two-dollar hall rental and a part of the expenses for the plane used to bring Mr. Coldwell. One of the things which impressed Allan Blakeney years later, when Sandy had perfected his fund-raising approach, was

> the vigor with which he went out to raise money for the CCF. He made absolutely no apology for asking people for money. He used to argue that when he asked somebody for money he was doing them a favour. Sandy would explain this by saying that the CCF was a cause that they should support and that they knew in their hearts they should support. If he persuaded them to make a substantial donation they would be doing something which they knew they should be doing and would feel better within themselves for having done it. In this way he was conferring a positive benefit on anyone who he persuaded to make a substantial donation to the CCF. Sandy could put this argument with a great passion and conviction. I have heard him do it several times complete with the smile and little chuckle which was characteristic of Sandy.[15]

In the villages and towns where residents' activities were an open book, few secrets could be kept about political alignments. Attendance at CCF events often resulted in strained friendships and severed business connections. Sandy recalled,

> John Sykes, an insurance agent from Winnipeg, came to hear Coldwell. One of the local merchants cancelled a life insurance policy with him when he learned he had been at the meeting. When a CNR conductor — a CCFer — heard about the loss of the five thousand-dollar policy, he took out one for ten thousand dollars to compensate. So the insurance

agent didn't do too badly that time. The first visit of Coldwell to Hudson Bay Junction made a deep impression on everyone, including my wife and me.

The day before the provincial election, Sykes and Sandy took the train to Prairie River to canvass the town. They walked the four miles to Frederick's Mill where the men worked shifts around the clock. At the supper break they arranged to speak to the members of both crews and had an excellent hearing. Sykes predicted a 100 percent vote for the Farmer-Labour party from this mill. After they left, the owner held a meeting to undo their good work, saying, "Now if there's anybody who is not satisfied with conditions here and you want to vote for this new party, fine, but you'll be out of a job the day after tomorrow." Ballots indicated one vote for the Farmer-Labour party at Frederick's Mill. The party fared badly all across the province on 18 June 1934, electing only five of its candidates, who became known as "the Quints" after the Dionne quintuplets born in May that year: Andrew MacAuley, Cut Knife; Herman Kemper, Gull Lake; Louis Hantelman, Kindersley; Clarence Stork, Shaunavon; George H. Williams, Wadena. Coldwell would be elected the following year and would serve for twenty-three years in the federal Parliament.

Sandy believed that the party's inexperience at the polls contributed to the Farmer-Labour defeat. For example, in those days, there were no printed nomination forms and the nomination papers for Joe Phelps, Farmer-Labour candidate for Melfort, had been filed without his written consent. Poll officials discovered this discrepancy two minutes before the closing time for nominations in Melfort riding and Phelps, who lived fifty miles away could not be reached, so his candidacy for the Farmer-Labour party became invalid. Then, in the Yorkton riding, where Llewellyn Foster ran on the Farmer-Labour ticket, troubles arose when it became known he had changed his name from Fletcher to Foster, due to health problems suffered during his tenure as a United Church minister; some voters suspected that this was not the real reason for his change of name, and cast their ballots for other candidates. Sandy said, "Thus we had a candidate who ran under an alleged name and another who didn't know how to file papers properly."

When it became apparent he would enter the political arena, Sandy bought his first car, paying $150 for a second-hand Model A Ford. Before he allowed his name to stand as a federal candidate in Mackenzie, he visited Myron Feeley at Preeceville, finding him busy delivering grain to the elevator. Sandy made two trips with him in the cab of his truck, talking non-stop "Nicholson-style," about the political situation. When he asked Feeley if he would be the candidate for the next election, Feeley declined. Working his way into the monologue, Feeley told Sandy he had taken a thrashing during the Mackenzie byelection, "when it was all over, I was out-of-pocket $1,500," he said. Feeley had been the key person for the area until Stubbs's nomination, then an organizer arrived from Winnipeg announcing "there would be lots of money." However, this organizer had incurred numerous debts, while Stubbs travelled east on a speaking tour with the intention of bringing back "thousands of dollars," but failed to cover even his expenses. Creditors complained to Feeley and forced him to pay the bills personally before voting day. This put him in the hands of the debt adjustment board. Had he not been able to prove the money belonged to his wife, he would have lost his land. Nonetheless, Feeley encouraged Sandy to accept the Mackenzie nomination. Four years later, having recuperated from his earlier financial setback, Feeley became member of the Legislative Assembly for Canora and held that seat for ten years.

Sandy sought reassurance from another quarter. He heard that in 1933 the board of governors of the United Theological College in Montreal refused to renew King Gordon's appointment on the grounds of economy. Many thought the real reason for Gordon's dismissal in 1934 was his radical views.[16] In a letter to Gordon dated 14 October 1934, Sandy shared his concerns:

I have read the account of your case in the *New*

Outlook and I want to tell you that you have a great many admirers in the West. How long can you endure the struggle in the Church? There are so few within the church who have any vision about a Christian social order, that I feel like spending my energy along other lines. There is a possibility that I might be asked to take the CCF nomination in the now famous Mackenzie Constituency. Although it seems certain that a Liberal will be elected, I have been seriously thinking of undertaking the educational work of a campaign. It would mean resigning from the church, and what would happen to my family and myself after an unsuccessful campaign, I cannot say. It seems certain that a crisis will come during our lifetime, and it seems urgent to me that as many as possible should know the nature of the economic conflict.

The head office of the United Farmers organization in Saskatoon at that time arranged nominating conventions for the CCF, and called an executive meeting of the Mackenzie constituency in Preeceville to set a date in that riding. Sandy attended the executive meeting and agreed to the 23 November date, announcing that if he was nominated he would tender his resignation to the United Church to take effect at the end of December. Campaigning for the next federal election, expected in 1935, would be a full-time undertaking. Mackenzie constituency, an old and historic one and the only one left known by its original name, ranged 104 miles east and west and 621 miles north and south, including 26 towns and more than 28,000 electors.[17]

By 23 November roads were frozen and it was possible to travel from Hudson Bay Junction to Preeceville without too much trouble. Sandy took a carload of observers to the convention.

Next day Art Menzies, editor of the *Junction Judge*, nominated Sandy and he was unanimously elected as candidate for Mackenzie constituency.

In his acceptance speech, Sandy said that if he was elected he would do his best to get the government in power "to enact legislation to provide that the wealth and work of Canada shall be distributed more fairly and equitably."[18] He promised to do his share "in the world's work and the world's struggle" — the nucleus of Woodsworth's philosophy which had impressed him so much at SCM conferences. Sandy celebrated his thirty-fourth birthday on Sunday 25 November by having friends visit the Nicholson home after church, and by announcing his resignation to the United Church, to take effect at the end of the year.

United Church officials responded in various ways to Sandy's resignation, although all expressed sorrow at his leaving. The Reverend Charles Endicott wrote:

> I should like you to feel that I have greatly admired your character and your devotion to duty. I would like to wish you success but I cannot honestly do that in your political work. I am not sure that is because I am a strong Liberal, but you see I hope if you are not successful you will be back with us in the work of the church again.[19]

The Reverend J.L. Nicol, who had recruited Sandy and had witnessed his devotion to the people, acknowledged his resignation saying that "it [would] require a man of fine spiritual enthusiasm, strength of body and one who is not afraid of hard work to carry on his ministry."[20]

Acutely aware of the destitute settlers in Sandy's district, R.B. Cochrane offered the one positive note regarding the choice of Sandy's political career. He said, "No one who knows you can question for a moment your motives, and I am sure you are convinced that if elected to Parliament you can serve the people on the frontier and the Kingdom of God in a very unique and special way. Well wishes."[21]

Besides the regrets expressed by the church, the Massey family and Sandy's sisters were unhappy about Sandy's decision. As he remarked, "So many made no distinction between the CCF and the Communist party . . . but Marian by this time was familiar with how so many had to live in poverty and she was in agreement with my decision."

At St. Stephen's annual meeting in December, the congregation presented Sandy with a leather briefcase and

Marian received a bouquet of flowers. An article in the *Preeceville Progress* quoted Sandy as saying that although "the capitalistic system had treated him well, his experience while working among the people led him to socialism. [He would] resign from the pastoral charge and give his time to the teaching of socialism."[22]

Sandy tried his best to educate the residents in his constituency. Oscar Sorestad of Buchanan recalled, "I wish it was in me to print on paper all the enthusiasm he so elegantly displayed while going from door to door with me telling the disheartened people what they could expect in social and economic change, if they would elect a CCF government."[23] The concentrated educational effort, the distribution of party literature, and the calling of regular meetings were all designed "to win support for the CCF as a political instrument of the people." The party "had an internal constitution and structure which gave its members considerable control and made its leadership and parliamentary group accountable in a way totally unknown to other Canadian parties at that time."[24] Although "the keen group of intellectuals who lent their support" came from McGill and Toronto, "the LSR led by Frank Scott and Frank Underhill included such westerners as Graham Spry and King Gordon."[25] Still, the Saskatchewan CCF sustained the entire national party to a large degree, both financially and in proselytizing zeal from 1933 onward. Sandy took on the "essential individual mission work" needed then to spread the political gospel, stepping into January 1935 with a new purpose and an uncertain future.

Sandy travelled to Regina to meet George Williams, leader of the CCF opposition in the Saskatchewan Legislature. He also had lunch with the Coldwells and met Mrs. Coldwell for the first time. Mrs. Coldwell suffered from multiple sclerosis and had been to the Mayo Clinic in Rochester where the diagnosis offered no expectations of recovery. She seemed a very brave person to Sandy, and she expressed genuine interest in this young United Church minister with a wife and child who had given up a secure future in the church to be a CCF candidate.

Both Williams and Coldwell offered Sandy helpful advice, although Coldwell lacked in organizing skills, had less time to spare, and fewer financial resources available. Williams, however, suggested a practical approach to the problems Sandy might face. He understood that Sandy had saved some money, and he admonished,

> Whatever you do, don't let the people think you don't need their money. In every poll you should have a chairman, a vice-chairman, a secretary-treasurer and a committee. These committees should meet on a regular basis. You should get the names of people in the poll who would have a spare bed or could serve a meal. Tell them that when the leaders of this party — Mr. Woodsworth, Mr. Coldwell or I — go to a riding, we'd far rather stay in a home of one of our supporters than go to a hotel. You make no friends in a hotel. You're talking to people who are not likely to be supporters. But every home where you stay you'll leave some ideas, and that's very important. Keep track of these names.

> People will say, 'Our place isn't up to much, but if you're satisfied with what we have you're welcome and don't go to a hotel, don't go to a restaurant. If it's two o'clock and you haven't had a meal, my wife will always fry some eggs or something — you're working for us.'

> Now it is very important that you start from poll to poll as soon as possible. Since there's going to be an election in June [the election was not held till 14 October 1935], you'd better get a full-time organizer.

Williams had free telephone service as leader of the opposition, and, using this privilege, he arranged for Sandy and George Hope to canvass in the Wadena area in the first week of February.

Fred Stansfield, who lived in Hudson Bay Junction, expressed interest in becoming a full-time organizer for the CCF in Sandy's riding. The Dominion Electric Power Company granted him a leave of absence, and his wife and daughter went to live on her parents' farm enabling Stansfield to manage on the fifty dollars a month paid by

CCF supporters. He accompanied Sandy to George Hope's farm where the two men arranged to buy a team of beautiful white horses for one hundred dollars. Hope agreed to lend the men his harness and *caboose* (a sleigh with a little board shack built onto it, the construction of which resembled a railway caboose) until spring. With their newly acquired transportation, Sandy and Stansfield travelled from Hendon to Paswegan and Wadena, following the railway and stopping at every settlement on the line.

Sandy found the Bert McClure farm near Sturgis to be a perfect headquarters, and he formed a lasting friendship with the McClure family. The reminiscences of Berta McClure Campbell, from the view of a teenager during the 1930s,

> are of a man who seemed to care a great deal about his fellow men; who was well-versed in current affairs, but who could be just as interested in the weighty concerns of small children; who could pause during a public meeting at which he had been discussing world or national affairs and ask about the dogs and cats (by name) which he had encountered when he last visited a family.

She recalled

> that those who knew him had no qualms about firmly denying the attempted rumour that 'there would be no meeting [because] Sandy Nicholson and Bert McClure were drunk in a nearby beer parlour.' Such a stretch of the imagination!

Not only that, Berta continued,

> later when my parents found it questionable if they could afford to send me to normal school, they discussed the situation with the Nicholsons. In some way, they managed a loan and I was able to go . . . Men such as Sandy, aided by women such as Marian . . . have won respect for the CCF and [their] influence still generates a trust in the New Democratic Party.[26]

When Bert McClure learned how successful Sandy and

Stansfield had been in collecting money for the CCF in the Preeceville area, he believed the Sturgis district could do better. Sandy recalled, "We kept going till we had called at thirteen homes. There were no problems. No one said they couldn't afford the five-dollar annual fee. People thought it was a bargain if my wife and I could stay around until the next election."

The competitive collection spirit carried into the Norquay district where John Auguston felt confident the many Scandinavian settlers would readily support a canvass. Sixteen families contributed when Auguston argued that the annual fee needed to maintain a CCF organizer in the district was a bargain. Sandy soon realized they would readily find the two hundred families needed to support his salary. During the period before the election, the Saskatchewan CCF suggested a one-dollar annual membership. By this time the weekly CCF paper, *Saskatchewan Commonwealth*, had begun and it offered a year's subscription for three dollars. A number of supporters gave five dollars, saying "keep the change."

Prime Minister Bennett had changed his mind about calling a June election and delayed making a decision on a new date, finally announcing 14 October 1935. As Sandy would be campaigning for a longer period than he had expected, he decided to establish his office in centrally located Canora, which had good telephone and railway services. Relocating to new homes and storing furniture would become an integral part of life during Sandy's political career. In this first move, druggist Don Hood rented the Nicholsons' Hudson Bay Junction home. The Nicholsons and Stansfields rented a cottage in Canora large enough to accommodate the two families. Running water came from the town tap. Sandy said, "In due course we farmed out our furniture, leaving our piano with the Butcher family. We didn't want to move too much furniture and left some of the heavier material in the Junction. Stansfields left theirs in storage." When Stansfield received a promotion offer from Dominion Electric to be manager at Biggar, the CCF party agreed he should accept.

Barney Johnson, a married man with three children, who had worked previously for George Williams, became Sandy's new campaign manager in May 1935. During the campaign, as Myron Feeley had anticipated, Sandy learned there were still outstanding byelection debts. Sandy said, "We paid out more than one thousand dollars for by-election expenses, but we wound up with all our bills paid. We tried to get every poll to undertake some fund-raising project. I was still able to get buyers for a carload of wood at seventeen dollars. Amateur hours were quite popular on radio, and communities sponsored them to raise money. One community served turkey at a fowl supper for twenty-five cents a meal. So we paid our debts and balanced the budget." Such local money-making activities became a hallmark of the CCF grassroots approach to fund raising.

The Social Credit Party began to make inroads into Saskatchewan and approached Sandy with a saw-off deal. The *Canora Courier* reported that the Social Credit "told Mr. Nicholson they would guarantee him a seat in the next legislature in the next provincial election if he would consent to withdraw . . . Nicholson made it quite plain that he stood foursquare on the CCF platform and would not compromise with any other political group, nor could there be any question of withdrawal."[27] When Sandy refused to co-operate, the Mackenzie constituency candidate dropped out, and Benjamin F. Graham from Alberta became the Social Credit candidate.

The CCF brought in every big-name politician available to impress the voters and to win their confidence. Sandy visited a neighbouring constituency in Yorkton in May 1935, where he and his colleague King Gordon addressed the meeting. A guestbook signature of M.J. Coldwell confirms 25 July 1935 as the first time he stayed overnight at the Nicholsons'. At the Canora headquarters, Sandy said, "We had no indoor plumbing but we had a lot of beds. Coldwell did not object to having breakfast in bed after the others had eaten. Most times he visited us, you will find he had 'breakfast in bed.' Marian liked to cater to him because she saw how exhausted he looked each time he visited."

Coldwell came especially to attend the CCF picnic and rally at Crystal Lake on 24 July. Located south of Sturgis, near Stenen, Crystal Lake would later become an important CCF summer school site. At this first rally, Myron Feeley occupied the chair. A crowd of more than five hundred had gathered to hear Coldwell and Sandy speak. Women's voices were heard early, and many of them played an important part in the movement. Later in autumn Gertrude Telford spoke at a Canora meeting about the many difficulties and fears which beset people at that time because of the unequal distribution of wealth. Marian Nicholson made an appeal to the women to take a greater share in the responsibilities of citizenship. She said that the Liberals and Conservatives were not entirely to blame for the current conditions — they were merely tools of capitalism. Marian reiterated that the CCF party had no strings attached to it — it was a people's party. [28]

The Telford family became very active in Saskatchewan CCF politics. CCF speakers who came through Pelly generally stayed at the Telford home during the 1930s. *The Commonwealth* later carried a commendation to Gertrude Telford, saying: "During her years of service in the CCF [she] has served on the provincial council and executive; has been a candidate and constituency organizer; has managed CCF camps at Crystal Lake and instructed at Kenosee and Greenwater Lakes."[29]

J.S. Woodsworth also made a special trip to Hudson Bay Junction during the 1935 election campaign to speak on Sandy's behalf. Hugh and Kay MacKinnon owned the largest house in the community, and Kay wished to have the meeting at her home because her father had been in jail with Woodsworth at the time of the 1919 Winnipeg General Strike. In accordance with custom, the women served lunch after the meeting. Sandy provided a glimpse into Woodsworth's genteel character, revealing that he took him aside and whispered, "They'll not miss us if we slip out to the kitchen to see the women and say thank you for the work they've done. You see they go to a lot of trouble and we male folk talk and never take time to say thank you."

Out in the kitchen, Marian was impressed with Woodsworth's sincerity and the way in which he made the women feel the importance of their contribution.

All the enthusiasm generated in local CCF circles was not enough, however, and Sandy was defeated in the October 1935 federal election by J.A. MacMillan of Wadena, the Liberal candidate.[30] Indeed, the Liberals gained 170 seats to defeat R.B. Bennett's Conservative government, which had ruled for five years, while the CCF fell short of expected gains, winning only eight seats. The two elected in Saskatchewan were Coldwell for Rosetown-Biggar and T.C. Douglas for Weyburn. Sandy was convinced that the CCF would have won more seats in Saskatchewan "if Social Credit hadn't swept Alberta in August. William Aberhart was elected without even running. [Promising] twenty-five dollars a month for every man, woman and child" made a tremendous appeal to those in Saskatchewan who were on welfare. Aberhart had built up a huge radio audience with his "Back to the Bible" programme, using his fundamentalist approach and an appealing radio voice. The farmer from Alberta who ran for Social Credit in Mackenzie garnered 3,059 votes without making a public speech. These votes would have significantly added to Sandy's 4,312. The Liberals won with 6,595 ballots.

Sandy had learned a lesson about the ironies of elections. Although he had a reputation as a person who cared for people's welfare and carried projects to successful conclusions while he ministered to his flock, he suffered total defeat in Reserve Junction, where he had called on everyone in the village and annually had distributed gifts at Christmas. The secret ballot allowed people to vote for candidates from other parties, knowing the CCF would not form a government then. Sandy said, "If there had been one vote it would have been different, but it so happened there wasn't a single vote there. These things happen."

In a tribute to the Nicholsons, published in *The Commonwealth* about twenty years later, Mrs. Stewart Hawke said that after Sandy's defeat in 1935, "having set his hand to the plow he did not look back, but carried on with public meetings, study groups and organizing at every opportunity. One of his first fund-raising schemes was to dig a basement for a merchant (CCF of course). The farmers supplied the horse power, while the townspeople fed and billeted them. [The group] earned about $40 on the deal — pretty fair money in those days."[31]

Lloyd Shaw, appointed research director for the CCF national office in 1943, said of Sandy's skills,

> There is a period in the late 1930s, 1940s and early 1950s when the CCF Party put down strong organizational roots nationally that have contributed immensely to its survival as a significant CCF-NDP force in this day . . . One of these colleagues who played a key role in building the founding of the party is A.M. (Sandy) Nicholson . . . prior to and along with his six terms in political office, Sandy pioneered and set the standard for the organizational and financial base of the CCF movement, without which, on a people basis, no social democratic parties can survive and grow. And it's a difficult, tough and time-consuming role from which most of us shy away in most organizations, and particularly neglect in the political arena. But not Sandy Nicholson!"[32]

Chapter 7

Hiatus and Recommitment to the CCF, 1935-1940

Myron Feeley provided the impetus for Sandy to continue his CCF work. He convinced the Nicholsons that a nucleus of CCF supporters wanted Sandy as their representative in Ottawa and that there would be no problem collecting money to keep his family financially secure until the next election. Further, Feeley would guarantee them one hundred dollars a month if the expected support did not materialize.

Sandy said, "Marian and I recalled that the Stansfields and the Johnsons had worked for fifty dollars a month. We owned our house in Hudson Bay Junction. We thought we could manage on fifty dollars a month salary and fifty dollars a month expenses."

This decision had barely been made when a telegram arrived from President Walter Murray of the University of Saskatchewan in Saskatoon. The St. Andrew's College minister was dying from leukemia. Would Sandy be available to be their assistant minister and would he reply immediately? Marian agreed that Sandy should send a telegram stating he already had accepted a position with the CCF to remain until after the next election.

Other CCF members had confidence in Sandy's chances of being elected next time around. When Dr. Hugh MacLean[1] of Regina heard that Sandy was staying on in Mackenzie, he wrote and suggested that Sandy come instead to Regina. MacLean was planning to retire and move to California and he would not be running as a candidate again. Sandy opted to continue working in Mackenzie.

Feeley persuaded Sandy to begin canvassing for funds in Preeceville to test his theory that people were willing to support him. Sandy began to have second thoughts about this idea, believing the canvass to be "just sort of begging." He voiced numerous excuses, all of them dismissed by Marian, and at length, like Shakespeare's schoolboy, he went unwillingly to Feeley's farm. Finding Feeley busy with harvesting, Sandy seized on this as a legitimate excuse for delaying the fund raising ordeal, but everything had been arranged and the two men set out. After so much foreboding, Sandy arrived home feeling exhilarated, announcing to Marian, "We made twelve calls and nobody said they couldn't afford the five dollars. In a few hours we collected sixty dollars. And several people said, 'Don't throw in the towel, call again if you are short.'" Although the next federal election would not be called for five years, the CCF would reap the results of the intensive educational programme and campaigning directed by Sandy in the northeastern part of Saskatchewan.

Sometime in November 1935, Marian received a letter from Toronto indicating that her mother was seriously ill. The Nicholsons decided to drive to Toronto and they approached Feeley, now president of the Mackenzie constituency committee, regarding a two-month leave of absence. He agreed.

The CCF had called a meeting of all elected CCF members and defeated candidates early in December at Winnipeg. Because of his involvement in the byelection, Feeley wished to attend, and he accompanied the Nicholsons to Winnipeg. Sandy recalled this CCF conference as being depressing — so many defeated candidates and so few elected. The CCF had run only 118 candidates in fewer than half of the 245 ridings across the country. The party polled just under 400,000 votes (8.9 percent of the total cast). However, conference discussions revealed the CCF had not done too badly considering the circumstances — "no money, a weak organization, relatively few candidates, a new party with an ideology foreign to Canadians, and serious rivals for the vote of the discontented and disadvantaged." On the positive side, the CCF "had succeeded in laying, in three short years, a sturdy foundation on which to build."[2]

Sandy met Tommy Douglas, Stanley Knowles and Graham Spry for the first time. Woodsworth and A.A. Heaps had been elected in Manitoba, although Heaps would lose his seat in the 1940 federal election when Sandy won Mackenzie constituency for the first time. Ontario had not elected any CCF members. Ted Garland, a participant in the founding of the CCF, agreed at this Winnipeg meeting to accept the post of national organizer. This meant that the CCF now had two paid national officers — David Lewis as full-time secretary and Garland. Besides these two men, Sandy was the only other person in Canada at this time to have a guaranteed salary provided by CCF supporters. Not until the autumn of that year would the CCF have an office — a basement room on Wellington Street in Ottawa. There, H.W. (Herb) Dalton, a pensioner paid five dollars a week by the CCF, took care of the daily duties of running the office.

At the Winnipeg conference, the delegates' commitment to the party made a profound impression on Sandy. Although Tommy Douglas had financial difficulties, he returned 10 percent of his earnings every year to the CCF, continuing the tithing commenced when he became a church member. Later Sandy recalled, "While the MP's salary of four thousand dollars looked like a lot of money, you must realize you had to keep a home in your constituency and one in Ottawa. In 1944 I wound up very much in debt."

After the conference concluded, the Nicholsons and Feeley headed south into the United States. Feeley remained with relatives in Iowa and the Nicholsons drove on to Madison, Wisconsin, to spend a few days with Bunny Bunce — Sandy's college friend who shared the cattleboat experience. The Nicholsons arrived in Toronto a week before Marian's mother died. Sandy said, "We were not in Toronto very long before we decided to extend our leave without pay." A United Church in Port Arthur, Ontario, needed a supply minister. Sandy had no immediate plans, and as this opportunity to preach would bring in some money, he accepted. Upon his return to Toronto he received the following letter from D.F. Young, editor of the *News Chronicle* and church board member:

> Your congenial and sympathetic personality, your ability to make friends quickly and your exposition of gospel subjects in a manner which serve[s] not only your acquaintance with human nature but also gave evidence of scholarly attainments are in my opinion the qualities which assure a success in your chosen profession. I have no doubt that in due time you will be known generally as one of the most valuable men in the work of the church and there will be rich rewards for you in it.[3]

Sandy did not reach for the "rich rewards" in the church. His calling to the social gospel predominated and he laboured as a missionary for the CCF, although in early 1936 he seemed to be in limbo.

Marian visited Dr. Marion Hilliard, a prominent Toronto gynecologist at the Women's College Hospital (and friend of the Massey family), to find out if it would be safe to risk having another child. The women's friendship had begun in 1921 through their mutual interest in the SCM. Now Dr. Hilliard learned about Marian's recurring rheumatic fever, the loss of the Nicholsons' first son, and Marian's close call when Anna saved her life. After examining Marian, Dr. Hilliard believed she could safely have another baby. "But not in Hudson Bay Junction. If you'll stay in Toronto, I'd like to look after you."

While the Nicholsons debated about their future, Professor Frank Underhill issued a call for help. He knew of Sandy's successful fund raising in Saskatchewan and he asked for Sandy's assistance in raising money for the League for Social Reconstruction (LSR) — an organization of professionals and people not in the labour or farm movements in eastern Canada, but who were "critical of monopoly capitalism and demanded economic change by parliamentary means."[4] One of the organization's supporters, King Gordon, had canvassed the area before the 1935 autumn election. Now, Underhill said to Sandy, "We think instead of going back to Saskatchewan you should stay here in Toronto. Nearly any riding in Ontario could do what you're supposed to do in Saskatchewan. We'll pay you one hundred dollars a month and you 'cover the waterfront.' Select some place in Ontario where you'd like to put your roots down." With Marian's welfare in mind, the Nicholsons opted to remain in Toronto. Sandy wrote Feeley regarding their decision.

It was at this time that Sandy formed a lasting friendship with Graham Spry, whom he had met at the Winnipeg CCF conference the previous autumn. Also a defeated candidate in the federal election, Spry still served as secretary of the Ontario CCF. A graduate of the University of Manitoba and a Rhodes scholar, Spry had been instrumental in formulating many of the CCF's early policies. As Shona McKay later pointed out in an appreciation of Spry, "Tainted by his socialist political connections Spry found it difficult to secure a job in Canada and eventually [he] accepted an executive position with Standard Oil in London, England."[5] Later he served in India as personal assistant to Sir Stafford Cripps, and during the Douglas and Lloyd governments, as agent-general for Saskatchewan in the United Kingdom. In early 1936, Spry helped Sandy locate possible financial sources for the LSR in Kitchener, London, and some Toronto ridings. Sandy and Underhill drove around making contacts.

Besides fund raising for the LSR, Sandy worked closely with the Ontario CCF, bringing in memberships, attending conventions and making appeals for financial assistance for the party. He met Andrew Brewin, described by David Lewis as "a young lawyer, rapidly becoming a respected counsel by dint of hard work, incorruptible honesty and an engaging personality [who] had come into the CCF through the LSR and to the LSR through his religious principles."[6] Brewin became a member of Parliament and held high offices in the national as well as the Ontario party. Sandy also met Ted Jolliffe, later a leader of the Ontario CCF. Another Rhodes scholar, and a lawyer, Jolliffe had identified with the CCF, playing an important part in the 1935 federal election, and then as a member of the provincial executive and various committees.[7] Sandy added another valuable friend to his widening circle of colleagues — William Dennison. Dennison had a seat as a CCF member of the Legislative Assembly in Ontario, then as a Toronto city alderman and eventually as mayor of Toronto.

Graham Spry had been only one among many qualified people discriminated against because of party affiliation. During his association with the Ontario CCF, Sandy learned how business treated those with socialist political connections. He accompanied Garland to Cobourg for a meeting at the home of Bill Shenson, to organize a Cobourg CCF club. Shenson worked as a chartered accountant for the Cobourg Tannery, sat on the local school board, and served as an elder in the church. He agreed to be chairman of the club. An account of the meeting appeared in the local paper. Along with Shenson's next pay cheque came a memorandum stating, "Your services are no longer required with the company. We cannot have on our payroll a person who is the chairman of a party like the CCF." The Shensons were forced to leave Cobourg and to seek work elsewhere. The CCF had no funds to help him relocate, "the national treasury was empty."[8]

Although Saskatchewan led the way in CCF campaigning and proselytizing, progress in Mackenzie seemed slow. Feeley wrote to Sandy stating that the financial commitment previously offered remained effective. Would he return for a few months at harvest time on those terms, and would he consider returning permanently once Marian had her baby which was expected in February 1937? The party needed someone energetic to offset the loss of dynamism evident since the beating the CCF had received in the 1935 election. Sandy and Marian missed the west and the friends of their early married life, and they found life in eastern Canada less enjoyable. They agreed to return, and bought back their Hudson Bay Junction home, which had been sold in the meantime.

Coupled with the season — harvest is a good time to seek funds, as the grain has been sold and bills have been paid — Sandy's charismatic fund raising approach resulted in the replenishment of the CCF coffers. The *Preeceville Progress* reported on the annual CCF convention for Mackenzie held in the Preeceville Hall in October, with E.J. (Ted) Garland attending. The account also stated: "A.M. Nicholson has returned from Ontario and outlined plans for further activities."[9]

As soon as the provincial CCF office learned that Sandy was on hand and ready to work again, George Williams asked him to attend a meeting in Tisdale. Williams anticipated changes to constituency boundaries prior to the expected 1938 provincial election. Uncertain where the changes would occur, he wanted the party to field as many candidates as possible. He felt certain that there would be a Tisdale constituency, so he called a regional meeting there. At least four commendable candidates resided in the area — John Brockelbank, a former school teacher and now a homesteader and farmer at Steen; Dorothy Pope, a federal candidate for Melfort in the previous election; Percy Wright, a successful farmer; and O.W. Valleau, who was to hold the provincial constituency of Melfort from 1938 to 1948. Wright "didn't really want a political career," but Sandy would be instrumental in convincing him to participate later and to represent the Melfort constituency in the House of Commons from 1940 to 1953. At the end of this meeting, Brockelbank agreed to be the candidate for Tisdale.

Sandy's organizational philosophy parallelled Williams's — he believed that at least a year should elapse from the time the person was nominated until an election, allowing the candidate to visit every poll in the constituency and to set up committees. (A poll is an area comprising the population voting in one place. Any party contesting a constituency is represented at every polling place on election day. The average number of voters residing in a poll is about two hundred.) In the heyday of the Saskatchewan CCF the party had viable permanent organizations which consisted of dues-paying members in many polls of rural constituencies. Sandy arranged that money collected in each area would be credited to that provincial constituency. Out of the one dollar annual membership, the national office received ten cents, the provincial and constituency associations fifty cents and forty cents respectively.

By the middle of December, Marian had told Sandy by mail that she felt well and she encouraged him to stay in the west longer than the two months originally agreed upon. In a circular letter to his constituents, Sandy summed up the autumn's activities and projected his hopes for the future:

> We had a splendid executive meeting in Pelly at the home of our President, Mrs. G. Telford. The response to our financial appeals has been so encouraging that it would seem as if funds are to be forthcoming so I can continue as your fulltime organizer. Since I returned October first my salary has been paid in full, all expenses met, $25 contributed to the national organization, $32.20 to the Saskatchewan section of the CCF, $2 to the radio fund and $89.50 towards the 1935 election deficit. In addition, promises totalling more than $400 have come from poll committees and individuals . . . At Barford, arrangements have been made to have a 'bee' to take out a carload of green poplar. Seven men have promised to come with teams and sleighs, one man offered the use of his 'buzz' saw, a storekeeper gasoline to run the saw and a number of men with their strong arms so they hope to

haul, cut, split and pile the 17 cords in a single day. Another supporter offered to load the car when we should realize about $30.[10]

The letter also outlined plans for the development of a CCF summer school at Crystal Lake, near Stenen, stating, "We are inviting Mr. Woodsworth and Mr. Williams to attend, planning lectures and discussions on the CCF program."

Sandy was slated to spend the first three weeks of January 1937 in the Tisdale provincial constituency, but in the midst of this organizing period he received word that Marian had fallen and fractured one arm, so he returned to Toronto by train. Their daughter, Mary Anna, was born 24 February at Women's College Hospital with Dr. Hilliard in attendance. The doctor said it would be safe for Marian and the new baby to travel by mid-March.

Each year the CCF held a provincial convention in Regina, Saskatoon or Moose Jaw, where members voiced suggestions regarding policy. Part of Sandy's work entailed setting up committees in every poll to meet on a regular basis and report at annual conventions.[11] At this time, the whole of Mackenzie could boast of only seven miles of gravel road. For two winters Sandy travelled with a team of horses and a caboose. He said, "With two sticks of wood burning in the small stove you'd be comfortable. Although I had a fur coat, one could be in shirt sleeves in a caboose."

In the four provincial constituencies which made up Mackenzie, people would plan a week's programme in preparation for Sandy's arrival. Ukrainian communities usually preferred to have meetings on Sundays. When possible, Sandy liked to schedule a dance or box social on Friday evenings and then he would return home to Hudson Bay Junction for the weekend. Sometimes during bad weather, when his itinerary took him to the southern part of the constituency, he planned on being away three weeks.

Besides his winter activities in 1937, Sandy helped John and Gertrude Telford to establish the CCF summer school in Crystal Lake. This school held in Mackenzie constituency — the first one to be organized by the provincial party — ran for five days in early July. To plan the agenda, Sandy drew on experiences from his teaching stints and from his attendance at SCM conferences. Mrs. Telford had training as a leader at church camps. Facilities included "two small rented cottages and several tents and rough picnic tables under the trees for meals." A former army and lumbercamp cook, attracted to the CCF philosophy, turned out appetizing meals on a small stove. About forty young people, sixteen years and older, came from Tisdale, Wadena, Kelvington and Pelly provincial constituencies. Advertisements for the camp asked individuals to bring "a pillow and bedding for one, with a bed tick, dishes and cutlery for one, flashlight, pencil and paper for notes, bathing suit, toiletries."[12]

Marian, Ruth and Mary Anna accompanied Sandy to Crystal Lake, participating in as many activities as possible — "hours of earnest study, then sports, swimming, pageants, bonfires, sing-songs and the unique experience of having our great leader, J.S. Woodsworth, for two full days. No one who attended will ever forget his simple yet penetrating analysis of the economic system under capitalism" delivered with the backdrop of his charts and pointer stick.[13] The young people who attended brought lots of enthusiasm and ultimately worked for the CCF. In particular, Sandy remembered Alex Kuziak, later elected to the Saskatchewan legislature, who became the first cabinet minister of Ukrainian descent in Canada, and Margaret Telford, Sandy's secretary in Ottawa for one term, who later worked for David Lewis.

The next summer the Stenens lent the CCF their cottage at Crystal Lake. Mrs. Telford remarked in her reminiscences, "The roof leaked — not in drops but in streams. We borrowed two huge tents from the Stewart Lumber Company of Arran, but when the midnight downpour came it was a bit grim, especially for the girls, whose tent was on the side of the hill directly in the path of the down-coming rivulets." Even this failed to dampen the campers' enthusiasm. George Williams stayed for several days, "giving not only inspiration but most careful and constructive help in organization methods."[14] From such small beginnings, the Crystal Lake CCF summer camp developed into a major training ground for future CCFers. National and provincial leaders could always be persuaded to lecture if camp dates coincided with summer schedules.

In 1939 the Saskatchewan CCF decided to buy a permanent site of ten acres on the east shore of Crystal Lake. The acreage was partly a gift from the estate of the late D.M. Frederickson of Minneapolis. A co-operative association was organized to hold the property in trust for the CCF executive of Mackenzie constituency. At Crystal Lake that year, M.J. Coldwell served as special lecturer and main platform attraction for the annual picnic, the "platform" being an open truck. The picnic crowd swelled to five hundred. Five years later, attendance reached twenty-five hundred and remained at that level for years. Camp facilities improved, augmented by a "fine dining and lecture hall erected in just one day by a small army of devoted volunteers."[15] This building later became known as Nicholson Hall.

In 1937 the CCF party across Canada required funds. The CCF provincial treasury in Saskatchewan resembled Mother Hubbard's cupboard. Tommy Douglas had many friends in the west, so Sandy suggested to George Williams, "If you can arrange to have Douglas come and spend four days in my area, we'll send you two hundred dollars."

Douglas agreed to the idea, travelling on his Parliamentary railway pass, and held his first meeting in Preeceville where Sandy made the financial appeal. "Tommy's here," said Sandy. "It would not be a good meeting unless we took a collection. We want this to be one of the happiest days Tommy's had. I know money is scarce. No coin is too small. But if some of you have paper money, it counts much faster. And Tommy's been under tremendous strain. It's much more pleasant hearing the paper drop in than coins."

Sandy recalled,

Those were the best meetings we had. The two hundred dollars came in, and a great many memberships. We had a heavy rain that week, but people came miles across ungravelled roads to see and hear Tommy again. They felt wonderful about being part of the organization that had sent Tommy to the House of Commons. Tommy had great skill in getting the audience in a good humour. He had a wonderful collection of yarns, though he never spent too long on them. He was especially good handling hecklers and drunks. I've never known anyone else who could say the right thing without hurting and leave the audience in a good mood after the incident.[16]

Of this period in Sandy's political life, Magnus Eliason, CCF organizer and later a Winnipeg city councillor, said Sandy's contribution "to the party — and consequently to Canadian society — was that he just simply went out to build a party . . . Sandy played a major role in organizing that northeast corner which was virtually delivered to the party — four of the five seats" in the provincial election of 1938.[17]

Eliason referred not only to Sandy's work for the party in the Mackenzie constituency, but also to his tenure as provincial organizer for the Saskatchewan CCF. Sandy had been appointed organizer at seventy-five dollars a month to take effect in the new year, at an executive meeting in November 1937. Sandy treated the position as an extension to the work in his own constituency. Among the candidates he encouraged to run was Gladys Strum who carried the CCF banner in Cannington provincial constituency. She lost but would come into her own in 1945 when she defeated Major General Andrew MacNaughton, Minister of National Defence in the Mackenzie King government, in the federal constituency of Qu'Appelle. Sandy said, "Gladys later found while women do get elected occasionally, it's very difficult to stay there."

In the Battleford district, a controversy developed about "saw-offs."[18] Sandy did not agree with arrangements to refrain from campaigning in some constituencies. CCF executive minutes for 19 and 20 March 1938 contained a motion "withdrawing" A.M. Nicholson as provincial organizer and suggesting he be placed in some other work. Objections from other CCFers precipitated a motion to reinstate Sandy at the provincial council meeting in April.

In the Saskatchewan provincial election of 8 June 1938, the CCF had run only thirty candidates, refraining from fielding them in the three major cities of Regina, Saskatoon and Moose Jaw. Douglas said "Williams got the idea that the government was impossible to defeat and the only way to save the CCF from annihilation was to enter the saw-off relationships with Social Creditors and Conservatives." When the Liberals won thirty-eight seats, leaving ten to the CCF, "it was clear that Williams's strategy had gone awry."[19]

Sandy believed the Social Credit Party to be the greater threat to the CCF's success in these early years, but the activities of Communists had to be closely monitored also. During election campaigns throughout the years, Communists would state that they supported the CCF generally and sometimes Sandy in particular, claims which made Sandy angry. One battle the CCF fought in Saskatchewan was to counter the smear tactics of other parties which asserted that CCFers were Communists in another guise, intent on nationalizing farms and introducing other extreme socialist ideas. Sandy never participated in Red-baiting, and in 1940 he counted as his friend Dorise Neilson, the Labour Progressive member of Parliament for North Battleford. At a practical level, however, he had to demonstrate his anti-Communist beliefs, at the same time constantly guarding against Communist infiltration of constituency executives.

Shortly after the 1938 election, the Liberal candidate in Humboldt, James King, resigned to make way for C.M. Dunn, minister of highways, who had been defeated in Melville. Sandy said, "I happened to be through with my duties as provincial organizer but this was an important by-election. I conceived of the idea that if all the elected MLAs would come to Humboldt area as soon as they could and remain as long as possible, we might defeat Dunn. It was summer and the farmers weren't too busy. We asked for volunteers — I carefully avoided being the campaign manager for that byelection." On 4 August 1938, CCF candidate Joe Burton edged out Dunn by about two hundred votes — giving the CCF eleven seats in the legislature. Burton came from a pioneer family in the Humboldt district, and was one of the few Roman Catholics active in the CCF.

At the autumn executive meeting of the provincial CCF, Sandy had tendered his resignation as provincial organizer. Mackenzie constituency thereupon appointed him organizer. Nominations were often held at constituency conventions, and since portions of the Melfort and Yorkton federal constituencies comprised some of the area Sandy covered, he attended their annual meetings. He remembered the Yorkton annual meeting at which Mrs. Hugh Castleden's speech on her husband's behalf resulted in his nomination. Castleden taught at the Yorkton School Board which promptly dismissed him upon learning he had accepted the CCF nomination. Fortunately, the Melfort School Board was not as narrow-minded and willingly hired him. Percy Wright, who had successfully spearheaded the campaign which elected John Brockelbank in Tisdale, agreed to be the candidate for the Melfort federal constituency.

Mackenzie constituency held its nominating convention in October, with T.C. Douglas coming from Ottawa to speak in Sandy's favour. Sandy reiterated the beliefs of Coldwell and Williams "in the principles and practices of co-operation. They didn't restrict the application of co-operation to the commercial aspects of buying and selling [but] applied it also to relationships between people."[20] Sandy and his campaign manager, Sam Sookocheff, toured the countryside, urging each poll to initiate some fund-raising project. They sold memberships at these local functions. Sandy received a monthly statement from the provincial office, and he noted year after year that he had sent in a quarter of all memberships from the province.

When Sandy visited the federal constituency of Assiniboia, he discovered Sam Rogers of Wawota working to spread the CCF philosophy. Rogers's daughter, Madge, said her father "had a desire to explain it simply . . . [so] the uneducated farmer and labourer could understand what advantages [the CCF] would give to them. He felt that teachers, preachers and professors talked 'over their heads,' and that an uneducated carpenter like himself could put the Democratic Christian Socialist philosophy into more simple wording."[21] Rogers learned Sandy practiced a common touch, too. Sandy's "social gospel had meaning — like Jeremiah and Amos, those marvelous prophets of old — he too left the temple to answer the call for justice to the people."

Madge continued, "He touched our hearts — and our purses (which were lean, indeed, in those days). But we all realized how very important it is that the CCF be financed by The People and *not* by . . . Big Business."

In 1938 the Nicholsons employed Gladys Byrnes as housekeeper while Marian took employment as a school teacher for several months. As well the Nicholsons gave lodging to two high school girls. The housekeeper recalled that Sandy

> was away much of the time with his campaigning . . . In the summer when he was home for a longer period, some of his co-workers came and brought their wives, staying for a few days or a weekend — always finding warm hospitality. [Friends were] not limited to any certain position, creed or nationality. Persons from many different walks of life could and did find a warm welcome, a helping hand or a kind listening ear.
>
> I recall the weekend Charlie Quan visited. He quite impressed me at the time, his neatness, and polite, gentle way. I learned years later something of his hard work and the struggle to bring his family here from China, and of how successful they all became. Before he left that weekend, he came to the kitchen and spoke to me for a few minutes. He said, 'We should not say *I will never forget* — rather we should say *I will always remember.*' Charlie Quan I will always remember.[22]

The housekeeper remembered Marian as being a strong supporter of her husband's work. She recalled a trip Marian made that winter to a remote part of his area to speak in support of the CCF. After she returned she sent a box of clothes from her own wardrobe to those she felt needed them more. At home, Marian was active in church and community work. A sick mother often had Marian to thank for a hot casserole for her family's supper.

William Boschman, a store owner at Battle Heights in the Carrot River area, recalled "the summer of 1939 was very wet and the roads often impassable by car." Late one Saturday evening, about to extinguish his gas lamp and retire for the night, he saw a car-light far up the road and soon two men knocked on his door:

> One introduced himself as J.H. Brockelbank, MLA and the other as Sandy Nicholson, a federal candidate for Mackenzie . . . There are times when we can look back and see events that are landmarks in our lives. That visit with Sandy and 'Brock' was one of them. Experience had left me disgusted with the old parties and I was floating around in a political limbo. These two men were talking about a sort of economic and social change that I wanted to see. They represented a political movement of the people that could bring it about. That talk restored some of the idealism in me that had been giving away to cynicism. I had been on the edge of the CCF and now began to support the movement openly (being careful at the same time not to get into arguments with my customers). It seemed to do my business no harm.[23]

When the Canadian government declared war on Germany in September 1939, the CCF National Council met. Sandy said, "While the party had been built up by quite a high percentage of pacifists, it was felt the party couldn't accept Hitler dominating the world. So the party agreed to give wholehearted support to carrying the war to a successful conclusion. Mr. Woodsworth was given permission to state his personal position while Mr. Coldwell delivered the party's." The abandonment of pacifism, although cushioned with the CCF's campaign against an

Sandy Nicholson with the team and "caboose" used to visit polls in Mackenzie, northeastern Saskatchewan, for at least six weeks each of the winters from 1935 to 1938.

Sandy Nicholson and Charlie Quan, photographed at the Hudson Bay Junction railway station in 1938.

Sandy Nicholson, member of Parliament for Mackenzie, stands beside the parish priest after a meeting with voters in Island Falls new church building, August 1943.

Ruth, Sandy, Marian and Mary Anna Nicholson in 1940.

Sandy Nicholson (second from right), took part in a Citizens National Bank Forum broadcast, 10 January 1946, at CBS-KNX, Hollywood. With him (left to right): Dr. Walter Wallbank, University of Southern California; Dr. Dean McHenry, UCLA; and Dr. Wallace Sterling, moderator, California Institute of Technology. (KNX Photo)

A group of members of Parliament, among them Sandy Nicholson (far left), leaving a Royal Canadian Air Force plane on their visit to Churchill, Manitoba. (Saskatchewan Archives Board S-B3856, Department of National Defence (Canada), #PL-101847)

Sandy Nicholson (third from right, front row) played with the 1948 Parliamentary baseball team. Other players included: (front row, left to right) Paul Emile Coté; Robert Winters; Donald Fleming; Joe Tremblay; the Reverend Dan McIvor; Maurice Bourget; Hughes Lapointe; and Jimmy Gardiner. Standing, left to right: William Wylie; Bucko McDonald; Douglas Abbott; John Sinnott; Ross Macdonald; Ian Mackenzie; Tom Reid; George Cruikshank; Evelyn Tufts, a Press Gallery member; Gaspard Fauteux; Brooke Claxton; and Stanley McKeen. (Photograph: John Daviault. Saskatchewan Archives Board RB-2986(2))

When he visited California in 1946, Sandy Nicholson was the guest of Dr. and Mrs. Hugh MacLean in Los Angeles. In this photograph Nicholson is seated far right; others are (left to right): Mrs. MacLean, Mrs. Dean McHenry, and Dr. Hugh MacLean.

Sandy Nicholson (far left) converses with (left to right) Sam Sookocheff, Jack Midmore, Charles Mitchell, Ted Moritz, and Hugh Mitchell at the back door of the Nicholson home on the co-operative farm at Sturgis, Saskatchewan.

M.J. Coldwell (centre) was a frequent visitor to the Nicholsons' home. Here he is seen with (left to right) Sandy, Marian, Ruth and Anna at their home on the co-operative farm at Sturgis in June 1952. Coldwell wrote in the Nicholsons' guest book: "As in 1935, a wonderful welcome, rest __and__ breakfast in bed!"

India's Prime Minister Nehru greets Sandy Nicholson and an Indian delegate at his reception for delegates to the Commonwealth Parliamentary Conference in New Delhi in December 1957. Nicholson was the only CCFer in the thirteen-delegate Canadian party. (Archives of Ontario)

Sandy Nicholson talks to Indian President Rajendra Prasas at a reception for delegates to the Commonwealth Parliamentary Conference in New Delhi, December 1957. Others in the party (left to right) are the Honourable Winston Mahabar, Trinidad Minister of Health; the Honourable Hugh Downer, Speaker of the Ontario Legislative Assembly; and an African delegate. (Archives of Ontario)

Sandy Nicholson (far right) shares a joke with Prime Minister Nehru and Ontario MLA Tom Bate at the Prime Minister's reception for delegates to the Commonwealth Parliamentary Conference. (Archives of Ontario)

expeditionary force, profiteering, and infringements on civil liberties, was a major turning point for the party. The decision "removed the largest barrier to its association with the world and for the first time aligned itself with the overwhelming majority of Canadians against a common enemy."[24] On 25 January 1940, Mackenzie King moved the adjournment of the House, Parliament was dissolved, and an election called for 26 March 1940.

Marian worked in Sandy's Canora office and commuted between there and Hudson Bay Junction. On election day, the Nicholson's joint campaign resulted in Sandy winning in the Mackenzie constituency by almost one thousand votes more than his Liberal opponent. The five elected for the CCF in Saskatchewan were: T.C. Douglas, M.J. Coldwell, Percy Wright, Hugh Castleden and Sandy. At a celebratory banquet, Sandy said that as the member for Mackenzie constituency, "he now represented all citizens of whatever political views and invited everyone to discuss with him any problems they may have for which he promised careful attention."[25]

Among the letters of congratulation on winning the election came P.S. Quan's from China:

> I am very pleased to hear frequently the news about
> you from my father's letters, and am very pleasure to
> send my best wishes on your success of election.[26]

Following the election, officials of the United Church contacted Sandy and suggested that clergymen who were not active as ministers should not take the revenue which came from marriages. Sandy, seeing that such activities were unfair to other ministers in the area, agreed to have his name withdrawn from the list of ministers in the Saskatchewan conference eligible to perform marriages. Thus, the move into the formal political arena necessitated a complete break from official church association. Realizing vital Christian concerns were being met by neither church nor state, Sandy had been challenged to embrace the social gospel and to embark on a drive for direct legislation to spearhead social reform. He said he never looked back.

Chapter 8

Member of Parliament for Mackenzie, 1940-1949

Three newcomers from Saskatchewan — Nicholson, Wright and Castleden — and Nova Scotian Clarie Gillis, the first and only coal miner elected to the House of Commons, added colour and debating strength to the CCF caucus in Parliament. "We lost Grant MacNeil in British Columbia," Sandy recalled. "Angus MacInnis was the only one elected there. And we lost A.A. Heaps in Manitoba, where Woodsworth's constituents elected him despite his frail health and pacifist stand."

Woodsworth suffered a stroke during a meeting of the new CCF members and the national executive the first weekend following the opening of the nineteenth Parliament. He made "a fairly good recovery and came back to Parliament on several occasions, but wasn't able to make speeches again," Sandy recorded. Tommy Douglas acted as CCF Whip. Sandy and his colleagues followed policy set by their national executive, national council and provincial bodies and "concentrated their attention on studying and debating the essential features of a better society which [they] felt should be built in Canada after the war."[1]

A profile of parliamentary personalities said of Sandy's debut:

> If you had been in the House of Commons gallery in 1940, you would have seen an earnest young man talking down to the members. You would probably also have had the idea that any moment he was going to launch out into a sermon or, when the bells rang to conclude the session, would be asking a serious young group to remain for a quiet word of prayer . . . [This was] just his pulpit manner, and he was using the evangelical stance because he knew no other.[2]

Life on the Hill taught Sandy a great deal and he soon spoke in as off-hand a manner to the House as he would to a service club.

Sandy's maiden speech delivered on 21 May, suffered several interruptions.[3] "Generally in your first speech you have quite a sympathetic audience," Sandy commented, but he read a critical quotation about Jimmy Gardiner, minister of agriculture. "A bit of an exchange" developed between Sandy and Gardiner with the Speaker coming down on Gardiner's side. Later, Prime Minister Mackenzie King questioned Sandy's lengthy remarks in relation to the matter before the House. Sandy replied that the welfare of the Canadian people was very important, and he told the Prime Minister that he represented a large percentage of farmers producing food for the nation who were not receiving a fair share of the value of their produce. This was his first opportunity to say something about their needs.

Clarie Gillis had only an elementary school education, and he wondered what a coal miner could say that would interest doctors and lawyers. Woodsworth said, "Tell them about the life of a coal miner."

"Can you get away with that?" asked Gillis.

"Of course you can, that's what you're sent here to do."

Sandy remembered Gillis being interrupted by a lawyer who asked, "Wouldn't the member admit there are a lot of people who are too lazy to work, and wouldn't he also admit there were a lot of people who were agitators and no employer would have them?"

Gillis replied,

> You're quite right, I have known a lot of people too lazy to shine their own shoes. But they were the sons and grandsons of the owners of the coal mines. I also know of people who were agitators. My own father couldn't get a job as a coal miner in Canada because he was an agitator. He had to go to the States. I remember one of the foremen coming to our house and saying, 'Gillis, if you keep your mouth shut you can have so and so.' My father replied, 'I don't want what you've got. I want the right for the miners to organize.' You know while conditions aren't perfect, they're a lot better than they would have been if there hadn't been people like my father who were agitating for the rights of coal miners.

In Sandy's estimation, Gillis had conducted himself admirably.

For the first few months after the opening of Parliament, Gillis, Castleden and Sandy lived together in Ottawa. Sandy and Castleden shared an office at the House of Commons as well as the stenographic services of a secretary from the government secretarial pool. Initially, CCF members were dependent on Ottawa area secretaries who were not necessarily sympathetic to their political views. Later, Sandy found "it was possible to recommend someone from the constituency familiar with the names" to be one's personal secretary.

The CCF appointed Sandy as the party's housing spokesman and to quest for better housing for Canadians. Keeping up with developments in this field consumed a large portion of his time throughout his parliamentary years. He said, "When the National Housing Act was passed it was assumed it would be of interest to places like Vancouver, Montreal, Toronto and Windsor — the largest cities where there had been a great increase in labour force — but it wouldn't be of any interest in rural Canada." However, he became excited about the possibility of federal funds being made available for rural housing. He believed that the legislation should allow for the sharing of costs between federal, provincial and local governments. As he pointed out, "We had a very small percentage of people in Mackenzie who had running water in their homes. Many still lived in log houses. It wasn't difficult to convince the ministry responsible for housing that whether the provinces or local communities would ever take advantage of the legislation" it should still be put in place.

Zenon Park, a hamlet to the north of Tisdale, was the first rural community in Canada to take advantage of housing legislation, largely as a result of Sandy publicizing the new act in Saskatchewan. The CCF government in Saskatchewan had been the first provincial government prepared to assist, offering to pay 20 percent of the capital cost to any community, city, or non-profit organization willing to build and operate a project. The federal government loaned 72 percent for mortgage money. A parish priest decided that by providing only 8 percent of the capital cost, members could build low rental housing for elderly folk.

"Soon," Sandy said, "it seemed clear that this opportunity would be of interest to people selling their farms and moving to town. Instead of having to move to Regina or Saskatoon, they could now live in communities like Wadena, Tisdale or Assiniboia, adjacent to their former farms."

Sandy was critical of the quality of homes constructed under Wartime Housing Limited, established by an order-in-council 24 February 1941. He maintained, and supported his arguments with statistics, that Wartime Housing built houses of temporary calibre for approximately the same price that permanent houses could be constructed.

He cited statistics gathered in the United States indicating a definite relationship between poor housing and the crime rate, warning "we are building potential slum areas under Wartime Housing Limited . . . [supposedly] to be demol-ished when the war is over. Past experiences in every country however, have demonstrated that temporary houses will not be torn down" as long as people continue to occupy them.[4]

Party members worked long hours. "Things were more difficult for the CCF members in those days," Sandy said. "The CCF did not have any research staff paid by the government all the years I sat as MP. Initially, we had one telephone for the two members sharing an office. We never had long distance privileges. The salary in 1940 for an MP was four thousand dollars. It was increased to six thousand dollars in 1945. Times have changed. Now MPs have free telephone service anywhere in Canada. We should have had it, too . . . the phone bill was a major expense for MPs in my time." Members of Parliament did have free railway passes for themselves and their families, just as they have free air passes today. This perquisite would be beneficial when Sandy took on the duties of CCF national treasurer and campaigned for funds across Canada.

Sandy soon noticed that several weekly newspapers in his riding were not aware the parliamentary reading room paid for subscriptions. He immediately ordered subscriptions to all local newspapers in his constituency and began writing a weekly column for them, sharing items of interest from the House. One of his first letters indicated how much of a westerner he had become:

> Twenty years ago the familiar slogan, 'Go west, young man, go west,' lured me to Saskatchewan. Now I return to represent in Parliament a constituency in the province of my adoption. After being away for so many years, comparisons between east and west are inevitable. What a busy place Toronto is compared to our towns in Mackenzie. Judging by the expensive autos and well dressed people there is no depression in Canada's second city . . . an advertisement in a Toronto paper would seem to confirm this opinion. [Artcrete garden ornaments $158.98 for a fountain-figure] . . .
>
> Travelling by train to Bruce County where I was born, it is apparent that not many Ontario farmers are buying garden ornaments. Along 140 miles of railway there is scarcely a farm where buildings do not need

to be shingled, painted or repaired. Something will
have to be done to make life for the farmer more
attractive whether he lives in the east or west. At
present the work of producing the nation's food is not
being adequately rewarded.[5]

The parliamentary restaurant proved to be a comfortable
setting for discussing the nation's business with other
members of Parliament. Party issues were discussed with
colleagues at noon and in the evening. Sandy found
breakfast more informal, with members of all political
stripes associating freely with those from other parties,
reading the morning papers, and discussing general topics
of the day. The restaurant and other facilities offered in the
House are subsidized by the taxpayer. In 1940 Sandy could
have his hair cut at the parliamentary barber's shop for
twenty-five cents when the charge in the rest of the city
was one dollar; and he could have his suit pressed in the
tailor shop for a reasonable price.

In 1943 when William Boschman, who was then in the
armed forces, visited Ottawa with his wife and young son,
Sandy invited them to the House of Commons. Boschman
remembered the occasion well:

> Sandy met us and took us to his office. He introduced
> us to other MPs including Joe Burton, Tommy Douglas,
> M.J. Coldwell, Angus MacInnis, the rest of the CCF and
> A.H. Bence, Conservative member for Saskatoon. He
> took us on a tour of the buildings, the Peace Tower,
> the library. Then we had lunch in the parliamentary
> restaurant and met more people. We sat in the gallery
> and tried to absorb as much of the atmosphere as
> possible in so short a time.[6]

People who visited the House of Commons once in a
lifetime would say to Sandy, "Well, this is a queer sort of
forum you have. Members make fairly good speeches, but
nobody seems to be listening. They're writing letters or
reading the papers or just talking to neighbours. How do
you justify that?"

Sandy responded that all speeches are taken down in
shorthand. A team of efficient *Hansard* stenographers each

work seven or eight minutes at a time and their precise notes are transcribed. After the House is adjourned for the day, members are given an opportunity to edit the resulting text. "You're not to change what you said. Once you make the corrections the text appears in printed form and it is available on members' desks next morning."

In this first year when Sandy made his debut in Parliament, his sister, now Norma MacIntyre, came to Ottawa with her twelve-year-old son Alex. Her Lucknow neighbours remarked to her that had Sandy been a Liberal member of Parliament she and Alex could have met the Prime Minister while they were in Ottawa. Norma mentioned this to Sandy when she arrived. Challenged, Sandy wrote a note to Mackenzie King, who knew that Sandy's father had been a keen Liberal supporter in Bruce County:

> My sister, Alex Nicholson's daughter, and her twelve-year-old son are here. If you could spare a minute I'd appreciate it very much if you could shake hands with them.

Mackenzie King replied in his own handwriting, suggesting that the visit take place in his office after the orders of the day. Sandy, Marian, Norma and Alex visited the Prime Minister's office where Sandy introduced the members of his family; as they turned to leave Mackenzie King dissuaded them, saying, "No, no, sit down. I miss the opportunity to talk with people." And for young Alex's benefit, the Prime Minister took up a sheaf of cables that had come through from London and said, "These are very difficult times." Then, "Your uncle is with the CCF, some time I hope he will return to your grandfather's party."

The many issues which had propelled Sandy into politics remained of great importance to him. When one member of Parliament stated, "Western farmers have talked until I am tired of listening to them," Sandy replied "that so long as there is a single individual in my constituency who is going hungry in this land of plenty, my voice will continue to be raised to see that the necessary action is taken to remedy that situation."[7]

The utilization of the port of Churchill was another subject in which he had a keen personal interest and which he raised often. He asked if the British shipping board had been appraised regarding the port's facilities because "a number of people in northern Manitoba and Saskatchewan have directed my attention to the fact that large supplies of pulpwood, timber and various mineral products are available in this part of the country and could be shipped economically through the port of Churchill."[8] When he spoke again in favour of the Hudson Bay route, government spokesmen argued that the operating expenses were too great. Sandy then cited the thousands of dollars spent on dredging the St. Lawrence River between 1935 and 1939, as well as the compensation given to the two major railways. He then suggested that the government's priorities were misplaced and he said that western Canada would like a fairer distribution of subsidies.[9]

Both Tommy Douglas and Sandy Nicholson spoke in the House against the large amounts of money funnelled into financing the war, "while denying to the people of western Canada the right to have enough food to eat." Sandy questioned the government's policy of dumping surplus wheat. He received a letter from one of his constituents suggesting that the government distribute the grain locally. The man "happened to be the legal attendance officer for his school district. By the teacher's report there were three children kept home during the month because their parents had no flour to bake bread for their lunches."[10]

Sandy directed many broadsides at liquor manufacturers and their wartime profits derived from the boatloads of beer sent to soldiers; he asked "the honourable members to picture a railway train with an engine in the city of Quebec and its caboose in Ottawa and the entire train extending from this city to the ancient capital, filled with cases of beer en route to the Middle East."[11]

An article in *Canadian Business* stated:

> Some of the boys in the Gallery and elsewhere are down on [Nicholson] because he objected to sending beer to the soldiers in Africa. That the Canadian troops

should have the choice of drinking the bottled brew or leaving it alone, he does not concede. Here is certainly no place to wave the flag of temperance, nor to fight out the prohibition issue. Sufficient to say, however, that most of our fighting men do not take kindly to Mr. Nicholson's "dry" viewpoint.[12]

Although he was aware that "certain members may think him a crank on drink," Sandy did not allow other people's viewpoints to alter his stance. He was critical that young people were being encouraged to consume liquor, and he quoted an article in *Brewers Magazine*, which stated:

One of the finest things that could have happened to the brewing industry was the insistence of high ranking officers to make beer available at army camps . . . Here is a chance for brewers to cultivate a taste for beer in millions of young men who will eventually constitute the largest beer consuming section of our population.[13]

In March 1942 Sandy spoke at a memorial service for J.S. Woodsworth at McDougall United Church in Edmonton. When Woodsworth died in Vancouver on 21 March, the national office requested provincial offices to arrange memorial services in the country's main centres, so that as many of his supporters and admirers as possible might be able to pay him their last respects.[14] In his eulogy, Sandy said,

J.S. Woodsworth will be remembered as a prophet of the Canadian people, and as one of the common people whose cause he always championed . . . Always, conviction, sincerity and courage were evident in his work. He always sought for high places, acknowledging his responsibility to his fellowmen and exploring new paths by which to benefit them. Because of him new worlds have opened up for others. During all his years in the House of Commons, from 1921 to 1940, he was a single voice which never wavered or modified in its appeals.[15]

Stanley Knowles contested Woodsworth's Winnipeg North Centre seat in the byelection in November. Because Sandy had helped to convince Knowles to remain in politics, he was jubilant when Knowles not only won but "received 70 percent of the vote and his opponents lost their deposits."[16] Stanley Knowles's defeat in Manitoba in the 1940 federal election had been a major disappointment for the party. The United Church had issued him an ultimatum, challenging him to decide once and for all whether his allegiance was to the church or to the CCF. Soon after Woodsworth's stroke, Sandy asked Knowles, "What are you going to do?"

"I don't know."

"Mr. Woodsworth is never going to be able to resume his seat in Parliament. If you could be around, you should replace him."

"Well, Sandy, I couldn't do it on fifty dollars a month like you did, but if I had one hundred dollars a month I might manage."

Of the arrangements to guarantee him a suitable salary, David Lewis wrote, "Both Nicholson and I were more than happy to help raise the money for the purpose. Thus Knowles, who was unpaid provincial chairman for a while, became provincial organizer and secretary in 1941 and held that office until his election to parliament."[17]

In 1942 the CCF expanded its staff, first by appointing Sandy as national treasurer, then, a year later, by adding Lloyd R. Shaw as research director. Shaw proved to be a great help to the party and to Lewis personally. About Sandy, Shaw wrote:

> It was not surprising that in 1942 Sandy was appointed the first CCF national treasurer. Up to that time there wasn't enough money in the CCF kitty to warrant appointing a treasurer. His main responsibility was not to look after party funds, but to raise the money . . .
> As a result of Sandy's organizational and financial efforts, he demonstrated that political party funds can be raised on a non-patronage basis. This enabled his colleagues, spear-headed by National Secretary David Lewis, together with Leader M.J. Coldwell, National President Frank Scott, Angus MacInnis, Stanley Knowles and many other CCFers in all walks of life to

start building the federal party for the first time on a much more solid basis.[18]

Coming from Saskatchewan, where farmers supported the party financially despite their disastrous years of Depression and drought, Sandy was appalled to learn about the paucity of contributions in other provinces. He set out to raise the financial sights of the party and to a large extent he succeeded. Lloyd Stinson remembered him being "bold and imaginative in his approach to potential donors." He recalled accompanying Sandy to the Childs Building in Winnipeg to see a businessman said to be both wealthy and sympathetic to the party — possibly good for a one thousand-dollar donation. Sandy made his pitch; the man refused. To Stinson's amazement, Sandy immediately suggested one hundred dollars. Relieved, the man wrote a cheque for the smaller amount. Later Stinson asked Sandy why he came down so far, so fast. He replied, "It was either one hundred dollars or nothing, and I wanted something."[19]

Sandy liked to tell about his first substantial donation which had occurred accidentally. In February 1942, when Coldwell was speaker at an Empire Club luncheon in Toronto at which Sandy was a guest, he "happened to be placed beside Joe Atkinson, owner and publisher of the *Toronto Star.*" In the course of the conversation, Atkinson told Sandy of his offer of five thousand dollars which had been rejected by Woodsworth. Sandy responded that "times have changed. If you should feel like doing that again, I'd be sure you would not be offended by having your cheque returned." Atkinson suggested that Sandy should visit him at his office and he subsequently made several generous contributions to the CCF. The two men became friends, as implied by correspondence from Atkinson to Sandy a year later, saying, "I have yours of the 21st and note what you have done with my cheque. I enjoy our too infrequent talks — why not oftener?"[20]

Margaret Telford's arrival in Ottawa coincided with Sandy's appointment as national treasurer. She worked as secretary for him and Percy Wright. She believed Sandy's "most important contribution has been in human relationships, and the demonstration that politics is an honourable occupation." He conscientiously cared for his constituents, following up "on their requests and writing as quickly as possible to let them know what he was doing and what success he was having."[21]

Another secretary of Sandy's, Pat Armstrong, spoke of the "voluminous correspondence" that kept her typewriter clacking. Armstrong added, "Marian was sometimes in Ottawa and sometimes in Saskatchewan," where she sent Sandy notes from his constituency "about who had died, been born, married . . . information on which he based letters to his constituents, showing them he had not forgotten them while in Ottawa."[22] When she was in Ottawa, Marian spent hours in the House Reading Room gleaning the same kind of news from the Saskatchewan weekly papers.

Sandy and the other six Saskatchewan members of Parliament spoke often and loudly about the plight of westerners. Making a point about the penury of prairie people, Sandy called attention to a situation parallelling the Biblical widow's mite — an old age pensioner over eighty who "every month buys a war savings stamp for each of his 18 grandchildren [$4.50 a month out of a $20 cheque]."[23] Sandy's philosophy dictated acknowledgement of coins whether for the CCF or other commendable causes.

His exasperation at the "eastern mentality" gave rise to this speech:

> It has been suggested that we in the west are like poor relatives, always coming to the treasury and saying gimme, gimme, gimme . . . Many years ago the poor manufacturers in Canada found themselves competing in a ruthless world with more powerful groups in the United States prepared to flood their markets and force down prices. So these poor manufacturers came to the rulers of the day and said, 'We want help.' And they got it."

He continued,

"The minister of munitions and supply (Mr. Howe) has gone on record repeatedly that it is unreasonable to ask any manufacturer to manufacture at a loss, and I have yet to hear anyone tell of a manufacturer of machine guns or tanks or munitions or any other war equipment who is losing money. The farmers are engaged in the production of food to feed our own people and allied peoples of the world. Is it fair that those who are engaged in this necessary activity should have a return for their services that is not on a parity with the return that is going to these other groups of society?

He explained parity price for farm products as "a price that will enable the farmer to buy in the market an amount of goods similar to what he was able to buy during a basic period."[24]

When Sandy spoke in the House he was reiterating CCF policies which called for protection and assistance to farmers by providing them with the opportunity to earn a fair share of the national income. This would enable them to maintain equity in their land, home and equipment, as well as permitting them to improve their living conditions. Sandy had traced the origin of economic parity of agriculture with industry, primarily an American concept, to the depression of the early 1920s in the United States. Although Canadian farm unions and the CCF advocated parity prices constantly, the principle was not accepted readily by other political parties.

Some CCFers decided that if the party was to survive it would be essential to elect a government in some province. "To go with Tommy Douglas in Saskatchewan seemed to be the best prospect," Sandy recorded.

He rallied support in Saskatchewan for Douglas to be the new leader of the provincial CCF. Following the 1942 provincial convention where Douglas was elected leader, Sandy continued collecting funds for the party. He seldom asked anyone to do more than he was willing to do himself. Being used to church tithing, he gave "5 percent to the federal organization, and 5 percent divided between provincial and constituency offices."

Douglas said, "Sandy could raise money like nobody I've ever known. [He] became a legend."

Sandy recalled,

> We had to raise money. I went after $5,000 right away. I put it to the provincial executive — we needed ten people to give $100; 20 to give $50; 50 to give $20; 100 to give $10, and 200 to give $5. I didn't talk about paying off debts. This was a victory fund. I said, 'Tommy is our new leader, we have to do what we haven't done before.' And the way we got the money indicated to me we were going to form a government.

Sandy always gauged the health of the party by the response to appeals for financial aid. There were the Logans in Yorkton who always gave ten dollars when Sandy collected. This time Sandy said, "I need nine more like that." Impressed by Douglas, Logan made out a cheque for one hundred dollars. Even farm labourers earning twenty dollars a month boosted their contribution. In the course of his rural collections, if Sandy saw a farmer with a good head of cattle he asked, "Why not give one of them or a cash equivalent to the CCF?"

Within two years the CCF had an organization in every constituency in Saskatchewan, had candidates in most of them, and workers canvassing door-to-door and farm-to-farm, exhilarated by the response of the people they called on.

Besides his concentrated fund-raising efforts in Saskatchewan, Sandy covered Canada from coast to coast. He first toured the Maritimes in the autumn of 1942, beginning with a visit to Dalhousie, New Brunswick. Next he drew overflow crowds at Moncton, New Glasgow, Stellarton and Truro. He addressed a mass meeting at Sydney, Nova Scotia, and spoke to a joint meeting there of the CCF national and provincial councils; then he left for New Waterford and on to Sydney Mines, ending his tour in Halifax. A month later, Sandy paid his first visit to Vancouver.

Marian had been busy, too, working on a CCF

cookbook. Margaret Telford Thomas recalled, "After the 1942-1943 session I went to the CCF National Office to work on the cookbook — which Mrs. Nicholson was coordinating with a committee of Vida Knowles, Marjorie Mann, Sophie Lewis, other MPs' wives in Ottawa, and for which Sandy was soliciting advertising [during his cross-Canada fund raising]."[25] The cookbook, *Canadian Favorites*, published in 1944, contained a foreword in English and French (no common gesture then) by Lucy Woodsworth, widow of J.S. Woodsworth. Recipes had been supplied by Canadian women from coast to coast, and they reflected the cuisine of at least two dozen countries. The cookbook brought in ten thousand dollars on the first printing and another ten thousand dollars on the second. In the 1960s, building on past experience, the women of the New Democratic Party (NDP) would issue another cookbook as their first national fund-raising project.

To encourage more people to contribute to the CCF coffers, Sandy prepared pamphlets for distribution, aimed at parting CCFers from their hard-earned dollars. In a two-page appeal, "How to win friends and influence history," Sandy made light of his onerous task stating, "Contrary to popular belief, the soliciting of funds for the CCF is one of the most fascinating assignments anyone could accept."

Magnus Eliason remembered:

> Around the mid-forties, I think a new method of fund raising by the United Church was emerging on the scene and Sandy adopted that method . . . for the party . . . being roughly that you discussed seriously with the person what they could afford based on their income and their expenses and arrive at some sort of approximate amount . . . And Sandy was the instrument of getting the first one thousand-dollar contribution for the Party from an individual — another Reverend Nicholson in Nova Scotia.[26]

Following the 1944 CCF sweep in Saskatchewan, Sandy "found it easier to find ten in Saskatchewan who gave one thousand dollars than it was to get the first one hundred dollars in 1942."

To help mail financial appeals and other CCF promotional material, Sandy found supporters in Ottawa. Nettie Forsiuk wrote,

> My first contact with Sandy Nicholson was in 1944 . . . I was then employed in the Dominion Bureau of Statistics . . . I got a call from Sandy Nicholson at my place of work (which was a surprise) because one, I did not know my MP, and two I would not have expected anyone to have taken as much trouble as Mr. Nicholson did to locate me . . . On the first call, Mr. Nicholson invited me to the House of Commons for dinner. At the dinner, if I recall correctly, there were three other guests all of whom stayed to help Mr. Nicholson's secretary stuff envelopes. After that initial introduction, I would get a call from him whenever he was sending out a householder [mailing] . . . We would dine in the parliamentary restaurant and then assist with the envelope stuffing.[27]

CCF policy at this time was based on the principle of equality of sacrifice during the war and of creative postwar planning. Sandy's speeches hammered home these points, always incorporating the Liberal war slogan with regard to the CCF's peace plans, insisting "whatever is physically possible must be made financially possible."[28] He remained adamant that if the government could provide health care for men and women in the armed services in wartime, "it is equally important in time of peace to be concerned about the health of our people."[29] He deplored the ratio of patients to doctors in his riding. He said, "We have 11 doctors practicing now, each looking after an average of 5,217 people. Our three practicing dentists look after an average of 19,131 . . . [I can't see] why it is necessary to have a dentist for every 535 in the Canadian army, and why the people of Mackenzie riding should have to get along with so few."[30] To serve the area, dentists in Mackenzie led an itinerant life. An announcement in a 1943 issue of the *Kelvington Radio* stated:

> Dr. W.J. Olmstead, dentist will be at his Kelvington
> office from January 23 to February 10 for the practise
> of his profession . . . will be in Rose Valley for the
> practise of his profession two days.

During the 1944 Saskatchewan provincial election campaign, Sandy remembered that Liberal party tactics became rough as its politicians began to smell defeat. The Communist party had become respectable, so the Liberals created a new calumny by labelling the CCF as national socialists, intent on farm take-overs, business confiscation, and driving industry out of the province. Newspapers augmented this campaign by publishing full page editorials attacking the CCF. However, prairie people were less vulnerable to this type of political libel than they had been during the previous election. Most farmers were off relief; economic conditions had improved slightly; farm wives and parents were receiving army pay from members serving overseas. And, said Sandy, "June 15, 1944, dawned clear and warm, bringing our predominantly rural supporters out to the polls. We won forty-seven of fifty-two seats."

Although Sandy had spent much of his free time fund raising in 1945, he had allowed a sufficient number of hours to campaign in Mackenzie for the federal election called for June 11. He defeated his nearest opponent by almost 4,000 votes. The CCF took 18 of the 21 ridings in Saskatchewan and 44.4 percent of the vote — more than the Liberals and more than double the Conservatives.

Tom Bentley, elected member of Parliament for Swift Current, had been one of the people involved when Sandy set up successful CCF organizations in the province. Another member from Saskatchewan joined Sandy as a colleague in 1945 — Robert Ross Knight (better known as Roy), member of Parliament for Saskatoon City. Mrs. Ellen Knight reminisced about those days,

> We all joined the women's group — the parliamentary
> wives' association. For all the wives — Liberals,
> Conservatives, Social Crediters and CCFers. We sewed
> baby napkins by hand. We sent parcels overseas . . .
> Sandy was so kind to us . . . he remembered

everything and everybody — a marvelous organizer. Marian was always behind Sandy — a marvelous help to him in her quiet way. She was a lovely person, no fanfare at all . . . I'll never forget a meeting in Saskatoon [while campaigning for the June federal election where] Sandy was the money man. And there was so much money he went to some room and took a drawer out and filled it with money. Sandy walked up to the front with it. It was full of money and cheques, this bottom drawer of some dresser at the Bessborough Hotel — and Roy got elected. Sandy knew just what to say when he got up to ask for money.[31]

In March 1945, Sandy spoke on the importance of Canadian participation in the San Francisco Conference, held there from 25 April to 26 June to formulate world-wide plans for a new society after the war. He said, "In Canada, we have found from experience that working together for the greatest number has been" far better than each province looking after its own needs. He went on to state that of the thirty-three national groups within Saskatchewan, the largest was of Ukrainian origin. Sandy's own children went to a school where more than half of the children were non-Anglo-Saxon, a miniature league of nations. He believed "children growing up in that sort of environment will not be handicapped by prejudices that frequently are deep-rooted in countries where it is assumed that all virtue is to be found in those who are of the race or colour or creed of one particular group."[32]

Sandy made his first trip to California in January 1946, embarking on a speaking tour to take the socialist message to interested groups in the United States. He had "sixteen busy days in Los Angeles, where Dr. Hugh and Mrs. MacLean were his hosts, and two weeks in the San Francisco area." In most cases Sandy spoke to the converted. He said, "The United States got the Roosevelt New Deal about the same time as we got the CCF in Saskatchewan. Those who invited me to speak were active in hoping to get a new party similar to the CCF in California."

One large audience in Los Angeles — a weekly luncheon assembly of business and professional men who met at the Biltmore Hotel — was not particularly sympathetic to CCF ideas, but gave him a friendly hearing. A letter from the vice-president of the Hollywood Bowl Association acknowledged:

> Again I wish to express the deep appreciation of the members of the [Severance] Club and myself personally for your generosity in giving so freely of your time and bringing such a fundamental message. Canada is to be congratulated in inaugurating this wonderful movement for human amelioration and constructive development . . . [33]

While he was in California, Sandy arranged to meet Charlie Quan's son, Ping-Shao who "along with six other engineers, [was] sent by the Chinese government to study irrigation and drainage at the University of California at Davis." The men were "to be in charge of a large water conservation programme after returning to China."[34] Before departing for the United States, Sandy had engaged in negotiations with the Canadian Government and the Chinese Embassy in Washington, soliciting permission for Ping-Shao Quan to visit his father in Saskatchewan before returning to China. Thanks to Sandy's intervention, a passport proved unnecessary and letters from the Canadian immigration department authorized Quan's entry.

Sandy seldom did things by halves. His arrangements included forwarding a map to Charlie Quan marked with his son's route. He also invited them both to Canora for Easter Sunday dinner. In the Nicholsons' guestbook, Charlie Quan listed his address as Texas Café, Assiniboia, Saskatchewan. Ping wrote in Chinese characters:

> Appreciate highly for your invitation of coming to your home on Easter Sunday, hope to have the pleasure of your nice family to come to our home in China in the future.

In February 1946 the Saskatchewan air ambulance service had been inaugurated. Sandy had discussed this with Douglas as soon as the CCF formed the Saskatchewan government in 1944. Both men had experienced near tragedies which strengthened their determination to make such a medical service a reality. They believed that health should not depend on the ability of people to pay for care nor on whims of specialists. At the first opportunity, Sandy spoke in the House of Commons about this innovation:

> Saskatchewan is the only province on this continent who [has] the good fortune to have a publicly-owned and operated air ambulance service available for anyone in the province, if a doctor, nurse, or justice of the peace or any responsible citizen expresses the opinion the air ambulance service is necessary. There is a $25 fee charged for the ambulance, with a trained nurse to go with it. It is available to go anywhere in the province to move a patient to the hospital. If the patient cannot pay the $25, the air ambulance makes the trip in any event."[35]

As a member of the CCF National Council, Sandy attended the March conference at which council accepted "the recommendation to expand the national office and the idea of a national membership." Lorne Ingle became research director; Donald MacDonald, publicity and education director; and Helen Peart, librarian. The increased staff required larger office space, leading Lewis and Sandy to look into purchasing a modest building. They chose a three-storey residence on Metcalfe Street, which the officers of the Canadian Brotherhood of Railway Employees agreed to buy in trust for the CCF; the party named the building Woodsworth House and moved into it in September 1946.[36]

The CCF continued to advocate that the government's duty was to plan the use of the country's resources for the benefit of all Canadians. The national office launched a "nation-wide petition pleading for a pension of $50 a month at age 65, without a means test and with cost-of-living supplements." Within three months volunteers collected some half a million signatures.[37] Sandy recalled the excitement among CCF members as they carried the signed petitions into the House on 16 May 1947.

Dispelling the Communist bogey and promoting better relationships between Canada and Russia became one of Sandy's continuing concerns. A 1948 letter from Dr. MacLean told of the anti-Soviet feelings then rampant in the United States:

> I expect the hysteria that is found here is to some extent existing with you. Here one can hardly express a progressive thought without being called a communist . . . I am afraid that because of the ensuing hysteria democratic socialism will be pushed into the background for some years to come . . . As in Saskatchewan, and in parts of Canada the old parties will go so far as to try to get the people to believe that to vote CCF will ultimately bring about communism.[38]

At this same time, Sandy began a lengthy correspondence with Alexander Fishman whom he had met in California. Fishman had written *Bells of Russia* under the name of Alexander Morskoi. Sandy promoted the book in Canada. He contacted W.S. Lloyd, minister of education in Saskatchewan, noting the book was written "without any note of bitterness and very definitely to break down American anti-Soviet prejudices." Lloyd sent the letter to the provincial librarian, giving her authority to order two hundred copies for the province's travelling libraries. When Fishman learned this, he wrote that many copies deposited in a library "are far more important than trice this number sold to bookshops . . . I cherish the idea that you have in mind not only myself but the great cause of bringing at least morally the great peoples of the East and West a bit closer to each other."[39]

Since Russia formed the basis for the friendship, Sandy replied to Fishman, "Had I mentioned previously that my wife is taking Russian for the second year at Carleton College? She has prepared a brief speech, which she plans on giving in Russian during the Saskatchewan election campaign." Explaining this, Sandy said he enjoyed good Russian support in several communities, "where older folk liked to hear CCF speakers who could tell our story in

Russian."[40] The ability to speak a second language helped Sandy's colleague, Alex Kuziak, to become elected as member of the Legislative Assembly for Canora in the June provincial election. Kuziak's fluent Ukrainian earned him the Ukrainian vote. Until then, numerous older people of Ukrainian descent felt it was their duty to vote Liberal evermore as they had come to Canada when the Liberals were in power.

In 1947 and 1948 Sandy pursued his sideline of fund raising. On weekends and during recesses, his journeys took him to "the coal fields on Vancouver Island, in northern Alberta, in New Brunswick, on Cape Breton Island and on the mainland of Nova Scotia."[41] He also made appeals for funds to run candidates in three federal by-elections — Ontario county; Yale, British Columbia; and Vancouver Centre. The appeal in CCF newspapers stressed that without support "CCF workers within the con-stituencies would be unable to match the unlimited funds which would be spent by the old parties during the campaigns." Sandy reminded readers, "as a result of contributions from old age pensioners, from veterans, farmers and workers, ample radio time was purchased, pamphlets distributed and victories achieved in other by-elections such as South York, Winnipeg North Centre, Selkirk and Humboldt."[42]

During the year both David Lewis and M.J. Coldwell incurred huge hospital bills as a result of their wives' illnesses. Because their salaries did not allow for any added expenses and "lack of funds in the national treasury and the critical financial position in provincial sections of the movement ruled out any increase in salary," Sandy spearheaded a drive for a benevolent fund and turned over sizeable cheques to both men. Writing to an official in Douglas's Regina office, acknowledging a donation to the Lewis fund, Sandy stated Mrs. Lewis "had a very critical period last June and July when her life was in danger for several days. Later on in the year the twins were born." Not often expressed, but intimately experienced, Sandy con-fided that he sometimes felt "guilty in bringing our financial problems repeatedly to such a small group but one would not discover all the fine qualities of CCFers without these practical tests."[43]

Sandy's services as fund-raiser and campaigner were stretched to the limit in 1949. He blamed his long absences from his own constituency for his defeat in the June federal election. On the campaign trip to the Maritimes in February, to help in the Digby-Annapolis-Kings byelection, Lloyd Shaw wrote:

> Ice froze in the bedrooms of this "summer" hotel overlooking the Bay of Fundy in Digby County, Nova Scotia. The chef had left for the winter so Gladys Strum grabbed a frying pan in the hotel kitchen. Soon Warner Strum and I sat down near a huge cook stove to a breakfast of tasty bacon and eggs.[44]

Sandy, Coldwell and Brockelbank joined the fray for the last week. Shaw, now secretary of the Nova Scotia section of the CCF, registered disappointment at the CCF vote, although it showed a sizeable increase.

On the hustings in New Brunswick, Sandy met Dana Mullen, CCF provincial secretary, who gave up a university teaching position to work for the party. Mrs. Mullen's husband was a veteran finishing his last year at university. Although the national office was unable to subsidize the New Brunswick operation, the Mullens insisted they would "make this year's work a contribution to the CCF and turn over any money available to enable students to campaign in rural counties in New Brunswick" in summer. Sandy recalled that the work done by veterans at the University of New Brunswick was not being parallelled anywhere in Canada. About ten men and two women on campus, all outstanding students, wanted "to remain in New Brunswick to help elect a CCF government there."[45]

Speculation ran high regarding a June 1949 federal election, although no date had been announced. Before Parliament adjourned in April, Sandy witnessed the ceremony in connection with the entrance of Newfoundland into Confederation. On 1 April, Newfoundland became the tenth province.

During the ceremony the Prime Minister cut the first line on one of the ten shields at the entrance to the Peace Tower. He mentioned that when the new buildings were erected following the disastrous fire in 1916 the main tower was dedicated to peace and on the arch were inscribed the Coats-of-Arms of the nine provinces of Canada. The architects carved ten shields instead of nine. One was left blank for the day which the Fathers of Confederation had foreseen when Newfoundland would join Canada. The day had come.[46]

Following the dissolution of Parliament at the end of April, Sandy began a concentrated campaign in his constituency. He tackled his itinerary with an optimistic approach. During his tenure in the House he never compromised his integrity and he believed his record reflected this. The Sturgis local paper supported him:

[He] had earned a place as one of the prominent pioneers of the party . . . [As CCF national treasurer since 1942] he has made an outstanding contribution in building the movement through the organization of its financial base, working always on the principle that great numbers of Canadians, each contributing according to their ability, can build a party which truly represents them and which can effectively challenge the privileged few who can back the old party machines.[47]

On the other hand, despite all his years in the Hudson Bay Junction district, Sandy had to contend with being a prophet not accepted in his own country. Campaign cullings in a June *Commonwealth* stated:

If Sandy Nicholson gets re-elected in Mackenzie it won't be due to the publicity he gets in the *Hudson Bay Post*. Last week Mr. Nicholson got one paragraph on an inside page to Jimmy Gardiner's three columns starting on the front.[48]

Pat Armstrong, who continued to work occasionally for Sandy in Mackenzie constituency, remembered "working in the CCF office in Sturgis one sad night when he conceded defeat." He had been "much more cheerful in appearance" than the rest around him that night of 27 June 1949. The fact that it had not been an isolated regional defeat for the CCF provided no balm for the beating. A CCF newspaper reported Conservatives and CCF alike shared defeat "when a wholesale flopover of Canadian voters sent at least 193 Liberals to fill the government side in the new 262-seat House of Commons." Not unexpectedly, the Liberals took fifteen of the seventeen new seats created by redistribution and Newfoundland's admission.

Besides learning that his colleague Clarie Gillis had retained his seat in Nova Scotia, Sandy was delighted with Roy Knight's substantial win in Saskatoon. Knight's success was attributed to the fact his candidacy was the first to be officially endorsed by the Trades and Labour Council (TLC).[49] The Saskatoon *Star-Phoenix* said in an article on "The New Parliament" that "the nature and calibre of the opposition is no less important to parliamentary govern-ment" than the party in power. It agreed that the CCF had lost a few of its leading figures: "Mr. Nicholson and Mr. Wright from Saskatchewan and Mr. Zaplitny from Manitoba were good government critics. Their loss will weaken the Party."[50]

Magnus Eliason remembered Sandy saying after this election that he "realized to hold a seat in the House of Commons meant staying at home when you had time and working with people, rather than circulating across Canada raising funds for the party — that didn't bring you votes." Defeat did not mean he would quit promoting CCF principles. Up to this time he had been honorary national treasurer, giving his spare time to the job "no charge." Percy Wright, now CCF national president, persuaded him to assist in eliminating some of the debts incurred in the 1949 election. The national council confirmed Sandy as full-time national treasurer in October.

Lewis suggested Donald MacDonald try his hand at fund raising in co-operation with Sandy, as Sandy had indicated he probably would not continue after one year. The two men travelled throughout the province of Ontario "from

Cornwall to Kenora, from Windsor to Cochrane, sometimes together, more often fanning out" on their own. MacDonald said, "Up to that point I had never been engaged in fund-raising work; in fact, I viewed it as a rather distasteful activity! Certainly not one that attracted me. But I was able to learn the basic tricks of the trade from Sandy. And I added the component of organizing as a coordinated effort with fund-raising [and] soon found [this] very much to my liking."[51] MacDonald succeeded Sandy in the newly designed capacity of federal treasurer and organizer at the 1950 convention. After his relentless pursuit of nickels, dimes and dollars for the party, Sandy looked forward to starting a new segment of his life as a full-time participant in the co-operative farm at Sturgis.

Chapter 9

Co-operative Farm Venture in Saskatchewan, 1945-1953

A n address at a prairie provinces wheat pool convention held in Regina in 1944 supplied Sandy's friend, Elmer Sjolie, with the idea of a co-operative farm venture. Sjolie took the idea back to Sturgis and consulted Sam Sookocheff and Sandy, both of whom became interested immediately. They contacted other farmers in the area and called a meeting at the home of Albert Sjolie in Hassan on 28 January 1945.

Incorporation of the Sturgis Farm Co-operative Association Limited took place on 15 March 1945. Members listed on the 1945 financial statement included: A.M. and Marian Nicholson; Charlie and Beda Mitchell; Hugh and Olga Mitchell; Elmer and Lena Sjolie; Sam Sookocheff; Hannah Sookocheff.

In the economic sense, Saskatchewan is considered Canada's banner co-operative province. From the beginning, farmers were dependent mainly on the wheat crop, experiencing recurrent failures and fluctuating prices. Powerless then, as now, to control prices, they could and did form co-operatives eliminating the middlemen. Once in power, the CCF government improved the climate for co-operatives in the province. In 1941 the percentage of the population that held membership in co-operative organizations was 5.7; by 1946 it was 15.4 and it continued to increase.[1]

The first efforts at co-operative farming emerged in 1943 at Round Hill, followed by Hepburn and Sturgis. It took months of organization to get the Sturgis venture underway. Initially, farmers interested in forming the farm co-operative were scattered throughout the district. Members soon realized that matters would be facilitated if the group could farm adjacent lands. Most believed that the men would work together well, but some wondered how, as Sandy put it, "the women folk would agree," while others anticipated trouble when the children "started tearing into each other." Such arguments soon dissolved when it was decided that each family would live in its individual home, have its own vegetable garden and perhaps a few hens and a cow. Seeking organizational information, the Sturgis group visited Regina for interviews with staff members of the new Department of Reconstruction and Co-operatives. Writing from Ottawa to Alex Turner, deputy minister of the co-operative division in Regina, to introduce the group, Sandy said, "While I am not going to have a great deal of time to spend on the farm in the initial steps, members are all anxious to assist in finding a solution for some of the rural problems in our country, and are joining this undertaking with a view to working together for the greatest good of the larger community as well as for this particular association."[2] In drawing up the association's bylaws, provision was made to accommodate members by granting "time off with full pay to perform various community duties which may, or may not, give such member a net return."[3] The group learned to its dismay the Saskatchewan government had not formulated specific information on farm co-operatives, leaving the Sturgis group to lead the way. In fact, the government departments concerned with co-operatives requested the group to forward pertinent material for departmental files.

In April 1945 members pooled their labour, land and machinery and acquired three thousand acres near Sturgis. Each member was allowed the appraised value of his land and machinery in credit as loan capital in the association. Together, they had more machinery than needed and by disposing of the surplus, they netted four thousand dollars. The co-operative farm idea took on a more concrete form when the regulations and articles were drawn up. [See APPENDIX III for bylaws.] Within a few years the association had perfected its means of operation, but it commenced by appointing several farm managers who undertook the work by rotation for short terms. In this way, farming practices were not frozen in time, as each new manager experimented with his pet theories. At the beginning, as Sandy remembered, "Around two thousand acres were usually under cultivation and the field work done by a 120-horsepower Cle-trac caterpillar tractor, two John Deeres, one International Diesel WD 9, two self-propelled combines and one team of horses."

Sandy sold his Canora home in April 1946 and vacated it in June. The Nicholsons put the entire revenue from the sale into the co-operative where it became available for the proposed building programme. In a letter to Elmer Sjolie, Sandy sought a solution for the perennial problem of furniture storage, asking if he or the Mitchells might have an empty granary for use until the Nicholsons' living quarters were ready. Sandy explained, "Marian and the children will be coming down after school is over and will make their headquarters here [in Ottawa] until houses are built at Sturgis."[4]

While he was still in Parliament, Sandy watched for legislation which might be advantageous to the co-operative, and he asked about the availability of loans for co-operative farms, under the proposed Central Housing and Mortgage Corporation. "Would the minister [The Honourable James Lorimer Ilsley, minister of finance] indicate whether a co-operative farm, for example, wishing to embark on a co-operative housing programme, would be eligible for a loan under the act now that this section has been added? . . . We will say there are to be ten houses on the co-operative farm which they wish built as a unit, where they might have central heating?"[5] The minister replied in the affirmative. When Sandy spoke in the House of Commons that day in 1945, the co-operative hoped that between ten and twelve families would be joining.

However, as Sandy noted, "when it came to investing all [we] had there were just five families. Sam Sookocheff was a bachelor, the rest of us were married with spouses keen on the idea."

Contractors who were questioned about the feasibility of a four-family unit under one roof, advised Sandy against that concept. Separate units would be preferable, with resale likely to be a factor in the future. In the end, the association neither applied for nor received any funds from either provincial or federal governments.

The association's assets totalled more than $59,500 by the end of 1945. The $19,000 crop consisted of: wheat, 351 acres; oats, 502 acres; barley, 123 acres; tame hay, 67 acres. Summerfallow amounted to 627 acres for that year. The Sturgis co-operative sold $18,988 of their 1945 crop. Other income from custom combining, members' outside work and miscellaneous sales brought in a further $1,247.95, making a total income of $20,236.89. Operating expenses amounted to $14,418.81 (which included all wages to members and outside help), leaving a surplus available for distribution to final returns of labour, interest on membership loans, and statutory reserves of $5,818.07.[6]

The principal owners of the Scandinavian Land Company, Olga Fredericksen and her husband, who considered themselves socialists, had a large tract of land in the district. The association bought and located on eight acres of this land north of Sturgis, the west half of 9-33-5, selecting this building site for the co-operative because of its good water supply, its highway and railway connections, and its proximity to the village.

After Olga Fredericksen moved to the United States, Sandy kept up a correspondence with her concerning the co-operative housing plans on the land which had been purchased from her. As he explained to her in one letter,

> There are very definite savings available if materials
> can be purchased on a wholesale basis, and a number
> of units can be built at one time. Title to all the
> houses would be held co-operatively. Should anyone
> wish to withdraw at any time, arrangements would be
> made so the co-op would reimburse them for the
> value of their equity. If property values increased all
> would benefit; should they decrease, all would share
> the losses. The land would be included as part of their
> capital cost, valued at the amount we paid you.

He went on to say that members probably would agree
on one general style of architecture, and would make
provisions in case some "families wished some additional
frills, these extras would either be advanced in cash or paid
for by higher rents." He added, "We all take a great deal of
pleasure in speaking in terms of 'our' land and 'our' crop
rather than using the first person."[7]

Although he was disappointed at the slow pace of
construction on the site (the Nicholsons' house was built
last), Sandy enjoyed having his family in Ottawa. Marian
took advantage of the city's night school courses to learn
drafting and design which enabled her to make the
blueprints for the Nicholsons' Sturgis home. Sandy, Marian,
Mary Anna and Alexander were not to move to Sturgis until
after the election defeat of 1949. During the intervening
summers, 1946-1948, Marian and the younger children
returned to the Sturgis area "living in granaries, a tent and
other temporary housing."[8]

Sandy's experiences "down on the farm" would later
provide grist for political arguments in Parliament. He
would call attention to the healthy profits made by farm
equipment distributors, and pounce on this in his perennial
pleas for parity prices for farmers which would enable
them to purchase the expensive machinery. Referring to a
self-propelled combine bought in 1946, he told members,
"As a result of an error made at the factory, the invoice for
this combine was sent to us direct, instead of to the
Canadian Co-operative Implements Ltd . . . factory price at

Brantford, Ontario [was $2,308.25]. The price we paid was $3,421.35." He added that the difference lay not in freight charges, as papers showed two combines could be shipped in one railcar at a cost of $125 each.[9]

While Saskatchewan's CCF government encouraged the development of co-operatives, federal legislation continued to put obstacles in their paths, arbitrarily classifying associations as corporations under the tax laws. During 1946, Sandy and the other CCF members of Parliament fought a running battle in the House arguing against this unfair concept. A CCF pamphlet issued that year stated:

> As a result of their opposition, several improvements were gained. These included an increase from six months to one year as the period within which a co-op must pay its dividends; the retention by co-ops of dividends if authority is given by members; the taxation of profits from non-member business; and exemption for three years of all newly organized co-ops.[10]

W.B. Francis, solicitor for the Co-operative Union of Saskatchewan, was an expert on taxation matters, and his opinions were made known at a regional co-operative meeting. Francis had stated that although all corporations with an income were then (and still are) subject to income tax, some groups were entitled to certain deductions. He explained:

> The new amendments to the income tax legislation were not designed for production co-operatives, as they do not specifically cover exemption on labour dividends. However . . . individual members of these co-operatives might sign a special agreement with the co-operative to cover handling of any surplus payable to each member and thus place the co-operative in a position where it would have little or no income under the general income tax law. The individual members would then be taxable on the three-year average basis for farmers on these amounts if they, as individuals, were taxable.[11]

Unfortunately, the Sturgis Farm Co-operative Association

could expect no deduction except under contracts.
Crippling taxes would eventually result in the co-operative's closure.

In October 1946 Sam Sookocheff represented the Sturgis
co-operative at the meeting of production co-operatives in
Saskatoon. Reporting for the association, he said his land
had been twenty-five miles from that of the other members
until he had sold it recently. By this time, the association
operated three sections of land, not all under cultivation.
He believed that through pooling all capital resources,
many of the difficulties of partial pooling were eliminated.
Sookocheff said, "The Sturgis farm pays its members a
monthly wage [and] the manager is not paid any more than
the other members; the lady members got along very well
together; five basements had been dug on the site of their
co-operative community, but lack of material was holding
up building operations; the livestock operations had been
pooled only recently; part of the dividends from last year
had been retained in the co-operative. Membership consisted of five men and six women."[12] Doreen Sookocheff,
his new wife, was added to the membership on the 1946
financial statement. Each family received $105 a month as
return for labour, plus interest on capital.

By March 1949 four new homes had been built at a cost
which dug deeply into the co-operative's financial reserves.
The building programme called for one new home to be
constructed each year until all members had been housed.
Sandy's daughter Ruth recalled, "For several of the families,
it was [their] first home with electricity and insulation."[13] As
well, each house had a cistern with a pressure system, and
each had its own furnace.

The farm operated on a factory time basis with set hours
for all facets of work, except during harvest. Although
operating the farm kept them busy, the members proved to
be an asset to the Sturgis community. Every worthwhile
project had their backing, "not only in spirit, but in cold
cash and hard work."[14] Until he was defeated at the polls,
Sandy's parliamentary duties had absorbed most of his
time, but he, too, was to become active in community

affairs, serving as president of the local horticultural society and the Sturgis Memorial Rink. The Mitchell brothers and their wives were ardent curlers as well as members of the Sturgis Credit Union and co-op store. Elmer Sjolie's time as a member and delegate of the Saskatchewan Wheat Pool left him with few leisure hours, but he found time to participate in local school meetings and some bonspiels. Ted Moritz, a World War II veteran from western Saskatchewan, was the handyman around the farm. Being a licensed electrician and adept with hammer and saw, he sometimes accepted work in the village. He and his wife, Margaret — a Scottish war bride — joined the co-operative in 1947.

The bylaws guaranteed each member a minimum wage of $240, provided a member was available for service to the association for at least nine months of the year.[15] Sandy explained that when the bylaws were drafted, members anticipated that they also would take jobs other than their association work. This seldom occurred as work around the farm kept them fully employed. Another bylaw stated that "net earnings of members for services rendered to other than the Association should be paid out to the Association and such members shall receive standard wages."[16] This affected Elmer Sjolie. As a Saskatchewan Wheat Pool officer he drew a salary which he turned over to the farm. The same bylaw allowed a member to apply for a leave of absence "without pay or benefits from the Association if outside labour services" exceeded six weeks in any one year — in which case the member retained his salary. Sandy fell into this category while he sat in the House of Commons. Periods between sessions, when he spent time on the Sturgis farm, served as vacations. In one letter to Sjolie, when a short recess prevented him from travelling to Sturgis, Sandy wrote, "I would give a great deal to get on my overalls and get out to the woodlot for a few days."[17]

Sandy's capital investment formed a large portion of the co-operative farm's assets so annual meetings were slated for times when he could be in attendance. A January 1947 letter from Sturgis stated,

The annual meeting of the Sturgis Co-operative Farm is being held today. Nineteen forty-six was an exceptionally good year with our wheat yielding over 29 bushels per acre, oats 25 and barley 48. The taxation passed last session unfortunately is going to take more from us for income tax purposes than we would have paid operating individually with the same financial return.[18]

In addition to the unfair taxation laws, the problems of living together compatibly plagued most co-operatives, and generally became a major factor in their eventual breakup. In the summer of 1951, T.C. Douglas addressed this issue at the second annual meeting of production co-operatives held at the Matador Co-operative Farm, about halfway between Swift Current and Rosetown. Delegates representing twenty-four co-operative farms and ten machinery co-operatives met there on a co-operative farm for the first time. Douglas pointed out that co-operative farms demanded "people who are grown up, whose personalities have matured," who have learned "something about group living."[19] As early as 1947, conscious of these necessary attributes for congenial business operations, Sandy urged caution in connection with enlarging the Sturgis unit. While the co-operative had had "two very good years" in crop production, he said, members had yet to experience "living in close proximity" and such adjustments "might become more complicated" unless there was some certainty that members would be congenial.[20]

Sandy had expressed the same idea a year earlier to Olga Fredericksen when she had intimated that she and another family would be interested in joining the co-operative. He believed that the members would have no difficulty dealing with them personally, but that the Fredericksens and their friends might dispose of their interests "to others who would not be as co-operative." He said, "We think it important that our program be on a strictly co-operative basis rather than having a number of families on a separate parcel of land."[21]

Bolstered by the encouragement and assistance of the

CCF government, the idea of co-operative farms caught on quickly. By the autumn of 1947, the eight Saskatchewan production co-operatives had assets that totalled $286,000. Besides the co-operative at Sturgis, the farms involved included Laurel, Matador, Turner, McIntosh, Algrove, Mount Hope and Round Hill.[22] An average of four co-operative farms a year had started in Saskatchewan following the incorporation of the one at Sturgis, making a total of sixteen by 1949.

Following his defeat in the June 1949 federal election, Sandy settled down to life on the Sturgis farm. In the autumn, he attended the ceremony at which Woodrow Lloyd, provincial minister of education, officially opened the Sturgis School Unit's new $100,000 vocational composite high school and dormitories. Alexander and Mary Anna attended this first composite school constructed in Saskatchewan, which had been open since October the previous year. Marian taught there part-time beginning in 1953, and permanently from 1955 to 1959. Ruth remained in eastern Canada, attending the University of Toronto, where she won the Urlich bursary on the basis of her first year examination results.[23]

Sandy combined work on the farm with continued campaigning for the CCF. In June 1950 Coldwell stayed with the Nicholsons when he came to attend the Mackenzie federal constituency convention. He wrote in their guest-book on 27 June: "The first anniversary of a disappointing day is marked by a very happy visit, encouragement and goodwill, with valued friends." At the convention Coldwell said his main purpose in coming was "to speak on the CCF movement, which has the common man in mind and makes representations to parliament on his behalf." But he had another important reason — to pay tribute to Sandy, whose "opinions and judgments were appreciated and valued by members of all parties in the House." Coldwell wanted the people to know that Sandy "was a member highly respected by all and his absence from the House [was] a definite loss to all who knew him there." Other speakers included Ruth Nicholson, who gave a report on the Co-operative Commonwealth Youth Movement (CCYM), and Myron Feeley with the constituency president's report.[24]

In August, Sandy and Ruth attended the eleventh CCF national convention, held in Vancouver. The Saskatchewan delegation travelled by chartered bus to the first national CCF convention held west of the Rockies. Although it meant an expensive trip from central and eastern Canada, David Lewis hoped that holding the convention there might help diminish "the alienation felt by our colleagues in British Columbia because of their distance from and occasional disagreement with Ottawa."[25] Grace MacInnis reminisced about early campaigning in Mackenzie constituency where the Myron Feeley home "was practically a hotel with every bit of floor space covered with beds at night and every bit of table room crowded with visiting speakers by day."[26]

Billed as the burly national party treasurer who would resign that week to devote full time to the farm in northern Saskatchewan, Sandy said, "We're only in our sixth year, so we're still in the experimental state. But we feel we're doing all right." By "all right" he meant that the six families had made enough money in the past five years to pay all the farm debts, to build new homes, and to buy new cars. And they found that their combined efforts had alleviated the drudgery of some of the more irksome tasks in farming.

"None of us likes to milk, but with our system a man does the chores only one week in five. That way we don't all have to get up in the middle of the night, and we're not tied down all the time by the cattle," Sandy commented. Both men and women received monthly wages based on the farm's earnings in the previous year. Sandy always believed in and promoted equality between men and women; although the women did not do much farm work, the men agreed that they deserved a wage for looking after the homes and raising the children. This co-operative principle of earning equality long preceded the feminist movement. In addition, all members received a 5 percent dividend on the basis of their capital investment, and the total added up to a comfortable amount. It was agreed that earnings were higher than when individuals had worked separately. Besides the financial benefits, Sandy explained to the convention that there were other advantages. "We've built our homes close together and it makes it easier . . . if one of us gets sick the rest of us can pitch in to help without travelling a long way to do it."[27]

During the Vancouver convention the CCF honoured several long-time workers. The party presented gifts to Sandy, retiring treasurer; Frank Scott, retiring president; and David Lewis, former CCF secretary. Lewis wrote: "the continuing financial crisis [in the 1950s] saddened me. After so many years of effort by Sandy Nicholson, Donald MacDonald, many others as well as myself at the national level, and hundreds of members and leaders at the provincial and local levels, the party was still unable to finance a minimum program of activity."[28] Sandy's friend Percy Wright became national chairman.

Although Sandy had resigned as national treasurer, he did not cease his fund-raising activities completely. William Boschman, now in Hudson Bay Junction, where he worked for the timber board division of Saskatchewan Forest Products, recalled Sandy's assistance. He wrote: "The Hon. J.H. Brockelbank was now minister of natural resources and chairman of the timber board. He visited the constituency often . . . Sometimes Sandy Nicholson was there and his appeals for funds managed to separate people from a few dollars that might otherwise have gone for special treats, beer for instance." During that period, the Boschmans attended CCF meetings at the Nicholsons' and "enjoyed the hospitality at their co-operative farm near Sturgis."[29]

Along with his farm duties, Sandy kept apace with the activities of his CCF colleagues. In July 1952 he read in *The Commonwealth* that Graham Spry, Saskatchewan's agent-general for the United Kingdom and Europe, had represented the province at the funeral of George VI earlier that year. The article also announced that a radio play written by Spry would be broadcast from London on 9 July by the BBC. The play about the life of Lord Durham, with a cast of twelve and produced by Rooney Pelletier, dealt with "responsible government in Canada and transfer of power from London to the Canadian legislature a century ago."[30]

Sandy's family took pride in their gardening on the co-operative farm, and the local newspaper reported the results of their combined efforts by listing their prizes in the 1952 Sturgis horticulture show. Marian took second and third prizes in nasturtiums, gladioli and table centres. Mary Anna won a first for her African violet and also for four gladioli grown by children. Not to be outdone, Alexander took a first for his weed collection.[31] But Sandy's sojourn on the farm would soon be terminated. A federal election was expected to be called in 1953, and a nominating convention for the Mackenzie constituency was organized in November 1952.

Chapter 10

Back in the House of Commons, 1953-1958

With a federal election pending, the CCF looked for winners and chose Sandy Nicholson as its candidate in Mackenzie at the nominating convention in Preeceville on 3 November 1952. Delegates attending the convention numbered 219, representing 161 polls of the huge constituency extending from Buchanan, in the south, to the Northwest Territories. More than five hundred people taxed the capacity of Preeceville's new Legion Hall to hear Premier Douglas and other speakers at the evening meeting. Douglas told the audience that when he had returned to Saskatchewan to assume his duties as provincial leader, one of his stipulations had been that Sandy Nicholson assume the duties of treasurer for the provincial CCF. He added that the money raised in every corner of the province by Sandy had been an important factor in building CCF morale and winning the 1944 election.

In his speech, Sandy recalled that it had been eighteen years since he first contested the Mackenzie riding, and he said he believed still that the CCF would be the liberator of the large contingent of Canadians who lived in "daily fear of hunger, unemployment, sickness, old age and war."[1]

Redistribution had reduced the number of Saskatchewan seats from 20 to 17 in the 1953 federal election. Sandy's

Mackenzie constituency had become slightly larger, taking in some area formerly in the Melfort and Humboldt ridings. Under Sandy's guidance, a round of fund-raising fowl suppers, raffles and whist parties whipped up support. Sandy took the seat from incumbent Liberal G.M. Ferrie by a margin of 555 votes. Percy Wright who left his safe Melfort seat to contest Melville "to perform a valiant public service in retiring the Rt. Honourable J.G. Gardiner from the House of Commons" did not do as well. Although Gardiner beat Wright, the intensive CCF campaign in Saskatchewan paid off. The party won eleven seats, six more than in the previous election, restoring the parliamentary group to twenty-three. Sandy's colleague, Clarie Gillis, who had represented the coal mining constituency of Cape Breton since 1940, doubled his majority.[2] A few weeks after the election, more than 150 friends and neighbours gathered at the CCF Crystal Lake grounds to celebrate Sandy's win and the Nicholsons' twenty-fifth wedding anniversary.

Before Parliament met that autumn, Sandy sailed by ship from the port of Churchill to the United Kingdom to obtain up-to-date information on some of the problems connected with the marketing of grain. A long-time member of the Hudson Bay Route Association, Sandy opted to travel on a freighter, the SS *Begonia*.[3] Thus he became the first member of Parliament to travel from Hudson Bay to England. In Parliament he explained:

> I went entirely on my own. I was not representing any government or any organization. I went as a farmer. I thought that, as a member of this House, I should have the best information available about two things: the development of the port of Churchill — a resolution on the order paper will give me a chance to say something about that a little later on — the present and future needs of our customers.[4]

Through the courtesy of a former colleague in the House of Commons, Colonel Alan Chambers, by then resident in the British capital, Sandy was able to visit the Canadian cemetery at Dieppe and the World War I memorials in the

Vimy and Arras districts. He also spent two weeks with Ruth in England, where she was attending the London School of Economics on a Lord Beaverbrook scholarship. On his way home, this time by ocean liner, he paid a brief visit to United Nations headquarters in New York where he attended several sessions of the General Assembly.

A shortage of high school teachers in Sturgis encouraged Marian to upgrade her qualifications at summer school in 1953, and she started teaching at the composite school that autumn. Alexander lauded this arrangement as it allowed him to continue his education in Sturgis. Mary Anna was at Regina College, where she was preparing to obtain a music degree. So Sandy set off for Ottawa alone.

Delivering his first speech of the first session of the twenty-second Parliament on 19 November, he said, "I should like to thank my honourable friends for welcoming me back to Parliament. Four years ago the people of my constituency apparently had complete confidence in this [Liberal] government. I accepted their verdict cheerfully and spent four pleasant years on the farm."[5] He would later remind the House he spoke from personal experience when he fought for farmers' rights, as all his worldly possessions were "tied up in farmland and equipment."

Seldom did Sandy miss an opportunity to use past experience for current arguments. As soon as the order paper permitted, he referred to his ocean voyage to England, constructing a strong case for better usage of the port of Churchill. He said, "The captain had come into the port of Churchill on half a dozen occasions and with radar, the gyrocompass and the excellent aids to navigation provided by the department of transport," and that he had indicated the entry to the harbour there was no more hazardous than going into Montreal. Sandy continued, "I think we should have more cargo coming into Churchill so that the people who live on the plains may have the advantage of the short rail haul and be able to get goods from overseas markets by the most direct route." Sandy is credited with playing an active role in securing additional elevator space at Churchill, but this time the government acted speedily and accepted the accolades. Before Sandy could have his resolution debated for increasing elevator space and upgrading port facilities, "the minister was kind enough to announce that the facilities were being doubled."[6]

While Sandy believed it important to look to the future, he cautioned about forgetting the past. Twenty years later this penchant for preserving Canadian history would motivate him to begin collecting oral accounts on tape. In the autumn of 1953 he said, "When I travel over the northern part of my constituency by air with all the ease and pleasure of modern travel, I never forget that two and three hundred years ago people travelled through that country by very different methods." He suggested members could refresh their memories by reading Kelsey's papers describing his 1689 journey, available in the parliamentary library.[7]

Visiting remote areas in his constituency reduced the amount of time Sandy spent with his family. Conscious of this, he initiated other occasions to be with them. The Massey family had not been in favour of Sandy's choice of a political career, but they knew of his devotion to Marian. Her brother, Norman Massey, recalled the time in December 1953 when Sandy met Alexander in Toronto for a brief holiday. Massey said, "Sandy and Alexander were visiting my wife and me in Cobourg where I was teaching. As a special treat to mark Al's twelfth birthday Sandy had arranged for Al to come east in order to attend an NHL [National Hockey League] game in Maple Leaf Gardens. Before the hockey game Alexander was talking about the upcoming Maple Leaf game and he asked his father, 'Is Conn Smythe the cleverest person in the world?' Sandy thought a moment then answered, 'Oh! I think Mother.'"[8]

In the new year, Sandy opposed a raise for either senators or members of Parliament, saying, "I simply cannot go back to my people and say that I could not get along on $6,000 a year and had to have an increase."[9] Before such legislation was carried, Sandy insisted the government should "provide social security or payments of increased amounts" to people in need, since that was one reason he came to represent the people in his constituency.

Speaking to the Vocational Training Co-ordination Act on 16 March, Sandy made evident his interest in the disabled, which would later occupy him both inside and outside the Saskatchewan Legislature. He said, "I think it is quite obvious that it is in the nation's interest that those who are disabled should be given the opportunity to make a useful contribution to society. I feel that the federal government would be only fulfilling its duty in co-operating with the provinces and the municipalities with a view to establishing training projects for the purpose of rehabilitating disabled persons." Being familiar with the Sturgis Composite School, he was able to explain to members that the addition of woodworking shops had given rural students "a new interest in education." He believed that providing incentives for disabled persons would prove just as beneficial.[10]

Long before it became fashionable, Sandy promoted equal rights for women in the workforce. He remembered that married women were not allowed to teach in 1928, so he and Marian were forced to postpone their marriage until he had graduated. In the House Sandy referred to an article in the *Financial Times*, 12 March 1954, by "Tempus," which had been critical of women voters. Commented Sandy, "We have the misfortune to have . . . only four women out of a total membership of 265 [and] we have had only five other women who have been in parliament since Confederation . . . I think it is childish for anyone in the middle of the twentieth century to suggest that for the most part women have no political savvy." Sandy further believed "that to handicap individuals because they are women and make it impossible for them to occupy the most important positions in the country because they are women just cannot be justified in this day and age."[11]

More than a year later he objected to an announcement from the Civil Service Commission of Canada which stated in part:

Married women may apply, but will be listed for

temporary employment only unless they can satisfy the commission that they are required to be self-supporting. An affidavit to this effect must accompany the application.

Sandy argued, "Surely in the year 1955 we should not be stipulating that while there must be no discrimination regarding race, national origin, colour or religion there may be discrimination regarding sex . . . There are a great many capable women in the civil service. Does this mean that if these women decide to marry they will not be permitted to carry on their employment?"[12]

Discrimination manifested itself in many ways. Sandy promoted both CCF and SCM policies in seeking better understanding between nationalities, and in preparing for peaceful ways of working together with those of other political ideologies. Solon Low, leader of the Social Credit Party, angered Sandy when he said, "This afternoon the CCF leader said that we have got to live with the communists . . . Should it be our policy to resign ourselves to the hopeless future of trying to live with the Devil himself?" Sandy objected. He said "the Devil was a naughty word" in his home when he was a child. He went on, "I have over 2,000 people of Russian origin living in my constituency and I have no reason to think that their cousins, uncles or aunts who are behind the Iron Curtain are beasts of people who would not be responsible."[13]

Both in and out of the House Sandy worked to create a climate of brotherhood, regardless of culture or colour. As a member of Parliament he was able to assist many immigrants, among them Ping Quan, in arranging for their families to join them in Canada. Ping had emigrated from his homeland in 1947 and was living with his father, Charlie, in Toronto. Ping wrote:

> My family arrived in Hong Kong in May 1954. An interview was scheduled to take place sometime in September, which meant that they would have to wait for four months. Since Hong Kong was a crowded city they shared a room in a friend's apartment, but accommodations were not too comfortable. Mr.

> Nicholson wrote to the immigration department in
> Ottawa [to J.W. Pickersgill], requesting an early
> interview. The interview was pushed ahead by two
> months. My family arrived in Toronto on July 4 . . .
> Mr. Nicholson has been a friend of my family for half
> a century. My father knew him in Somme, where his
> lonely life was enriched a great deal by his friendship
> with Mr. Nicholson.[14]

Ping's mother and sister were eventually allowed into
Canada, largely due to Sandy's persistence in intervening
on their behalf with the minister of immigration, and the
family all settled in Toronto. Whenever Sandy visited the
city he telephoned the family and, as Ping reported, "we
have had many occasions to be honoured and delighted by
his visits to our home."

Sandy's monthly letters to local newspapers kept his
constituents informed about House activities. He also
sought improved media coverage in northeastern Saskatchewan and lauded "the splendid service received from CBC
Watrous." He requested that the CBC "come into the TV
field in Saskatchewan instead of turning the field over to
private TV stations." Like Graham Spry, who had supported
the growth of a Canadian-owned radio industry in the
1930s, Sandy believed that "the people of Canada
collectively have to provide those services for the people"
in rural areas as well as in cities.[15]

During the summer recess, Marian and Sandy travelled to
Europe. When Sandy spoke about this trip later in the
House, or to constituents, he demonstrated how he
gathered grist for the political mill even on holidays. At a
public meeting in northeastern Saskatchewan he referred to
European fears of a third world war, and he urged intense
negotiation to avoid such a confrontation saying, "The
geographical position of Canada, situated between the two
giants of Russia and the USA, should make every Canadian
vitally interested in doing everything possible to avert a
third world war."[16] While he was in Europe, Sandy visited
countries facing economic problems similar to Canada's. In
Sweden, he learned that the government met annually with

representatives of the farmers to review the country's general economy and to decide "on what sort of deal should be best for the next year for agriculture." In this way, all producers should have for one year "prices which bear a fair relation to the wages and salaries that other people get." In France, too, prices were reviewed from time to time and farmers' income adjusted to take into account prices paid for machinery, fuel oil, and related costs. In West Germany, the government encouraged farm storage by paying farmers to keep grain on farms rather than filling up elevator space. Sandy hoped that the House would consider some of these solutions — among them recommendations that the CCF had advocated for years.[17]

Besides the thorny agricultural issues which plagued residents in Mackenzie constituency, they also faced grave water quality problems. Earlier, the pollution of the North Saskatchewan River affected the fish supply of the native people at Cumberland House. At that time Sandy· had support from John Diefenbaker, Progressive Conservative member of Parliament for Prince Albert, who argued, "We know the Canadian National Railway have found that using this water in its present state is the best means by which to scale the flues of locomotives. If it does that, what must it do to human beings?"[18] At the beginning of 1954 Sandy addressed the problem of flooding on the South Saskatchewan River and the necessity of a drainage system for adjacent lands. He said, "The situation in my own corner of Saskatchewan is more critical that anywhere else in the province . . . The last three years have been unparallelled in our history in that we have had so much rain each year that a great many farmers have not had any crop at all."[19] This meant that farmers were unable to pay their taxes, and the consequent loss of revenue in municipalities deprived school teachers of proper wages and hindered progress in providing other amenities in rural areas.

Upon his return to Parliament following the Easter recess, Sandy attempted to educate eastern members of Parliament about the farmers' plight. He sought a positive response to the Saskatchewan government's plea that the emergency created by the flooding be regarded as a national emergency and that sufficient funds be made available to help repair property damage. Farmers had tried to combat the elements, Sandy said. The previous year, many " . . . spent more than the worth of the crop in trying to get on the fields with a combine towed by a caterpillar tractor. Sometimes it was a combine mounted on a stone boat, with a small engine to operate the combine, while the whole equipment was hauled around by a caterpillar tractor."[20]

When the South Saskatchewan River Project appeared on the order paper a week later, Sandy said, "I believe we could not start too soon appropriating funds for a project such as the South Saskatchewan dam . . . as a beginning to conserve moisture and make water available in areas where they have recurring droughts" and years of flooding.[21] It would be three years later, in July 1958, when the project became a reality, with Saskatchewan entering into an agreement with the federal government.[22]

The need for flood control, irrigation, and potable water for his constituency had been one of Sandy's priorities, so he was grateful to see the construction completed. A short editorial in *The Commonwealth* regarding the naming of the dam appealed to Sandy's sense of humour:

> After thinking it over we can see that Mr. Pearson's decision to name the South Saskatchewan dam after former Liberal agriculture minister J.G. Gardiner was more appropriate than it seemed at first. Saskatchewan people, however, following their inclination to put the adjective after the noun as with Hotel Saskatchewan will no doubt in future be inclined to say Dam Gardiner, for that is the order in which words have been associated for many years in Saskatchewan. Particularly in the 1930s and early '40s, when people saw the pressing need for conserving water and developing irrigation and hydro power, the term "dam Gardiner" was frequently used, because the late Mr. Gardiner steadfastly refused to take any action.[23]

Ross Thatcher, Sandy's colleague, had served two terms in the House as representative for Moose Jaw, and was again elected by CCF supporters for Moose Jaw-Lake Centre in 1953, when Sandy returned to Parliament. Sandy expressed shock when Thatcher rose in the House of Commons on 22 April 1955, and announced his resignation from the CCF, stating he would sit as an independent. Others felt his action had been inevitable, since Thatcher had a good income "derived from his four hardware stores and farm of pure-bred Hereford cattle."[24] Lewis wrote: "Thatcher was an able and successful small-businessman who found it increasingly difficult to accept CCF demands for more social security and for higher taxes of corporations."[25] Thatcher moved from federal to provincial politics later, and Sandy himself would sit in the Saskatchewan Legislature when Thatcher became premier of the Liberal government.

Those who live in western rural areas where farmers deliver grain to local elevators are familiar with the farmers' complaints regarding the allocation of railway boxcars. Co-operative elevators, in particular, seem to receive less than their quota of the boxcars, which are used to move grain to points of sale. A true co-operative man himself, Sandy brought this issue before Parliament during discussion of the Canada Grain Act in May 1955, explaining "no subject has brought as many letters to my office." He cited a letter from a Kelvington farmer expressing displeasure over such discrimination against that town's wheat pool elevator. Sandy said, "I feel that the members of the wheat pool are being quite reasonable when they ask that boxcars be allocated in such a manner as to enable producers to deliver grain to the elevator of their choice . . . so they can receive the dividends which will come to them as a result of the volume of business."[26]

At the CCF national council meeting in Ottawa, 12-15 January 1956, Sandy listened as Tommy Douglas spoke about the possibility of forming a new federation encompassing farm, labour and socialist movements in Canada. The New Democratic Party would be born out of this idea.

Three months later, the historic convention in Toronto witnessed the merger of the Trades and Labour Congress (TLC) and the Canadian Congress of Labour (CCL) into one labour federation, the Canadian Labour Congress (CLC). When Sandy attended the CCF national convention in August, delegates showed support by adopting two resolutions. One greeted the CLC "as a great step forward in labour unity," commending the congress for establishing a political education department. The second "welcomed the legislative program of the Canadian Labour Congress and endorsed its twenty-nine points."[27]

In this same year, during the notorious pipeline debate, the Liberal government proposed to finance an American corporation "by a huge loan from the public treasury, to the tune of 90 percent of the needed capital."[28] CCF and Conservatives, although differing in policy, worked together to block the bill. C.D. Howe, minister of trade and commerce, implemented the seldom-used closure rule to halt debate. Sandy sat stunned, along with the rest of the opposition, on Black Friday when the Speaker reversed a decision made the previous day, allowing the Liberal government to pass the bill. Lewis reflected the CCF reaction to the issue of an American corporation building and owning a pipeline paid for with Canadian taxpayers' money, by saying it "offended CCF policy and commitment to Canada's independence [and was] an unforgivable sell-out."[29]

Sandy campaigned for the CCF's success in the June provincial election in Saskatchewan, determined to see stewardship of taxes more conscientiously administered by a CCF government. His efforts were rewarded when six of the eight constituencies in his area elected CCF members and Douglas continued as premier.

Many of the privileges Canadians today take for granted came about through hard fought battles for human rights. In January 1957 Sandy supported an amendment to the Canada Elections Act, made by Stanley Knowles, to allow a greater percentage of Canadian citizens to express their opinions on election day. Sandy acquainted the House with "problems which confront the people on the frontiers of the country." He pointed out that in Mackenzie there was "no provision for advance polling for railway workers . . . The trains must leave before the polls open, and when those men reach their destination they are outside their constituencies and are not entitled to register their votes," he said.[30]

In the spring Sandy began campaigning in earnest for the 10 June federal election. The previous autumn, Magnus Eliason, who had become full-time organizer for the Saskatchewan CCF in 1955, made a tour of Mackenzie with Sandy. Eliason said, "I spent the week up there with him. And [found] him a stubborn guy to work with. He had his own ideas — and [he was] very, very dedicated. His whole life was wrapped up in the party. He knew his constituency . . . like the palm of his hand. Not a striking speaker, but very methodical."[31] This time, Michael Kitchen of Sturgis acted as campaign manager. Several members of the Legislative Assembly accompanied Sandy on speaking tours. At the Sturgis Town Hall, during a "meet your member" banquet, Alex Kuziak, by now Saskatchewan's minister of natural resources, closed his remarks by paying tribute to Sandy for his "personal integrity and untiring devotion to the welfare of his constituents."[32]

"Nickels and dimes" collections at constituency gatherings reflected the paucity of party resources available to finance the campaign. Nonetheless, the CCF did reasonably well. Although the party "ran only 161 candidates, out of 265 constituencies [it] elected 25 members, two more than in 1953."[33] In Saskatchewan, Sandy held his seat in Mackenzie, receiving two thousand more votes than the Liberal candidate. Roy Knight was defeated in Saskatoon, while Thatcher's former constituency of Moose Jaw-Lake Centre was won by the CCF. Across the nation the CCF experienced gains and losses. In Port Arthur, Ontario high school teacher Douglas Fisher defeated C.D. Howe. Fisher was one of three CCF members elected in northern Ontario for the first time. However,

Sandy's long-time colleague, Clarie Gillis, lost his Cape Breton seat.

Sandy touched on all his priorities in his final major address to Parliament in October — he would be defeated in the 1958 Conservative sweep and would never return to the House. Still deploring the low level of pensions paid to the elderly at that time, Sandy challenged a Liberal member to try to live on the old age pension of forty dollars monthly, adding, "I myself would be glad to volunteer as a representative of the CCF, and I am sure the Social Credit group would wish to send a volunteer to try living on the [now proposed] $55 a month in any Canadian city which the minister cares to designate."[34] Sandy's challenge fell on deaf ears.

Sandy was soon to depart from federal politics, but he would enjoy one major event before this occurrence, as he had been named to the Canadian delegation attending the Commonwealth Parliamentary Association conference in New Delhi, India, slated for ten days at the beginning of December. The delegation left Canada on 27 November 1957.[35] The Commonwealth Parliamentary Association dates back to the organization of the British Empire Parliamentary Association at the coronation of King George V in 1911. Conferences are held approximately every two years in various parts of the Commonwealth. Sandy explained, "No decisions that are binding on any member countries can be made, but a most useful purpose is served by bringing together representatives of those charged with framing the laws in the Commonwealth countries."[36] This purpose parallelled Sandy's philosophy which had developed during his days in the SCM.

Senator Richard Donahoe wrote to Sandy twenty-seven years later, recalling the trip that took them to India via England

> to see the highlights of Pakistan (from Karachi to the Khyber Pass and points in between), Ceylon including Colombo, Kandy (Ceylon), Niuwara Eliya (Sri Lanka) — and all the points of tourist interest — Madras, New Delhi, Calcutta, Bombay — to say nothing of Nagpur

through which we seemed to pass each time we went from city to city. We had the privilege to meet Nehru and to see the Indian Continent in a state of ferment only ten years after it achieved Independence.[37]

The Commonwealth Conference sessions began on 2 December 1957 following three weeks of touring. Always an astute observer, Sandy expressed surprise when many speakers read from "manuscripts which seem to have been prepared thousands of miles from here, and were not modified to refer to the experiences of the past few weeks."[38] Speaking to reporters later Sandy said, "India is undoubtedly the most important underdeveloped democratic country in the world . . . It is impossible to appreciate the magnitude of the problems without actually visiting this part of the world. A million babies are born every month in India, so that in 16 months they will have as many babies as the entire population of Canada."[39]

Sandy visited Indian villages where no child had attended school until recent years. One of these schools, which accommodated ninety-five children who attended in shifts, had no classroom. Children sat cross-legged on sacks on the ground outdoors. School procedure operated on a parliamentary system with a student prime minister and youthful cabinet ministers. Sandy remarked, "The minister of education was the most beautiful minister anyone ever saw. She was just ten years old with jet black pigtails down her back, and her eyes were as bright as the artificial diamonds embedded on either side of her nose." Her daily duties included cleaning the blackboard set on an easel, and passing out books and newspapers.[40]

Such minimal educational resources strengthened Sandy's belief that Canadians should be participating more actively as world citizens, even though a great many pressing problems in Canada still needed immediate attention. He wrote, "The discussion of social services in the Commonwealth pointed up the very wide difference in standards of living in the different parts of the Commonwealth." He agreed that, "In a democracy it is not so easy to persuade governments to reduce the social services at home to increase give-away programs abroad. One of the Indian speakers was critical of Canada controlling immigration so rigidly when parts of the Commonwealth were so crowded, then at the same time refusing to move wheat which was spoiling when people were starving." It was not easy for him to make an adequate defence to these charges.[41] Many times in the House Sandy rose to propose the shipping of surplus commodities to distressed areas. It seemed appropriate that he happened to reach Bombay in time to attend the official ceremony in connection with the arrival of the first boatload of Canadian wheat sent as a gift from Canada to India. Under the Colombo Plan, Canada had responded to the food shortages created by recent drought and rice crop failure by donating $7 million worth of wheat.

One morning everyone arrived promptly to hear Prime Minister Nehru open the discussion on international affairs and defence. Sandy noted he was "without a doubt one of the greatest living men. He spoke for almost an hour with scarcely a reference to his notes. He had read the transcript of Mr. [Hugh] Gaitskell's speech . . . and speeches of the two USA senators, and had appropriate comments for each major point."[42]

Sandy's stamina surpassed that of most delegates, allowing him to keep pace with the round of arranged activities. Many delegates fell by the wayside when they read that the programme for the Calcutta to Bombay trip included a visit to the atomic reactor being built about thirty miles along the coast from Bombay, but Sandy "didn't want to go home without seeing what we are getting for $8 million." At the reactor Sandy and Senator Donahoe met a young Canadian engineer who greatly admired the late Mahatma Gandhi. "One cannot visit this part of the world," said Sandy, "without agreeing that Gandhi was one of the greatest men of all time." Sandy learned Gandhi "always travelled third class" on the railway,[43] and this reminded him of the CCF's greatest man, Woodsworth, who insisted on riding in the day coach across Canada.

On the final day of the conference, Prime Minister Nehru gave a dinner for the delegates. Sandy had missed few events during the conference, so the Canadian delegation gave him the honour of making the farewell speech on behalf of members.

When Diefenbaker dissolved Parliament on 1 February 1958, and called and election for 31 March, Sandy returned to his constituency. At the CCF nominating convention in Porcupine Plain Sandy was chosen as the local candidate. He spoke briefly, recalling his first visit there twenty-eight years before as a United Church minister, when the town was known as the Cordwood City of the North, and residents lived there without a school, hospital or doctor. Now, they had all three, enjoying "their fair share of the gross national product," thanks mostly to the provincial CCF.[44]

The 1958 election was a disaster for the CCF. As Lewis wrote in his memoirs, the party was reduced to eight members in the House and 9.5 percent of the votes cast. Coldwell and Knowles had been defeated and such prominent members as Colin Cameron from Nanaimo, British Columbia, Alistair Stewart from Winnipeg North and Sandy Nicholson from Mackenzie were also missing from the benches.[45] The Conservatives made a clean sweep of Saskatchewan, with the exception of Hazen Argue who held Assiniboia for the CCF. Argue temporarily became the CCF's leader in the House of Commons.

After Sandy's defeat, Marian revealed that she had been suffering some suspicious symptoms, which Dr. Sam Wolfe of Porcupine Plain diagnosed as cancer. He removed the growth, performing the operation at the Saskatoon University Hospital, and discharging Marian a month later on 13 May. By the middle of June Marian felt well enough to teach at the Sturgis School until the end of term. Meanwhile, Sandy had been offered two jobs, one with the provincial government, the other as a CCF organizer in Manitoba. He did not want to move to Manitoba, but he "did a few months organizing in Manitoba" assisting Magnus Eliason. At one public meeting Sandy said, "If we are going to effectively challenge the Tories at the next election, we must raise our sights and decide how much it would be worth to us to have a CCF government in Manitoba."

Lloyd Stinson wrote in *Political Warriors*, "Without Magnus Eliason in Manitoba our 1958 election campaign would have collapsed . . . We had little money, a handicap which we tried to overcome by enlisting more volunteer workers, supplemented by help from Ontario," and Sandy Nicholson from Saskatchewan.[46] Although the Conservatives, under Duff Roblin, won the Manitoba provincial election that June, Sandy was "jubilant about the outcome." The CCF had more than doubled its representation in the Manitoba Legislature.[47]

Again that autumn, Sandy returned to Manitoba to help elect Jake Shulz in the Springfield byelection called for December. Sandy appealed to all party members through the pages of *The Commonwealth*, telling how the CCF supporters in Springfield had rallied to Shulz's support. Then he added his plea to cover the cost of the radio broadcasts: "You have some neighbours who are most anxious that Jake Shulz should win. They plan on sending a dollar, but they have not got around to putting it in an envelope. Will you cut out the form below, see five of your friends, and then send what you have collected?"[48] Shulz lost the byelection, but the provincial party gratefully acknowledged the time spent by Tom Johnston and Sandy, saying "the belief in action as it is rooted in these two men from Saskatchewan really permeates your whole system and you cannot help but go home and work harder than ever."[49] In a little more than ten years, Manitoba would have an NDP government.

While Sandy had been busy in Manitoba, Marian found an advertisement in the *Star-Phoenix*:

> WANTED: A Male, full or part time worker for prisoner rehabilitation and secretarial duties at Saskatoon John Howard Society office.

Ready to settle into a less strenuous lifestyle, Sandy and some twenty other applicants answered the advertisement. The Nicholsons had planned to move to Saskatoon at the end of the school term, as Alexander would be ready to begin university. The John Howard Society offered a salary of three hundred dollars a month, and Sandy felt that this amount would be adequate for living expenses when combined with his parliamentary pension. He became the executive secretary of the Saskatoon John Howard Society in February 1959. The Nicholsons settled in Saskatoon at 828 Temperance Street, in a "very attractive bungalow with a basement area" that was later rented out. Bessie and Charlie Dunn, former friends from Hudson Bay Junction signed the guestbook on 3 July 1959, writing "So glad we are neighbours again."

A few years later, at the annual meeting of the John Howard Society held in Saskatoon in March 1963, Sandy, by now Saskatchewan's minister of social welfare and rehabilitation, was guest speaker. In this role he had the pleasant duty of announcing an increased grant to the society. He outlined the functions of the society as carried out while he had served it. He said that in addition to assisting discharged and paroled men and women to reestablish themselves there "continues to be the need for public education and a better understanding of the needs of the released prisoner, if he is to be accepted." Other activities of the society, Sandy said, included the task of finding employers who would provide job opportunities. He mentioned the "casework with the family of a person serving a term in prison which is given in conjunction with work with the inmate." The society also involved itself "in the interest of just legislation and crime prevention [giving it] a definite role to play in providing much needed services, and thereby [contributing] to an integrated correctional programme."

During his term as executive secretary for the society, Sandy's duties dictated visits to the Regina and Prince Albert Correctional Institutes and the Prince Albert Penitentiary, which served both Saskatchewan and Alberta. He said, "The Alberta [John Howard Society] worker came once a month and we tried to be at the penitentiary at the same time. It was our duty to sleep at these different places and to have our meals there." The Regina Jail had become the Regina Correctional Institute shortly after Tommy Douglas became premier in 1944, and had been placed under the jurisdiction of the provincial department of welfare. Before this, the department of the attorney general had supervised the jails. Douglas believed that the department of welfare would be familiar with many of the young people who ended up behind bars, and that there thus would be more likelihood of helping them change their outlook. Sandy's role as minister of social welfare and rehabilitation enabled him to continue as an advocate for those who were incarcerated.

Chapter 11

Saskatchewan Legislature, 1960-1967

A s the Saskatchewan provincial election approached, many people pressured Sandy to stand as the CCF candidate. Sandy recalled that "Marian and Al did not want me to run in Saskatoon in 1960, when I worked with the John Howard Society." However, with medical care the chief issue in the election, J.H. Brockelbank (who had entered politics at Sandy's behest) suggested that he enter the race. Tommy Douglas had not promised a cabinet post, neither had he approached Sandy to run. Again, as in his earlier life, Sandy had several options. At that moment, he stood in line for the position of provincial executive director of the John Howard Society, as the then director planned to return to his home in England.

The political call prevailed, however. At a nominating convention in the Bessborough Hotel on 23 March 1960, Sandy Nicholson, Arthur Stone, who had served in the Legislature since 1944, and Gladys Strum were chosen to be CCF candidates in Saskatoon ridings.

Years of service devoted to the cause of labour benefitted Stone in bringing to the Legislature "the knowledgeable acumen to present a rational brief in labour's behalf."[1] Regarding medicare, he believed that the people were ready for it and that the time had come for its introduction.

172

Since Gladys Strum's defeat in federal politics where, at the time, she was the sole woman sitting in the House of Commons, she had returned to studying and teaching. Like Sandy, she had other choices. Entering politics now would jeopardize her chance to complete her education degree, but Strum, too, believed in medicare and while she had been in the House she had pleaded repeatedly "with the federal government to implement its promises in regard to a federal health program."[2]

Of Sandy's candidacy, *The Commonwealth* stated:

> The provincial arena will be a new field for this Saskatchewan candidate. But so important and strategic has Saskatchewan become, so much has it become the social conscience of all Canada, that this redoubtable warrior for progress looks forward with understandable enthusiasm to participating in some of the most history-making legislation ever enacted in this or any other country . . . Tireless in his efforts to advance the ideals for which the CCF stands, this genial, vigorous worker has established one of the best records in the service of his constituents. Truly, Sandy Nicholson is a tower of strength in the great movement toward a better social order.[3]

One thing seemed certain — with the election of these three CCF candidates, the CCF government in Saskatchewan would become a much greater bastion of democracy and progressive administration.

Saskatchewan voters tasted modern 1960-style electioneering, with many candidates turning to advertising and television campaigning as their main sources of publicity. Only the CCF stuck closely to the old-fashioned brand of politicking — public meetings, informal meetings with candidates in private homes, and whist parties. The women of the Churchill and Haultain districts in Saskatoon introduced an auction, putting the candidates up for bid to perform light duties. Sandy served as window washer at the home of Mrs. Harry Link who won his services at the auction.

The CCF government campaigned on its record,

pledging "to make all medical services provided by physicians available to every resident for a premium which he can afford to pay."[4] As leader of the provincial Liberal Party, Ross Thatcher conducted a vigorous campaign focussing on the need for a plebiscite on the medical care issue. His main assault centred on the national CCF move to form a new party. He declared, "The socialists are selling out agricultural Saskatchewan for the interests of a few labour bosses in Eastern Canada. Farmers will be the junior partners in this merger because most of the money for the new party will come from labour."[5] To combat Thatcher's attack, Douglas spoke in the Legislative Assembly defending the national CCF in its drive to form a new national party, but promising such a move would not alter CCF status or policies in the province of Saskatchewan. When some Liberals railed against the CCF association with labour, saying that a party beholden to the trade unions could not serve all the people, the CCF candidates countered that a party beholden to big business could not serve the common people. The medical profession and the Saskatchewan College of Physicians and Surgeons, assisted by the media, joined the opposition parties in waging a well-financed campaign under the slogan Political Medicine is Bad Medicine.

Even with such sustained opposition, the voters returned thirty-eight CCF members, sweeping the party back into power, holding the Liberals to a small gain, and completely smothering the other parties. In Saskatoon, Sandy, Stone and Strum won their seats, with Gladys Strum becoming Saskatoon's first elected woman representative in the provincial Legislature. Following the election success, the Saskatoon winners were at the centre of celebratory ceremonies. *The Commonwealth* reported:

> A royal welcome extended to our Premier when 150 cars, gaily decked out with CCF banners and ribbons of gold and green escorted him in a convertible to Saskatoon from Sutherland [a division point on the CPR, in the Hanley constituency represented by R.A. Walker]. Following behind the Premier in open cars

were highland pipers and the three Saskatoon candidates Strum, Nicholson and Stone, and Attorney General R.A. Walker . . . spring flowers and CCF banners decorated the stage at the arena where Douglas spoke to the enthusiastic crowd of 1,000.[6]

Douglas requested Sandy to be in Regina on 11 July 1960 to become either speaker of the Saskatchewan Legislative Assembly or minister of social welfare and rehabilitation. Sandy preferred the cabinet post. Later in the Legislature he spoke of the history of his department: "Saskatchewan did not have a department of welfare until 1944. At the very first session [of the new CCF government] . . . although there were seventy-three bills passed, bill number one on the order paper was an act respecting the department of social welfare; bill number two was an act to amend the industrial school act; bill number three was an act to amend the education of blind and deaf children in Saskatchewan. These three bills do indicate something of the very high priority which was given to welfare at that particular time." The word "rehabilitation" was added to the department's title in 1948 in order to facilitate its role in the resettlement of World War II veterans.[7]

In taking over the portfolio from T.J. Bentley, Sandy said, "It is an honour to be appointed to this responsible position and in view of Saskatchewan's advanced concept of welfare services, and the scope of their welfare programmes, it is indeed a challenging appointment. We in Saskatchewan have in the past spearheaded new concepts of welfare services. These are being observed with considerable interest beyond the boundaries of our province, and are contributing to the overall strength of welfare services in Canada."[8]

One of Sandy's first actions was to break a long tradition which had seen cabinet ministers move to the capital city. He and Marian decided to retain their home in Saskatoon to which he returned at weekends, but he also rented a Regina apartment which provided shelter during the week. This arrangement was beneficial to both Sandy and the government, as it allowed him to represent the government at some Saskatoon events, while at the same time it diminished the need for other cabinet ministers to travel to Saskatoon from Regina.

During the summer and autumn of 1960, Sandy attended several memorable CCF meetings. From the first discussions on the subject, he had agreed in principle to the formation of a new farm-labour political party. The New Party entered the political scene in a setting similar to that prevailing in 1933. The problems of unemployment and lack of food remained, the latter as grave, but now on an international scale. As Sandy said, "The election results in 1958 were so disastrous for the CCF that many of us came to the conclusion we should try some new ideas. Stanley Knowles had a good connection with the CLC and was elected a vice-president [after his defeat in the election]. Knowles was given authority to spend full time if necessary to work on plans for a platform and programme for a new party which would appeal to both farmers and labour. He did a fine job."

At the twenty-fifth annual convention of the Saskatchewan CCF at Regina in July 1960, delegates endorsed the move to affiliate with the New Party, defusing some existing and potential opposition with a resolution "that the Saskatchewan CCF will continue to operate under its present constitution and will have, as heretofore, the fullest autonomy in determining its provincial policy and program . . . Resolved that the CCF party retain its present name and identity in Saskatchewan."[9]

In August, the CCF held its national convention in Regina. Tension centred on the position of parliamentary leader Hazen Argue who was seeking the leadership of the New Party, but as Sandy said, "T.C. Douglas had done an excellent job in building a strong socialist party in Saskatchewan. He was the best person on the horizon as leader of the New Party." Argue accepted the position of new national leader for the CCF, agreeing with the decision to leave the selection of a leader for the New Party until its founding convention in 1961.

Sandy Nicholson's services as a window-washer were auctioned off to Harry Link at a CCF fund-raising event in Saskatoon in 1960. Here his work is supervised by Mrs. Harry Link. (Saskatchewan Archives Board, Star-Phoenix Collection)

Four candidates for the CCF Saskatoon nominations for the provincial election in 1960 (left to right): Gladys Strum; J.E. Brockelbank; Arthur Stone; and Sandy Nicholson. Both Strum and Nicholson had experience as members of Parliament; both were nominated, along with Stone. (Saskatchewan Archives Board, Star-Phoenix Collection)

Lord Taylor and Saskatchewan cabinet ministers were entertained at the home of Premier Woodrow Lloyd in August 1962. Left to right: A.G. Kuziak; C.G. Willis; Sandy Nicholson; R. Brown; R.A. Walker; Premier Woodrow Lloyd; Lord Taylor; C.C. Williams; O.A. Turnbull; W.G. Davies; E.I. Wood; I.C. Nollet; J.H. Brocklebank. (Saskatchewan Archives Board)

In July 1960, the Honourable A.M. Nicholson signed the oath of allegiance as minister of Social Welfare in a ceremony at the Saskatchewan Legislature, while Premier T.C. Douglas looked on. (Saskatchewan Archives Board 60-263-04)

Among the other new cabinet ministers was (next to Sandy Nicholson) minister of Co-operation O.A. Turnbull. Next to Premier T.C. Douglas is Lieutenant-Governor F.L. Bastedo. (Saskatchewan Archives Board, Leader-Post Collection)

The University of Saskatchewan's fall convocation in 1962 was a particularly memorable occasion for the Nicholson family: Marian received her Bachelor of Education degree, while her son, Alexander, received a Bachelor of Arts with distinction. (Star-Phoenix)

"It was one of those golden days one has in the CCF, when we were at Lou Hentelman's for dinner and a long afternoon just talking things over." Left to right: M.J. Coldwell; Myron Feeley; Mrs. Hantelman; Mrs. Gillanders; Lou Hantelman; Mrs. Feeley; and Molly Feeley. (Mrs. Myron Feeley)

The Honourable John R. Nicholson unveils a plaque commemorating the Saskatoon Federal-Provincial low rental housing project, as Sandy Nicholson looks on. (Saskatchewan Archives Board S-3849)

Charlie Broughton and Myron Feeley rest between sessions at a Saskatchewan CCF convention in the Bessborough Hotel, Saskatoon. (Mrs. Myron Feeley)

The potash mine at Lanigan, Saskatchewan, received a visit from Sandy Nicholson and M.J. Coldwell in July 1967. (Saskatchewan Archives Board S-B 3857)

Former members of the Saskatchewan Legislative Assembly gathered for a reunion in Regina, December 1980. Left to right: Alex G. Kuziak; Anne Kuziak; Sandy Nicholson; Marian Nicholson; D.Z. Daniels; and Kay Daniels.

The descendants of Charlie and Yuet Wah Quan celebrate Mrs. Quan's ninetieth birthday with the Nicholsons on 9 September 1979. Left to right, back row: Lai Quan; Ping Quan; Taoing Ng; Mr. and Mrs. Sui Leung Law; Sui Ling Law; and Sing Wai. In the centre: Sandy Nicholson; Yuet Wah Quan; Marian Nicholson. Left to right, front row: Corinna Quan; Franklin Quan; Sherry and Jennifer Ng.

Sandy and Marian Nicholson celebrated their fifty-fifth wedding anniversary in Toronto on 15 August 1983.

The Nicholson family on 15 August 1983. Left to right: Ruth Dibbs; Sandy and Marian Nicholson; Alexander; and Mary Anna Higgins.

After dinner in the Parliamentary Dining Room in September 1983, old friends gathered in the office of Stanley Knowles. Left to right: T.C. Douglas; Irene M. Spry; King Gordon; Stanley Knowles; Sandy Nicholson; Marian Nicholson; Graham Spry; and Irma Douglas. (Betty Dyck)

Marian Nicholson celebrated her eighty-third birthday 1 September 1985 with a picnic in a Toronto park. She died one month later.

Before that happened, however, Clarence Fines's retirement as provincial treasurer produced some changes in the Douglas administration. Woodrow Lloyd became provincial treasurer and Allan Blakeney succeeded him as minister of education. Blakeney and Sandy were cabinet colleagues for four years and both sat on the opposition benches for another three years. Blakeney remembered Sandy as a passionate advocate for two causes. First, Sandy argued strongly for a more comprehensive welfare system which would help people who were in need, concentrating on alleviating their problems, rather than how the problems arose. Secondly, Sandy addressed the pressing needs of senior citizens. According to Blakeney, he "had a particular concern for pioneers who had spent their life on the farm and who because of infirmity could no longer continue to live on isolated farms but needed to live in a village or some other centre that had some measure of services not then available on most Saskatchewan farms."[10]

Shortly after his appointment to the social welfare portfolio, Sandy visited all the provincial geriatric centres, nursing homes and housing projects. In September he spoke at the opening of the Canora senior citizens' home, congratulating "the members of the Ukrainian Greek Orthodox Church in the eleven parishes" who had built the home to honour their elders and to celebrate the fiftieth anniversary of settlement in the district.

As guest speaker at the Catholic Hospital Conference of Saskatchewan, about a month later, Sandy chose as his topic the types of service required for the needs of the aging and chronically ill. He informed the group that, in addition to the federal old age security pension of fifty-five dollars, for those aged seventy, "the Saskatchewan financial programmes to help the needy include supplemental allowances which are granted to Saskatchewan recipients of old age security on a means test basis."[11]

Speaking to the Wascana Kiwanis Club in Regina about security in the senior years, Sandy's sense of humour surfaced. Saskatchewan Senior Citizens' Week, celebrated annually in October, "perpetuates the tradition of honouring the pioneers which was established in the province's 1955 Golden Jubilee Year," he told the audience. He added, "If a bug or a bumper or a bomb does not get us, we may all finally be senior citizens."[12]

In the new year, Sandy attended the official opening of the Melfort and District Pioneer Lodge. Seldom losing an opportunity to pay tribute to Marian, he said on this occasion, "Melfort holds a particular significance for me. My wife, who was formerly Marian Massey, taught mathematics at Melfort High School for three years and left that position some years ago to marry me. Melfort lost an excellent teacher — I gained a more than excellent wife." He expressed pleasure at the vision of the community in providing the facility, saying, "I feel it can be truly said that in so doing you have collectively given practical expression to the commandment honour thy father and thy mother . . . The town of Melfort is the first community outside of the major cities to have both a geriatric centre and a housing project."[13]

The first session of the fourteenth legislature opened 9 February 1961. At the Legislature in Regina, Sandy watched as Lieutenant Governor F.L. Bastedo, dressed in Windsor uniform and plumed hat, read the Speech from the Throne, and Ross Thatcher, leader of the Liberal opposition, took his seat in the Legislature for the first time. For the next six weeks the CCF government and the Liberal opposition would be locked in a battle of words.

In a letter to Sandy, commenting on an earlier opening, Dr. Hugh MacLean wrote:

> I was interested in the opening of the Legislature with all its archaic display of pomp and ceremony. It was a field day for the military coats in all its branches. I would have liked to have seen the Governor, if we must have him, accompanied by a Master Farmer, who would be chosen by the Grain Growers or some such body as the outstanding farmer who has contributed more to the peoples' welfare during the years, and a Master Laborer (similarly chosen from his group) on either side of him, as he entered the House to open it.

It would, I hope, be much more symbolic of the 'common man' whom we profess we wish to come into his own.[14]

The magnificence of the opening ceremonies were dictated by tradition, but Sandy himself preferred a common approach. A former secretary remembered Sandy as much more than a fair-weather friend, and one who kept abreast of the whereabouts and circumstances of all those close to him. She said, "In 1961 when I was hospitalized in Regina, he and Marian appeared most unexpectedly from the opening ceremonies of the Legislature, and presented me with an armload of beautiful flowers from that occasion. It was amusing how my stock went up with the nurses that day!"[15]

The Saskatoon *Star-Phoenix* frequently assigned Florence Pratt to write articles concerning Sandy's activities. Pratt said:

There could never have been any doubt as to the sincerity and devotion with which Sandy approached his cause, politically oriented or otherwise . . . for those of us less dedicated than Sandy, and also involved with a multitude of problems unrelated to his own particular field, we were tempted to wish, occasionally, that he might have been a little less energetic and manipulative. Without those qualities, however, plus his dedication and unwavering faith, the improvements in social welfare, rehabilitation and care of the mentally retarded in Saskatchewan would hardly have been achieved as quickly as they were.[16]

In his opening speech in the Legislature Sandy took the opportunity to honour one of his constituents. He called attention to Mayor Sid Buckwold, recently elected president of the Canadian Federation of Mayors and Municipalities, who "brought this honour to Saskatoon and to the province for the first time in our history." Then, partially to acquaint members with the wide-ranging responsibilities of his social welfare department, but also to make the point that he believed in small-scale economies, Sandy handed out pamphlets with his predecessor's name on them, saying,

"We have a number of these on hand, but my Scottish background would never permit me to destroy them." Sandy's philosophy and that of his department were founded on belief in the integrity and dignity of the individual. As Sandy said, "Every individual receiving public assistance should have the right to plan his own life as he chooses, even though he's lost his financial independence." He praised the co-operation of religious, municipal and service organizations in attacking some of the disheartening aspects of old age by assisting in building the forty residences for senior citizens in the province.[17] Always critical of the piecemeal manner in which social welfare had been handled between different levels of government, Sandy achieved another of his aims by piloting through the Legislature a bill to amend the Social Aid Act of 1959, in order "to permit municipalities to group together to facilitate administration of social aid."[18]

Besides raising the public image of social welfare in Saskatchewan and piloting contemporary legislation through cabinet discussions, Sandy's first term of office coincided with the foundation of the New Democratic Party (NDP). According to Sandy, "Our Saskatchewan cabinet was divided about Tommy Douglas seeking the leadership. Several feared that we would not hold the province without him. I felt that Canada was more important and that Tommy should do his best, which he did. We lost the next election in Saskatchewan, but it was close."

Although Douglas expressed a reluctance to leave provincial politics, he stated, "I am free and willing to serve as leader of the New Democratic Party if the majority of the Founding Convention delegates so decide, but I will definitely not campaign for the office nor seek it in any other way."[19] At the new party's founding convention, held in Ottawa the first week of August 1961, Douglas defeated CCF national leader Hazen Argue by more than one thousand votes. The new NDP platform contained no reference to socialism, but stressed economic planning, co-operative federalism, and a comprehensive national health plan. Historian Lewis Thomas wrote: "It was a victory for the eastern wing of the CCF, who wanted a new image: 'secular, accelerating, affluent, urban, American.'"[20] It was a short-lived victory, however, for as Sandy remarked the new party ended up being "much like the CCF in that neither party has been successful in enlisting the rank and file of either labour or farmers."

In November, the Saskatchewan CCF convention voted to keep its name, establishing itself as the Saskatchewan section of the NDP. Convention delegates chose Woodrow Lloyd as provincial leader, following Tommy Douglas's official resignation which left him free to begin his responsibilities as national NDP leader. Lloyd made only two changes to the cabinet, appointing Allan Blakeney, formerly minister of education, as provincial treasurer, and giving the educational portfolio to O.A. Turnbull, who also remained as minister of co-operatives. Sandy retained his portfolio.

When he was not otherwise occupied with ministerial business Sandy could be found among the public, where his ease of manner and natural charm made him many friends. In December he attended the Mackenzie constituency nominating convention to support Charles Mitchell, Sandy's official agent in many political forays, as NDP federal candidate. Both Charles Mitchell and Tommy Douglas lost to Progressive Conservatives in the June 1962 federal election, when Douglas contested the Regina riding. In order to give Douglas an opportunity to run for a seat in the House, Ernie Regier resigned in the British Columbia riding of Burnaby-Coquitlam. Douglas won the October byelection, and took his place in Parliament.

By that time Hazen Argue had departed the party, having shocked Saskatchewan party members by announcing his resignation from the NDP in a blaze of publicity on 18 February 1962. During the two previous days Argue had mingled with the provincial council and executive at the Coldwell Building in Regina in an apparently friendly manner, even discussing future party activities. However, he met then with his federal constituency executive to offer his resignation, after which he proceeded immediately to a press conference where he unleased a torrent of abuse upon the NDP.

Premier Lloyd commented that Argue's "deal with the Liberal Party — that group which no one accused in more extravagant terms than did Argue a few months ago — is undoubtedly complete." Lloyd believed Argue's charge of potential trade union domination would fall strangely on the ears of those who knew the situation. Out of twenty thousand CCF members then in Saskatchewan, only two thousand were affiliated through trade union memberships. Lloyd added, "Even if it were the wish of these groups to dominate — and of this there is no evidence — it would be an insult to the rest of us to suggest that they could."[21] Only a portion of the CCF farmers feared union domination, and it was to these that Argue addressed his remarks. David Lewis knew of many progressive CCF farmers in Saskatchewan who saw similarities between the long-term interests of farmers and labour. These staunch CCF supporters would not be swayed by Argue's tactics.

Sandy saved his public comments on Argue's decision to leave the NDP until much later. When Prime Minister Lester Pearson appointed Argue to the Senate in 1966, Sandy remarked that never in history "has any person been appointed to the Canadian Senate whose main quali-fications were that he betrayed the thousands of hard-working people who trusted him and elected him to be the youngest member ever . . . "[22] Sandy strongly believed that the Senate served no useful purpose. And, as he pointed out, Argue, unsuccessful in the last two general elections [1963 and 1965], would now cost taxpayers $750,000 if he lived to age eighty-five. This remark led to a challenge from Public Works Minister Gardiner in the Legislature in regard to Sandy's respect for the elderly. Sandy responded, "I have a great deal of respect for old-age pensioners . . . When the prime minister of Canada turns down $100 a month for old-age pensioners and votes three quarters of a million dollars for Senator Argue, I suggest I have much more respect for old age than the prime minister has."[23]

Sandy's entry into provincial politics gave him both the power and the opportunity to implement many of his aims. In March 1962 he announced that the new budget made provision for increased probation services in the province, allowing persons to be kept in the community at considerably less cost than in prison. He also informed members that provincial recipients of old age assistance, disabled persons' and blind persons' allowances would be increased ten dollars a month, retroactive to February that year. And he reminded them that Saskatchewan was the first province to introduce such supplements. In addition, said Sandy, "Saskatchewan recipients of supplemental allowances have since January 1, 1945 been given a wide variety of health services" at a cost borne entirely by the province.[24]

Sandy referred to a variety of initiatives taken by the CCF upon achieving power, all of them designed to raise the standard of social aid. In his essay on social aid, historian James M. Pitsula states, "One of the worst features of the relief system prior to 1944 was its intimate connection with the Liberal political machine. Voters who failed to support the government were in danger of losing their relief."[25] In 1945 the CCF had introduced free medical, hospital, dental and nursing services for recipients of mothers' allowances and their dependents, and old age pensioners and their dependents. No other province in Canada offered such benefits at that time.

Before Clarence Fines retired from provincial politics in February 1961, he had brought down a budget including an item for a planning committee on medical care insurance, also referred to as Medicare. Two months later, the Saskatchewan government appointed an advisory planning committee under the chairmanship of W.P. Thompson, president emeritus of the University of Saskatchewan. After eight months of acrimonious bargaining between the provincial government and Saskatchewan doctors, the committee issued an interim report recommending "a system of universal coverage, financed by direct taxation and general revenues, and run by a nonpolitical commission. Doctors would be paid on a fee-for-service."[26] Saskatchewan doctors vowed they would neither join the scheme nor co-operate with the government in its implementation.

In the Saskatchewan Legislature during a debate on the proposed medical care insurance plan in March 1961, Sandy reiterated his determination that there should be adequate medical care for all. He said, "One of the main reasons I became interested in the CCF/Farmer-Labour Party many years ago, was because of the medical problems that existed in northeastern Saskatchewan where I lived."[27] Sandy had a deep concern for his constituents, but his convictions in regard to health care stemmed from a series of personal experiences closely tied to the lack of health services at that time. One of these was the death of his four-day-old son, Norman, at Hudson Bay Junction in 1932, which he remembered as " . . . The most shattering experience in my lifetime." Within the next few years, Ruth's eyes became crossed after a severe bout of whooping cough. Although the Nicholsons could afford the necessary corrective surgery to straighten Ruth's eyes, Sandy believed it unfair that personal finances should determine whether or not a child suffered a lifetime handicap. Then, too, his memories of Marian's poor health and her brush with death added to his persistence in fighting for proper medical care for rich and poor, young and old. Addressing an audience of nursing home personnel in Saskatoon, Sandy said, "Health is the determining factor between living with zest, motivation and purpose, or just living the weary days away . . . These senior years are just as much a part of one's whole life as the teens or the twenties."[28] He questioned how "a doctor who considers it is quite all right to take a salary every month from the ratepayers in his municipality can think it is all wrong to take payment on a fee for service basis from a commission on which he will have a membership."[29]

Ruth, Sandy's older daughter, believed that the Medicare crisis in Saskatchewan was the most interesting and probably the most significant event of her father's political life. She said, "The whole province was unbelievably polarized with families splitting when they were on different sides of the debate." Certainly, relationships within the Nicholson family were never the same again and this was especially true of Marian's eldest sister, whose stepson was a doctor. Ruth remembered that her parents "lost friends over this issue. At the time they also got many crank calls and even threats over the telephone."

Along with his welfare portfolio in the Saskatchewan Legislature, Sandy served as acting minister of health during Walter Erb's absences. Erb's appointment by Douglas as minister of health had not been a popular choice with members of the Legislature. Sandy commented that he was not surprised when Erb resigned his cabinet post (he had been transferred to public works when Woodrow Lloyd shuffled the cabinet after Douglas left) and joined the Liberal Party.

Erb was responsible for one debacle during the Medicare debate when certain promises were made by the government to a delegation of doctors who met Premier Douglas, Woodrow Lloyd, Walter Erb, J.E. Brockelbank and Sandy. The doctors indicated that they were unwilling to go along with the majority report, and Premier Douglas made it clear that the government "had a mandate and it would be going through and the legislation drafted." The doctors then asked to see a draft of the measure before the legislation went before the Legislature and, as Sandy recalled, Walter Erb promised they would receive a copy. The promise was not fulfilled, however. Sandy said, "This was one of the mistakes — a responsible cabinet minister failed to keep a promise. The doctors concluded the government couldn't be trusted."

Sandy believed that several other factors added to the acrimonious atmosphere during the Medicare crisis. In the early years when the CCF government initiated free treatment for cases of cancer and tuberculosis in addition to free mental health services, the medical profession lauded the moves. However, by 1962 many of the doctors practicing in Saskatchewan were immigrants who had graduated from medical schools overseas. Among this group, the majority had immigrated to Canada from Britain to escape the British state health plan. In addition only half of the doctors in Saskatchewan had been practicing there for more than a decade and thus they had not experienced the Depression. Indeed, they came to the province in a period of prosperity and they had thrived. Another factor was Tommy Douglas's acceptance of the leadership of the national NDP and the opinion of some that his desire for the implementation of Medicare was, in reality, an attempt to gain a higher public profile.

In truth, Douglas believed that the time was right to proceed with Medicare. After the Conservative win in 1957, Diefenbaker moved to make federal funds available to assist any province ready to share the costs of a provincial hospital scheme. Preliminary preparations in the province prior to this included a programme whereby exceptional co-operation between the provincial government, and rural and urban municipalities resulted in the creation of a network of new hospitals throughout Saskatchewan. The stage was set.

Sandy remembered some progress being made in the morning session of a special meeting with government officials and doctors' representatives in March 1962. At a break in the negotiations representatives from the American Medical Association (AMA) met with the Saskatchewan doctors and managed to sow additional seeds of disquiet. Sandy said that the AMA had a vested interest in the discussions because of the effect on the insurance industry in America. "This was dynamite, you see — the first Medicare package in America — and the AMA was most anxious to kill it."

There was also a determined effort on the part of the Canadian Medical Association (CMA) which donated $35,000 to help cover any deficit incurred during the Saskatchewan doctors' campaign against Medicare. The Saskatchewan College of Physicians and Surgeons, too, sought a voluntary levy of $100, collecting more than $60,000 to aid the doctors in their battle.

Sandy said, "When the war chest of the college was compared with the total election expenses of candidates of the two principal parties ($89,000 for the CCF; $71,000 for the Liberals) one realized the doctors were spending more trying to prevent the introduction of Medicare than the political parties were in getting elected."

Early in May 1962 about three-quarters of the practicing doctors in Saskatchewan attended an emergency meeting of the Saskatchewan College of Physicians and Surgeons in Regina. They decided to print the following sign which would be used in medical offices across the province:

TO OUR PATIENTS: THIS OFFICE WILL BE CLOSED AFTER JULY 1, 1962. WE DO NOT INTEND TO CARRY ON PRACTICE UNDER THE SASKATCHEWAN MEDICAL CARE INSURANCE ACT.[30]

An advertising campaign, and the assistance of the press, which sided with the doctors, played a major role in soliciting public sympathy.

The Saskatchewan CCF government implemented the Medical Care Insurance Act on 1 July 1962 whereupon the Saskatchewan doctors withdrew to emergency services in strategically located hospitals. About 200 of the college's 625 practicing doctors continued to provide free emergency service at 41 of the province's 154 hospitals.

The government and the Medical Care Insurance Commission were ready for these tactics. They brought from Britain approximately sixty doctors, recruited with the assistance of Graham Spry. These volunteers, who received transportation to Canada, were to work for one to three months on fixed contracts. The commission also hired some American doctors, and located all recruits in areas not served under the doctors' emergency plan. Dr. Sam Wolfe, now a member of the Saskatchewan Medical Care Insurance Commission, began temporary practice in Saskatoon at the newly formed medical clinic operated by a citizens' co-operative.

Allan Blakeney was strongly critical about the attitude of the media after some of the Medicare problems had been solved. He cited one of many instances in which the press had suppressed pertinent information favourable to public acceptance of Medicare principles, but had printed a report about a Keep Our Doctors (KOD) committee which drew less than twenty people. Publications outside the province proved to be more objective, but this had little effect on Saskatchewan readers who tended to subscribe only to local papers.

On 4 July 1962, the *Financial Post* published on its front page a stinging attack on the Saskatchewan medical profession. Sandy quoted this article during a taped interview now housed in the Ontario Archives:

> The medical legislation . . . may or may not be good. But it is law . . . That's the way democracy works. But society finds revolutions — organized bands defying laws — intolerable . . . Strikes . . . are increasingly anachronistic . . . Whatever the medical politicians running the doctor strike think about the legislation, the strike they organized is an outrageous assault on organized society . . . No profession has, of itself, dignity, integrity, or any claim to public esteem . . . The American Medical Association . . . may be delighted with the Saskatchewan performance. Is anybody else? The striking Saskatchewan doctors in the months and years ahead will not be happy about their guinea-pigging for the AMA.[31]

Lord Taylor, a British medical consultant and former Labour parliamentarian, accepted Premier Lloyd's invitation to study the province's medical crisis. Taylor acted as a catalyst in his role as mediator between government and the medical profession. The government later amended the Medical Care Act, implementing the changes agreed upon by all parties. Among the points won by the medical profession was one which guaranteed the freedom of patients to select doctors of their own choice; doctors were to be permitted to practice within or outside the confines of the act. Existing insurance schemes also would be permitted to continue.[32]

Premier Woodrow Lloyd thus won the distinction of

being the leader of the first government in North America to sponsor a comprehensive medical care insurance plan. The CCF newspaper stated, "With him will be bracketed T.C. Douglas, who initiated the plan and whose government won the mandate from the electorate to carry it out."[33] The Saskatchewan CCF paid the price of opening the door to universal medicare, however, and lost the next election. Ironically, ten years later every province in Canada had implemented a medical care insurance plan.

Throughout Sandy's career, Marian "had proven herself [to be] a steady, supportive, yet quietly unobtrusive helpmate, adviser and counsellor . . . Social obligations were fulfilled equally well."[34] "Saskatoon Briefs" in the CCF newspaper reported a meeting of the Mayfair Caswell Hill CCF group where "Mrs. A.M. Nicholson, our guest speaker, gave an interesting talk on social welfare."[35] Marian, who had returned to university, graduated from the University of Saskatchewan in the autumn of 1962 with a Bachelor of Education degree. At the same convocation ceremony the Nicholsons' son, Alexander, received a Bachelor of Arts degree with distinction. Marian already had received a Bachelor of Arts degree from the university, but she needed a few more credits for the second degree. She said, "With two daughters each holding two degrees and a son already working for a second, I had to try for mine to keep up with the family."

Florence Pratt wrote, "How Marian found the time to be an excellent homemaker and yet participate in the many public duties and activities required of her, must surely indicate that she, like Sandy, was dedicated and unwavering in her determination to help the less privileged."[36]

Marian also played a role as a party fund-raiser. To swell the party coffers, Marian spearheaded the committee which would produce a souvenir calendar celebrating twenty years of CCF government in Saskatchewan. Marian accompanied Sandy to the Canora CCF convention in Preeceville, in June 1963, where she reported on the Saskatoon ladies' group calendar project. Ten thousand calendars were being printed by the CCF-NDP printing plant. More than forty-three hundred names and birth dates of NDP supporters were sent in to be included on the calendar, among them "names came from 558 places in Canada, USA, Germany, Australia and Scotland."[37] A coloured cover featured nine Saskatchewan scenes sketched by Kathy Brown. Messages featured inside the calendar included those from Premier W.S. Lloyd, federal leader T.C. Douglas, M.J. Coldwell, Mrs. J.S. Woodsworth and Mrs. George Williams. The project took fourteen months from conception to completion and netted the party eight thousand dollars.

Cabinet ministers were slow to order the calendars for distribution in their constituencies, however. To Sandy, who expressed his disappointment over their lack of support, this signalled that the party was in distress. Closely associated with party fund-raising throughout the years, Sandy had developed another Nicholson tenet: "When people stop spending money on their party, it's in trouble." He had seen the phenomenon before and his predictions proved to be true once again when the CCF went down to defeat in the Saskatchewan provincial election in April 1964.

Until election day, top-ranking Canadian journalists thought that the Lloyd government deserved the confidence of the electors and that it should win on the strength of its record. Even this positive support from the traditionally unfriendly media did not alter the outcome. The election of Liberal Sally Merchant broke a twenty-year tradition in Saskatoon and deprived Gladys Strum of her seat in that CCF stronghold. Sandy and his colleagues J.E. Brockelbank, Wes Robbins and Harry Link won the other Saskatoon seats, with Sandy recording the largest vote in any provincial riding. In Ottawa, Douglas said, "The seeming defeat of the CCF government in Saskatchewan has come about not through the desertion of its friends but by the re-grouping of its enemies."[38] The popular vote for the CCF indicated that the party had increased its vote slightly in comparison with returns in the 1960 election.

Sandy sat on the opposition benches once again as he had in the House of Commons. At the opening of the

Sturgis community clinic in August, he felt satisfaction in the fact that his former federal constituency had finally obtained better medical facilities. The project had been well under way before the provincial election, but the new Liberal government, led by Premier Ross Thatcher, was able to collect some political dividends because the clinic opened under its aegis.

While Sandy devoted the necessary time to his political duties, Marian returned to teaching, accepting a position at the Lanigan High School east of Saskatoon. She taught there for the autumn term of 1964, all of 1965, and six months in 1966, while Sandy continued to live in his Regina apartment during the week. The Saskatchewan CCF remained hopeful. In December, Sandy, Brockelbank, Link and Robbins placed the following Christmas greeting in *The Commonwealth:*

> Instead of sending personal cards to our friends in Saskatoon your members are contributing the cost of the cards and postage to the Fighting Dollars Fund. It is important that we speed the day when Woodrow Lloyd will be Premier of Saskatchewan again.[39]

By 1965 Sandy had spent thirty years battling for better living conditions for the poor and disadvantaged and had been in the forefront of agitation for the implementation of social welfare legislation. M.J. Coldwell observed that "neither the CCF nor its successor, the NDP has succeeded in electing a federal government, but our pioneer work in the political field is generally credited with laying the foundations for most of the social welfare legislation which Canadians now enjoy." He added that the Saskatchewan CCF "within its constitutional limits had built a welfare state which had become the third wealthiest province and would probably never again be known as the 'cinderella province' of Canada."[40]

Sitting in opposition for the last three years of his long political life, Sandy launched bitter attacks on the provincial Liberal government. He criticized the Throne Speech, delivered in March 1965, condemning the closure of Embury House, the withdrawal of funds from the Institute for the

Aging and the withdrawal of financial support to the Centre for Community Studies at Saskatoon. Sandy was disheartened by the diminishment of the CCF social service programmes. A year later, he charged the Thatcher government with the betrayal of trust in the fields of health, education, and care for the aging. He said, "Cancellation of CCF government plans for a two-stage $14 million addition to the University Hospital at Saskatoon . . . had brought about a low morale among senior personnel who have spent eleven years building up the hospital, resulting in resignations of several senior administrative staff."[41]

Sandy bristled with indignation and took the Liberal government to task for ignoring Saskatchewan's senior citizens in the 1967 budget. He commented, "It is cool comfort to them to hear the premier boast that 1966 has been the most affluent year in Canadian history; that liquor sales have reached an all time high — more than one million dollars a week sales — or that we are to have additional miles of four-lane highways."[42] He added, "The pinching of pennies to reduce our services for the aged is no way to plan for the celebrating of Canada's 100th birthday."[43]

When the Liberal government dissolved the Saskatchewan Legislature on 8 September 1967, and called a provincial election for 11 October, Sandy agreed to be a candidate reluctantly. He thought that the CCF would win two seats and lose three in Saskatoon, so he chose one of the seats which he had predicted would lose, saying that he had had a long spell in politics. As well as losing the three Saskatoon seats, the Saskatchewan CCF-NDP lost the election and the Liberals remained in power. The party gave a retirement dinner for Sandy and three other long-time members of the Legislature — Marjorie Cooper-Hunt, I.C. Nollet, and John Brockelbank Sr.[44] Adolph Matsalla, MLA-elect for Canora made the presentation of a copy of *Canada — Year of the Land*, published for the centennial by the National Film Board. The book's inscription read:

> Sandy — in recognition of your dedication to the
> service of humanity, and the vision of tolerance with

which you filled the role of elected representative and
minister of the crown.

Sandy responded, "My wife Marian has reminded me that
it is exactly thirty-three years since I burned a lot of bridges
and took on the responsibility of candidate for the CCF in
Saskatchewan. Thank you very much for your wonderful
co-operation through many years."[45]

Sandy's final retreat from politics coincided with the
laying to rest of the Saskatchewan CCF. At the thirty-second
annual convention of the CCF Saskatchewan section of the
NDP, members voted to change the name to NDP
Saskatchewan Section. Among others, Sandy expressed
regret "at departing from the name of the CCF which was
associated with so many legislative advances," but all
recognized the time had come to take the logical step of
making the name conform with that of the federal party.

Social welfare had been at the very hub of everything
Sandy stood for in representing the CCF. The party's
officials publicly praised Sandy's "eloquent fashion" in the
Legislature, stating "there has been no one more vigilant
and qualified to arraign the Liberals in this regard than A.M.
(Sandy) Nicholson." Although at the age of sixty-seven
Sandy ceased to be active in politics, this by no means
meant he would stop placing "top priority on the worth of
a human being in society."[46]

Chapter 12

Fund Raising and Other Activities, 1967-1976

Mental retardation with its multi-faceted problems had become a concern for Sandy about a year before he retired from politics, when he became involved with the Saskatchewan Association for Retarded Children (SARC). The association encourages the public to accept the mentally retarded, believing that "all people have the right of equal opportunity, dignity, respect and to share in all elements of life in their communities."[1]

Sandy admitted that he might have gone through life unaware of the complex health, welfare, educational and community problems encountered by the mentally retarded had not SARC involved him in its 1966 national crusade. Pearl Isabelle, SARC executive director at the time, attended the same Saskatoon church as the Nicholsons and was "impressed by their genuine warmth and friendliness, [and he was] not at all what one would expect of a successful cabinet minister."[2] Later, after she became more closely acquainted with Sandy, she would speak of him as being a great humanitarian.

Pearl Isabelle accepted the responsibility of forming a committee for the national crusade on mental retardation which would establish thirteen major research projects across Canada. The committee's goal was to set up more effective methods of treating, training and caring for the retarded. The two projects to be initiated in Saskatchewan were a mental retardation unit, now known as the Alvin Buckwold Unit, at the University of Saskatchewan in Saskatoon, and a co-operative school-work training project for the educable mentally retarded, based in Regina.[3] Saskatchewan's campaign goal was set at fifty thousand dollars. Harold Crittenden, vice-president and managing director of Transcanada Communications Limited, was named crusade chairman for the province, with Saskatoon Mayor Sid Buckwold as northern chairman. Pearl Isabelle said that Sandy's name immediately came to mind because of his success in fund raising for the CCF when it became apparent that there should be approaches to the public for donations as well as to wealthy individuals and corporations.

Sandy agreed to be co-chairman for northern Saskatchewan. He and Sid Buckwold travelled together throughout the northern area soliciting funds, often the butt of jokes about Sandy, the staunch NDP and Sid, the die-hard Liberal, making strange bedfellows.[4] The October 1966 SARC newsletter, *Outlook,* printed a progress report on the national crusade, lauding Saskatchewan for leading the way in raising the five million dollars required. By then the province had surpassed two-thirds of its objective.

Dr. G. Allan Roeher, executive director of the Canadian Association for Retarded Children (CARC), wrote to Sandy in December:

> This past year has been a most dramatic one for mental retardation. The single greatest happening for us was your coming on board the Crusade. In addition to realizing the financial goal, you have, with your good sense of judgement, evolved the best human interest and public education program of the campaign. This had a further side effect in boosting the morale of the Crusade team across the country and hence, your impact has been nation-wide.[5]

This involvement with the crusade brought Sandy into closer contact with the handicapped and aroused his humanitarian spirit which resulted in him conducting his own campaign in and out of the Legislature for the next few years. One of his first actions was to make a motion in the Legislature, which was seconded by Ed Whelan, to amend the School Act "and other legislation if necessary, to make mandatory the education of all educable and trainable mentally handicapped children, and to recognize in its grant structure the additional costs of such education."[6]

He acquainted the legislature with the story of Michelle, tiny daughter of Mike Sibas of Middle Lake, north of Humboldt, the first phenylketonuria (PKU) baby to be detected in Saskatchewan by the Guthrie blood test. Sandy explained that PKU is a metabolic disorder which results in severe retardation if it is not detected early and treated with a special diet.[7] Anxious to share their knowledge with other parents confronted by this affliction, the Sibas accompanied Sandy and pediatrician Dr. J.W. Gerrard to many meetings throughout the province to demonstrate the positive results of early detection. Dr. Gerrard stated, "Wherever we went Sandy was not only well honoured but he was also well beloved."[8]

As for the child, Michelle seemed to understand she had a mission to perform. Pearl Isabelle wrote: "This two-year old child was truly remarkable . . . She sat through long meetings, luncheons and posed like an expert model for photographs, all without a whimper."[9] Sadly, Michelle died that autumn as a result of complications from contracting measles.

Sandy had learned that in 1966 the John Dolan School in Saskatoon was one of only thirty-six facilities in the province for teaching and training of the retarded.[10] Focussing attention on the lack of educational facilities for the mentally retarded, Sandy mentioned that the John Dolans, farmers in the Girvin district southeast of Saskatoon, after whom the school was named, had their adopted mentally retarded girl for two years before they became aware of how severely she was retarded. The department of social welfare offered to take the child back, but the Dolans decided to keep her. They inquired about enrollment in special classes in Saskatoon, following the local school board's request to remove the child from her school. They had purchased a house in the school district and then drove the little girl back and forth from Girvin daily. Sandy continued, "She didn't fit into the class for slow learners, so we have the John Dolan School today."

Sandy and his team were questioned frequently as to the reasons why funds for the crusade had to be raised by public subscription, rather than being provided by the Saskatchewan provincial government. Based on his experience as minister of welfare, Sandy was able to respond, "I have never known of any government whether it be a federal, provincial or a municipal government that has ever had enough money to do all the things that the government would like to do. So governments must be influenced by public opinion to some extent."[11] He participated in the crusade collections because he did not believe that the parents of retarded children should have to "carry more than their share of providing educational facilities." At that time, only ten of the fifty-nine provincial school units provided facilities for the trainable retarded.

Sandy urged both provincial and federal governments to share the costs of educating handicapped children. As he said, "All children irrespective of whether or not they suffer from mental or physical handicaps, should have every access to the best medical advice and treatment and should also have therapeutic services, nursing and social services, education, vocational preparation and employment . . . They should be able to satisfy fully the needs of their own potentialities and become, as far as possible, independent and useful members of society."[12] Sandy's efforts, together with the pleas of a more informed public, propelled the Saskatchewan provincial government into action, and in March 1967 Sandy rejoiced in the "approval in principle to the building of a special vocational school by the Regina Board of Education" funded by both provincial and federal governments. The school would accommodate approximately seven hundred Regina area students incapable of profiting from normal academic programmes, but who would benefit from special school-work training vocational courses.[13]

At the close of the crusade, Pearl Isabelle commended those who had helped in making it a success and she made special reference to Sandy's role. "I have reserved a particular 'thank-you' for Sandy Nicholson who devoted full-time to the crusade for several months without remuneration," said Isabelle. She added, "I feel quite safe in saying that the outcome of the crusade would have been very different had it not been for the devotion of Mr. Nicholson and Mrs. Nicholson, who shares his concern for the mentally retarded."[14]

The benefits of Sandy's involvement were being reaped years later. During the crusade Sandy and Sid Buckwold met Mary McLatchie, a wealthy, elderly spinster living in southern Saskatchewan, who made several generous donations. Sandy realised that bequests from the wealthy could have considerable positive impact on programmes for the retarded. He therefore maintained his contact with Mary McLatchie, and a considerable portion of her estate was left to SARC at her death. SARC received another sizeable bequest from the estate of a bachelor who had an investment in oil. This bequest was made at the suggestion of Sandy and John Dolan, and SARC received about eight thousand dollars in annual payments from interests in oil royalties.[15]

In autumn 1967, Sandy became the executive director of SARC, acting in this role for one year. In his report at the annual meeting in March 1969 he described SARC "as one of the links which unites the thirty-five branches in the province, with similar branches in the other Canadian provinces. The provincial associations are affiliated with the Canadian Association for the Mentally Retarded (CAMR). The CAMR, in turn, is associated with similar organizations in many countries in the hope that discoveries made anywhere in the world might benefit those working in the field of mental retardation everywhere."

Sandy also reported that new branches had been

established in Tisdale, Preeceville, Kamsack, Meadow Lake, Langenburg and Outlook since he took office. New branches were established when the parents of six or more trainable children, along with friends of the retarded, met with a view to establishing a class in the community, he said. He also announced that Dr. Zaleski had been awarded research funds of thirty-five thousand dollars by the federal government, in addition to sixty thousand dollars already provided by the federal department of health. This award had resulted from the outstanding work already performed at the Alvin Buckwold Mental Retardation Unit, he said.

In announcing his resignation from the position of SARC executive director, Sandy said that as a result of his personal political involvement throughout the years, he preferred that the organization should not seek government grants to pay any part of his salary. However, he said, "in view of the fact that the federal government votes money to support our work on the national level and nearly all the provinces make grants to support our provincial branches, I think it not unreasonable to expect that the quantity and quality of work being undertaken by the SARC and our thirty-five branches should be supported by an annual provincial grant." He did not suggest that the association raise fewer voluntary dollars, he went on, because "no level of government accepts the major responsibility for providing research, training or suitable employment openings, [so] there will always be a need for an active voluntary association dedicated to providing a brighter future for this large group."[16]

Cheshire Homes of Saskatchewan, which provided housing for physically handicapped adults, was another organization in which Sandy developed a great interest. Founded in England by the distinguished World War II bomber pilot, Group Captain Leonard Cheshire, the Cheshire Homes movement spread to other countries. John Owen, president of Saskatchewan's Cheshire Homes, first encountered Sandy and Marian early in 1969, when they were members of a small, active Saskatchewan group then planning a Cheshire Home. Sandy's political experience and invaluable advice were to help the group in overcoming numerous obstacles and Cheshire Homes of Saskatoon was registered under the Societies Act on 19 January 1970. A year later, the society's first annual meeting was held at the Nicholsons' apartment. It was then that Sandy accepted election to the society's board of directors for a three-year term.[17]

Although the Saskatoon society had been the first to register with the Cheshire Home foundation on the North American continent, Toronto claimed the distinction of opening the first Cheshire Home towards the end of 1972. Sandy and John Owen visited the home shortly after it opened.[18] They carefully inspected the old but elegant house which had been donated to the society, noting the physical drawbacks of the four-storey building. The visit strengthened their belief that a custom-built house would be preferable in Saskatoon.

Sandy remained a member of the Cheshire Homes board until March 1973. During his tenure he wrote many letters and other documents to officials in various levels of government. One brief in 1972 resulted in provincial government support for an eight-bed unit. Sandy and Marian attended the official sod turning at the Arlington-Louise site in Saskatoon. "But it was not only with the tongue and the pen that Sandy aided our cause," Owen pointed out. "On 12 June 1971, at the age of seventy-one, he was one of ninety people who took part in the Hanley Walkathon which raised $1,640."

In May 1969, Sandy and Marian embarked on a world tour. Sandy said, "I had been away from home so much for so many years I wanted to make our remaining years as happy as possible for Marian." About their trip, Owen said, "It started with a visit to Britain where Sandy and Marian attended the First International Cheshire Homes Conference in London and met Group Captain Leonard Cheshire." Delegates had come from Asia, Africa and Latin America. During the coming months the Nicholsons visited homes in India and the Far East renewing these friendships.

The Nicholsons' world tour fulfilled Sandy's wish to take Marian to some of the various places he had visited as a member of Parliament. After selling their Saskatoon home and most of its contents, they purchased two all-inclusive tickets — air and shipping lines co-operated then with a special rate — good for a year, with as many stops as desired. Their 1970 Christmas letter stated:

> We did not plan too far ahead but were lucky in getting a cancellation to Orkney and Shetland Islands, in hitting New Delhi for India's Republic Day, January 26; Hong Kong for Chinese New Year, February 6; Japan's EXPO opening, March 15; Honolulu for the Easter sunrise service in the 'Bowl.' At international conferences . . . in Dublin for the Congress for Rehabilitation of the Disabled, and in New Delhi for World Literacy, we met old and new friends involved in challenging projects.

Sandy seldom took a holiday without making it a learning process. He and Marian visited schools, churches, hospitals and attended local productions in the arts. They found officials anxious to show and explain achievements accomplished in the field of social welfare. At Covelong, near Madras on the Bay of Bengal, the handicapped at the Cheshire Home had prepared Christmas decorations. Sandy, acting as Father Christmas, was warmly greeted by young and old of several faiths — Hindu, Moslem and Christian. Although all the countries they visited had problems of one sort and another, the Nicholsons found the common denominator to be that "people everywhere desire a world without war in which to live and raise their children." The general desire for peace led many to take a more active role in helping to establish permanent peace, as the Nicholsons noted with approval.

In Dublin Sandy and Marian had met the Indian Professor A.J. Selvanpadian, head of the Department of Orthopaedics and Leprosy Reconstructive Surgery at the Katpadi hospital. On their arrival at the hospital in India, they met the only Canadian on staff — a nurse from Halifax working under the Canadian University Services

Overseas (CUSO). CUSO operates in Canada through a network of volunteer committees involved in recruitment, fund raising and education.[19] This was Sandy's first encounter with CUSO, but it would not be the last. Both Sandy and Marian had been impressed by the CUSO volunteers they met and they felt that they would like to support the organization. Before returning to Saskatoon, they visited the CUSO national office in Ottawa. Sandy said, "The executive director, a graduate in law, was a friend of our son and knew of my fund raising. He reported they had never been able to get a committee in Saskatchewan to raise the necessary dollars." The question Sandy was asked was one by now familiar to him: would he help? Once the Nicholsons had settled into an apartment in downtown Saskatoon, Sandy slipped back into his old role as organizer and fund-raiser. He quickly assembled committees in Saskatoon and Regina, calling on local Rotary Clubs for their members' assistance. A guestbook signature of C.M. Williams in June 1970 is accompanied by the note: "The early discussions on setting up the local CUSO committee." Williams, a University of Saskatchewan professor, later became national president of CUSO.

Sandy recalled, "We were so successful in [fund raising for CUSO] in Saskatchewan that I went to Winnipeg, Edmonton, Calgary, Vancouver and Victoria where I knew premiers and cabinet ministers." By 1971, the CUSO letterhead listed Sandy as chairman of the Saskatchewan committee. The fund-raising method used by CUSO was simple. The CUSO headquarters supplied letterhead listing the provincial committees, on which were typed letters to those friends of committee members who would support the organization financially. As Sandy explained, "All we had to do was sign our name and get [the letter] on the way." Sandy's contacts for funds included the Atkinson Foundation, set up by his friend, the founder of the *Toronto Star*, who had donated so generously to the CCF. He succeeded in obtaining five thousand dollars for CUSO.

Stewardship for Sandy included time as well as money. He encouraged many people to put their talents to work for CUSO, among them Ernest J. Morris of Saskatoon, who told how Sandy had influenced him. Morris had worked in the logging industry around Hudson Bay Junction when Sandy represented Mackenzie constituency in the House of Commons. When the two men met in Saskatoon in 1971, Morris was retired but he was looking for a worthwhile occupation, so Sandy suggested that he consider going overseas with CUSO. Morris's skills as a gas turbine power plant operator were badly needed in developing countries, Sandy explained. By August 1972, Morris and his wife Pearl were embarked for Africa, where they worked at a large Zambian technical school for three years. Pearl taught English and mathematics while Morris taught welding and metal work, as well as helping to set up a new school. On their return to Canada in 1975, the Morrises suffered "the traumatic bout of culture shock which afflicts many Canadians who return to their native land after working for some years in an underdeveloped country."[20] They promptly returned to Africa where they spent another three years in similar work, this time in Botswana. Morris concluded, "We have never regretted acting on Sandy's suggestion that we go overseas. It was an interesting and, I think, useful way to spend some of a couple's later years."[21]

Sandy had no intention of sitting idle in his later years. In April 1972 he and Marian took part in a twenty-four member trade and goodwill mission to China arranged by Senator Donald Cameron, but with all delegates paying their own expenses. During a visit with Li Chang, the vice-minister of foreign trade in Beijing, Sandy learned that China was satisfied with the quality and quantity of Canadian wheat, but Chang expressed concern that Canada was not buying more commodities from China. Naturally, Sandy prompted the idea of importing more goods from China when he returned to Canada. While he and Marian were in China, he "had a chance to discuss the possible use of potash to increase production of crops." He carried soil samples back to the University of Saskatchewan for testing. Results indicated the soil lacked the necessary potassium to produce good crops. Sandy supplied this information to the

Potash Institute of Canada which would be attending the Canadian exhibition in Beijing. Saskatchewan subsequently sold potash to China.

The Nicholsons' network of friends included several who had moved to Australia and New Zealand — countries they had not visited. They left for the southern hemisphere in November 1972. William Boschman wrote, "Marian and Sandy arrived in Whakatane, New Zealand where we were in the process of settling. We had a car and were able to show them around the sea beaches, dairy lands and forest projects of that beautiful area." The Nicholsons then went to Australia, touring the continent and enjoying two visits with the former Mae Anna Quan and her husband, before departure for home in March.

Home meant Saskatoon, but only briefly. John Owen recalled, "Sandy did not seek re-election to the [Cheshire Homes] Board at the society's third annual general meeting in March 1973. He and Marian were planning to leave Saskatoon. We were sorry to miss them. To show its appreciation of his outstanding contribution to Cheshire Homes, the society made Sandy an honorary board member." The Nicholsons moved to Toronto in the spring. Fittingly, their guestbook records that Charlie Quan, his wife, Ping, and their family were among the first guests on 10 June 1973. Charlie's entry read, "We having nice evening visit. Thanks my old dear friends indeed."

Before moving to Toronto, Sandy discovered a new challenge — taping the reminiscences of those who had made important contributions to Canada's history. As John Owen remarked, "[Sandy] was particularly good at face-to-face communication. As a former United Church minister, he must have had a lot of experience talking to people." While he had been in the cabinet, Sandy had expressed interest frequently about the ways in which senior citizens might be honoured, and he became concerned about the preservation of Canada's heritage. In 1955, during discussions about the proposed National Library and Archives building in Ottawa, Sandy supported the project whole-heartedly. However, he remarked, "I cannot believe that we are to spend so much money on a project of this sort, without providing air conditioning . . . from the point of view of the valuable books to be placed in the building."[22] By 1963 Sandy had begun contributing audio tapes with interviewees of his choice, including M.J. Coldwell, to the holdings of the Ontario and Saskatchewan archives. By 1970, Sandy was devoting much of his time and energy to the collection of taped interviews.

Roger E. Nickerson, archivist of the Archives of Ontario audio-visual collection, who first met Sandy in September 1973, wrote, "Through the remainder of the seventies Sandy deposited with the Archives many important tape-recorded and transcribed historical records, so that his collection in the audio-visual section by 1983 numbered some 165 items." The tapes included many fascinating stories, among them those of Dr. Wilder Penfield, the famed neurosurgeon and founder of the Montreal Neuro-logical Institute; poet Edna Jacques; Nobel prize winner Dr. Gerhard Hertzberg; survivors of the nuclear weapons dropped on Japan; and five Canadian missionaries to China, including Dr. Robert McClure.

Nickerson believes that the Nicholson tape collection adds prestige to the Archives of Ontario audio-visual holdings. He said, "Wherever Sandy learned his techniques in oral interviewing, they are so far the best of any of the audio-visual collection's depositors. Nicholson tapes have been instrumental to me, and I have used them as prime examples of 'how to do it.'"[23]

Sandy is given special mention in one of the pamphlets of the Ontario Archives, *The Archives of Ontario Keeper of the Record*: "Notable collections are . . . autobiographical interviews with prominent Canadians by A.M. (Sandy) Nicholson."[24] On a CBC programme hosted by John Fisher, Sandy shared his interest in oral history with Canadian listeners, "The Ontario Archives are not like museums," he explained. "There are no three-dimensional objects. Every-thing is on paper except for the audio collections of taped interviews." Sandy mentioned a few he had secured: "You can hear Sir Frederick Banting reading a Christmas message; Manly Miner, the son of Jack Miner, talking about the pioneer bird banding work of his father; Jack Ayre, the last of the Dumbells on tape; and Syl Apps tells his story — athlete, Toronto Maple Leaf hockey star, MPP for Kingston, Ontario."

Earl Leard, director of media services for the United Church of Canada, recalled the telephone ringing in 1976 and a lively voice saying, "I'm Sandy Nicholson. I hear you're doing some oral history. I'm very interested. May I come to see you?" Two years earlier the United Church media services had begun an oral history collection for the use of congregations during the church's fiftieth anniversary celebrations. Leard wrote:

> Sandy's enthusiasm and willingness to work en-couraged us to continue to record interviews [and] was the motivating force leading to the setting up of a trust fund for oral history within the division of communication of the United Church. His contri-butions to the church and to Canada have been nothing less than outstanding. His insight, courage, motivation and persistence in worthy causes reflect the imagination and spirit of a disciple of Jesus and in that sense a servant of others.[25]

Epilogue

The Last Lap

On 16 February 1983 a *Toronto Star* reporter interviewed one of Sandy's long-time friends, Dr. Robert McClure. Learning of the many interesting projects McClure still participated in, the reporter said, "Sounds like you're not retired at all. Why not?"

McClure answered, "There's too much to learn. When you're coming to the last lap — that's when you have to run hardest of all."

Sandy Nicholson ran all his life — in one field or another, whether it was on sports grounds or in the political arena. Like Dr. McClure, he continued to participate long after most people would have retired. Sandy possessed the ingredients for a comfortable life — physically, mentally and materially. He could have chosen an easy life, but everything in his nature opposed that. He distinguished himself by being "both a man of the cloth and a man in government." He brought his concern for his fellow man into both fields and never compromised his basic principles.

If Sandy Nicholson had a compulsion, it was to alleviate ills. His convictions stemmed from a religious philosophy — early indoctrinated and later practiced with insight — and a political disposition towards equality for all people, which he dispensed on the principle of "no charge." His life became a crusade to help the helpless — whether on the mission field, in Parliament, in the Legislature, or through the many humanitarian associations in which he became involved. Contrary to the common image that politicians are cynical and materialistic, Sandy's "enthusiasm never flagged and his idealism never wavered."[1] Possibly he did not consciously associate his actions with the social gospel, yet he constantly concerned himself with the quality of human comfort here on earth. Until her death in October 1985, Marian stood by Sandy's side, encouraging him and adding to his contributions in her own self-effacing manner.

A reporter recently stated in *Macleans* that "Canadian heroes are hard to find — not because they weren't there in the first place but because we won't allow their reputations to survive."[2] Sandy's story is just one of many which might have lapsed into obscurity. Throughout his life he participated in many history-making events, not as an onlooker but as a "mover and shaker."

Sandy's varied vocations evolved not because he lost interest in what he had been doing, but because he continually accepted challenges to serve in other capacities. The common thread sewn through the fabric of his life's work was his practical idealism, expressed by a friend as "the prime example of why psychologists have called Man a social animal in the highest sense."[3]

Retirement years became as busy and as exciting for Sandy as his active years in church and in politics. In 1977 he examined the CCF files then in existence at the National Archives of Canada and literally "filled in the gaps," recording additional information which he had acquired through his long personal involvement with the party. The same year, he and Marian visited friends on the west coast, including John W. George, a former harness maker from Viscount, Saskatchewan, and later Saskatoon, on the occasion of his one hundredth birthday. Sandy taped the story of this many-faceted pioneer, adding another Canadian personality to his growing list of interviews being preserved in the archival collections.

Following a family celebration, honouring Sandy and Marian on their fiftieth wedding anniversary, in August 1978, the two set out for Saskatchewan with the idea of visiting all the places they had lived. They bought a ticket to Saskatoon, then rented an automobile to tour the countryside, because the interconnecting railway system of the 1930s was by that time extinct. They stayed in hotels. Sandy said, "For years I stayed with friends who gave every kindness you could ask, but then you do have to talk late hours and we had planned quite a busy pace and we thought we would stay in hotels." Early in this excursion, however, Marian suffered a fractured knee which abruptly terminated the trip. But they were to make two further forays into the area.

In August 1979 Sandy and Marian accepted an invitation to visit the Hudson Bay district to celebrate an anniversary of the Nixonville School — one built at Sandy's instigation during the 1930s. In his address as guest speaker, Sandy expressed gratitude at being part of the thrust to relieve rural suffering. He noted that the district had acquired modern medical and educational facilities, as well as better housing. He reminded the audience that such improvements had been made possible largely by the CCF government during its twenty-year term in the province. Well equipped buildings in the larger school units proved a contrast to the one-room log building at Nixonville where the reunion took place.

Besides celebrating Marian's eightieth birthday by travelling to Alaska, the Yukon, and northern British Columbia in 1982, the Nicholsons toured their Saskatchewan haunts again, renewing acquaintanceships. At Porcupine Plain Mrs. Barbara Machala, the first bride to be married in the Hudson Bay Junction manse in October 1930, brought her daughter and two grandchildren to greet them. The "missionary cow" baby, Eva Lukinchuk, now Eva Harris of Somme, also came to pay her respects. Sandy believed there was "a good deal of history of an important region of Canada which should be written about." He said, "We were happy we were able to spend the best years of our lifetime in Saskatchewan."

Wes Robbins, a former minister of finance in the Saskatchewan government and a long-time friend of the Nicholsons, had travelled with Sandy in the Hudson Bay area in the Dirty Thirties. He accompanied the Nicholsons on this 1982 junket, and said,

> The people I met and who knew him in those early days could not praise him sufficiently. One man told me of Sandy giving him his overcoat in the dead of winter when he was a returnee from hospital and poorly clad for a drive by team from the train to his farm home. Another told me of Sandy giving him his shoes (as he had none and this prevented him from cutting wood in the bush), with Sandy walking some twelve miles back to Hudson [Bay Junction] in his bare feet. The Good Samaritan according to these people had nothing on Sandy Nicholson.[4]

In September 1983 Sandy and Marian were the hosts at a dinner party in the House of Commons dining room at which guests included Stanley Knowles, T.C. Douglas and his wife Irma, Graham and Irene Spry, and King Gordon. The Nicholsons had known some of these friends since the 1920s. The conversation covered college days, track meets, fund raising for the CCF, politics then and now. Knowles thanked Sandy for arranging the dinner, and lauded him as the CCF's best organizer and for his steady support of the party. Knowles said Sandy

> . . . has maintained his definiteness ever since [the beginning] — stuck with it all through the years, as evidenced this evening in the stories around the table . . . Our CCF members have been few in total, but everyone is determined to make the party stronger. Sandy's determination and loyalty to his social conscience continues. Back in the thirties he helped me get elected. He was always helpful to me and he took politics seriously. Sandy and I sat side by side in Parliament. In a few words, I'd say Sandy is a man of determination.[5]

While the group enjoyed a quiet hour in Knowles's office following the dinner, the telephone rang. An official from the Vancouver NDP office had called to inform Knowles of Andrew Brewin's death. A brief pause followed, allowing the group to pay tribute to this man who had long championed the CCF cause.[6] Two months later, Graham Spry died of an apparent heart attack at the age of eighty-three. Spry, who had left a sick bed to attend the September dinner, had taken the opportunity to express his gratitude to Sandy for gathering the friends together. Spry will be remembered as a life-long advocate of public broadcasting, and he is known in some circles as the father of the CBC.[7] Within seven months, Douglas had suffered fractured ribs, a suspected concussion and internal injuries when he was struck by an Ottawa transit bus, while out walking. This was barely a month after he had received an honorary degree at the University of Winnipeg spring convocation.

Sandy said, "After our visit to Ottawa in September 1983, Stanley phoned me for my advice before he announced his decision to retire. I repeated again what I have said so often, that he has had a wonderful life, and he should take it easier." In October Knowles returned to Winnipeg to bid farewell to the political life. He had decided he would not represent the NDP in the next federal election because of the after-effects of a stroke suffered two years earlier, which seriously affected his speech and memory.

The new year brought improved health to both Douglas and Knowles, allowing colleagues to honour them further. Prime Minister Trudeau presented a motion in the House to make Knowles an honorary officer of the institution he had served for so many years. On 13 March, in an emotional ceremony that drew tributes from all parties, Knowles was made procedural adviser to the Speaker of the Commons — a post "tailor-made for Knowles, considered the leading parliamentary expert among sitting MPs."[8]

In April, Knowles served as guest speaker at a testimonial dinner in Toronto to honour Douglas. After he returned to Ottawa, Knowles wrote to Sandy (who had been unable to attend due to Marian's ill health), "Tommy, you and I are the only [ones left] of the CCF MPs who were in the House of Commons in 1940-1945. It has been quite a story — and the nine hundred or more who came to the dinner expressed their appreciation."⁹

Both Stanley Knowles and Sandy had earned a reputation as spokesmen for the elderly and as tireless fighters for improved pension benefits. Before his retirement, Knowles had assisted Sandy in his plea to have pensions reinstated for widows of members of Parliament who had retired before 1963, when legislation approved such payments. Earlier correspondence between Sandy and government officials had failed to resolve the problem, so Sandy took his own advice and enlisted Knowles in 1983. In one of his last official communications before his retirement in November, Knowles wrote to the Honourable Allan MacEachen, deputy prime minister:

> There are still about 24 members of Parliament whose wives will receive no parliamentary pension when those members die. I feel very strongly that this unfairness should be corrected. You have dealt with this issue a number of times. I urge that you now deal with it again. This time I hope you will correct this disparity. Because of my condition I know that I cannot run in the next general election, therefore I would appreciate having this matter resolved as speedily as possible.¹⁰

The issue still had not been resolved when former Liberal cabinet minister James Sinclair (one of the twenty-four members to whom Knowles referred in his letter), died in February 1984, leaving a widow.

Throughout his years in politics, Sandy championed women's rights and sought more recognition for them in the political field. He applauded the action of the NDP caucus in June 1984 concerning the creation of the Agnes Macphail Fund. This was established in order that more women would be able to run for election in the upcoming federal campaign.¹¹ It also aimed to increase the number of New Democratic women candidates in future elections. In the early years the Saskatchewan CCF had strong and influential women like Louise Lucas, Gertrude Telford and Gladys Strum. Marian Nicholson might have been among these women, but in order to advance his own political career Sandy left Marian to raise the family. The frictions this caused did not go unnoticed by their children. Marian struggled for her individuality, obtaining a second university degree, teaching, and taking holidays with friends like Edna Jacques, while Sandy performed his political duties. Marian's rewards did not come until Sandy retired.

Sandy's impassioned speeches in Parliament helped to push Canada toward more progressive ideals of greater equity, fairness and tolerance. He continuously voiced aversion to the "colour-blind immigration policy" practiced by Canada.[12] The confidence Sandy expressed in the 1940s about the value to the Canadian economy of immigrants' energy was upheld by the exemplary life of Ping Quan. Quan worked for Ontario Hydro till his retirement in 1980. He also served as a member of the board of the Mom Sheong Foundation for two years, and as chairman of the foundation's Chinese school committee from 1974. The Chinese community itself has assured the continuity of its culture and language.[13] Quan received a Senior Achievement Award recognizing his outstanding contribution to the quality of life in Ontario from the Province of Ontario in June 1984. [14] Ping's citation read in part: "Your dedication and commitment to others, and in particular to the older members of our society, is to be commended and merits this recognition."[15]

Sandy continued to keep abreast of current events. Part of his routine, even during Marian's illness, included watching the daily television newscasts. In November 1984, the assassination of Indira Gandhi came as a great shock. She had been her father's hostess when Sandy visited India in 1957, attending the Commonwealth Parliamentary Association conference. Sandy's diary entry at the time read:

> The Prime Minister [Nehru] had his reception for us at
> 4:45. He seems to have a tremendous amount of
> energy . . . His daughter was on hand to receive and

help look after the huge crowd of guests. We had tea
and sweets served out in the huge gardens behind the
residence.

Sandy had met and renewed his acquaintanceship with
Mrs. Gandhi again in 1970 when he and Marian spent
several weeks in India.

A closer friend, Frank S. Scott, died on 30 January 1985.
Scott had continued as a spokesman for socialism
throughout his life. The following year, on 4 February
1986, Tommy Douglas died at his Ottawa home, after a
lengthy battle with cancer. Prime Minister Brian Mulroney,
Liberal Leader John Turner, NDP National Leader Ed
Broadbent, and Saskatchewan NDP Leader Allan Blakeney
led the list of mourners at the funeral service. King Gordon
delivered the eulogy, saying, "Tommy Douglas is
remembered today as a man of integrity, clarity of thought,
commitment to values . . . " Gordon added dryly, "[and]
for his appreciation of the dialectical relationship between
truth and absurdity which we call humour."[16]

David Lewis, who died on 23 May 1981, was another old
friend who had nobly served both CCF and NDP, not only
as a party official, but as member of Parliament for York
South. Lewis also had gained political prominence as NDP
leader from 1972 to 1974 when the party held the balance
of power during the Liberal minority government. The
1980s had depleted the courageous band of early CCF
colleagues, leaving Stanley Knowles and Sandy Nicholson
as the sole survivors of the original group of members of
Parliament. On 2 October 1985, Marian Nicholson died
quietly in the Toronto nursing home where she and Sandy
made their home. The family tribute stated: "Marian and
Sandy Nicholson had a vision of a quality of life which
went far beyond their own personal well-being, and they
shared it with many, many others." An era has ended
perhaps, posing some questions: Will the giants of
socialism be adequately replaced? Will they be sufficiently
remembered?

Questioned about the changes he had witnessed
throughout the years, especially concerning public atti-

tudes, Sandy cautioned,

> People today are very cynical. We seem to live in a very selfish society. The name of the game seems to be 'get as much as you can, as quickly as you can, with as little effort as possible.' With this attitude in mind, people will get as good government as they deserve.

> There have been, and are today, good people in all political parties. But today, there is a greater need than ever for attitudes to change. The 'super-loto' concept of life cannot possibly lead to lasting happiness. You don't buy happiness.[17]

Sandy's life of service — "no charge" — has contributed to a fairer distribution of Canada's wealth for people in many walks of life. In the words of Lloyd Shaw, "All of us who have been privileged to serve in the CCF-NDP parties throughout all or part of the last 50 years and in the future, will always be indebted to Sandy, and his dedicated wife Marian, for their sacrifices and contributions to this great political movement."[18]

Appendices

Appendix I
General Election Results — Mackenzie Electoral District,
Saskatchewan
Showing Standing of A.M. (Sandy) Nicholson

General Election — 1935

John Angus MacMillan	Liberal	6,595
Alexander Malcolm Nicholson	CCF	4,451
Benjamin Franklin Graham	Social Credit	3,059
John Albert Padget	Conservative	1,234

General Election — 1940

Alexander Malcolm Nicholson	CCF	10,207
James Ross Barrie	Liberal	9,211
Walter Ernest Wiggins	Communist	819

General Election — 1945

Alexander Malcolm Nicholson	CCF	9,037
John Angus MacMillan	Liberal	5,306
Onofry M. Swystun	Social Credit	2,143
John Robeson Taylor	Progressive Conservative	1,580

General Election — 1949

Gladstone Mansfield Ferrie	Liberal	7,564
Alexander Malcolm Nicholson	CCF	6,209
William Michael Berezowski	Labor-Progressive	1,122
Frederick Albert Patrick	Social Credit	851
Samuel Edward Hall	Progressive Conservative	697

General Election — 1953

Alexander Malcolm Nicholson	CCF	8,021
Gladstone Mansfield Ferrie	Liberal	7,466

Frederick Albert Patrick	Social Credit	1,386
Samuel Edward Hall	Progressive Conservative	840
Mrs. Edna Juletta Williams	Labor-Progressive	554

General Election — 1957

Alexander Malcolm Nicholson	CCF	7,231
Joseph Marshall	Liberal	5,299
Stanley James Korchinski	Progressive Conservative	3,289
Robert S. Claypool	Social Credit	1,956

General Election — 1958

Stanley James Korchinski	Progressive Conservative	9,138
Alexander Malcolm Nicholson	CCF	5,559
Joseph Marshall	Liberal	2,511

Source: *Directory of Members of Parliament & Federal Elections for the North-West Territories and Saskatchewan 1877-1966*, p. 34. Published by The Saskatchewan Archives Board, Regina and Saskatoon, 1967.

Appendix II
Saskatchewan Provincial Election Results — Saskatoon
Showing Standing of A.M. (Sandy) Nicholson

Saskatoon City, Saskatchewan
General Election — 1960 (3 members)

Arthur Thomas Stone, CCF	16,159
Alexander Malcolm Nicholson, CCF	15,877
Gladys Grace Mae Strum, CCF	15,782
Herbert Charles Pinder, Liberal	11,582
William Loran, Liberal	11,346
Robert Andrew Heggie, Liberal	11,344
Lewis M. Brand, Progressive Conservative	7,042
Edward N. Hughes, Progressive Conservative	6,982
Thomas Park, Progressive Conservative	5,676
Earle Williams, Social Credit	3,035
Morris Chernesky, Social Credit	2,949
John K. Rodine, Social Credit	2,767

General Election — 1964 (5 members)

Hon. Alexander Malcolm Nicholson, CCF	16,701
John Edward Brockelbank, CCF	16,559

Wesley Albert Robbins, CCF	16,126
Sally Marie Margharita Merchant, Liberal	16,068
Harry David Link, CCF	16,041
Clarence Leslie Baldwin Estey, Liberal	15,761
Gladys Grace Mae Strum, CCF	15,741
Keith McLean Crocker, Liberal	15,661
Joseph Jeffrey Charlebois, Liberal	15,542
Victor Charles Hession, Liberal	14,770
Lewis M. Brand, Progressive Conservative	11,401
W. Hugh Arscott, Progressive Conservative	11,344
Ramon John Hnatyshyn, Progressive Conservative	10,874
Henry Clay Rees, Progressive Conservative	10,543
Irving Goldenberg, Progressive Conservative	10,240

Saskatoon City Park — University
General Election — 1967

Joseph Jeffrey Charlebois, Liberal	6,096
Alexander Malcolm Nicholson, NDP	5,410
Mel Mills, Progressive Conservative	1,356

Source: *Saskatchewan Executive & Legislative Directory 1905-1970*, p. 142. Published by Saskatchewan Archives Board, Regina and Saskatoon, 1971.

Appendix III
Supplemental Bylaws of the Sturgis Farm
Co-operative Association Limited

Membership

No. 1.   Any persons, either owners or tenants of land, or any persons who may contribute their personal service to the Association, in accordance with the bylaws, may become members of the Association.

No. 2.   Any person applying for membership in the Association shall be required to sign an application form, prescribed by the directors. The application form may include the following conditions:

    (a) An undertaking to describe and indicate the amount of capital and resources the prospective member will be prepared to subscribe and contribute to the assets of the Association;

(b) An undertaking to contribute whatever services, in the interests of the Association, may be required from time to time by the manager and the Board of Directors;

(c) An undertaking to agree to any special revaluation of assets or capital and resources of the Association from time to time as may be determined by the Board of Directors, subject to special arrangements set out in the bylaws for arbitration in cases of appeal by any member;

(d) An undertaking to sign an agreement to empower the Association to retain any loan made by the member, or his membership fee, for a period of time to be decided upon by the Board of Directors;

(e) An undertaking to abide by the final decision of the Board of Directors as to where, when and how the capital and resources subscribed, or the services contributed, to the Association may be used in the best interests of the Association.

No. 3.   No application for membership, transfer of membership or withdrawal of membership shall be valid unless approved by resolution of the Board of Directors, and duly recorded in the minutes of the directors' meetings.

No. 4.   The directors may, by a two-thirds vote, at a meeting duly called, order the retirement of a member from the Association:

(a) If the retirement of a member is ordered in accordance with the provisions of this bylaw, the Association shall repay the membership fee contributed by the member, and pay to him other amounts held to his credit, subject to the terms of any special contractual arrangements which the member may have made with the Association.

(b) The secretary of the Association shall, within five days from the date on which the order is made, notify the member in writing of the order.

(c) An appeal from the order may be taken by the

member to the next general meeting of the Association, provided that written notice of intention to appeal shall have been given by him to the secretary within thirty days of the receipt of the notice mentioned in clause (b).

(d) At such meeting a majority of the members present may confirm or rescind the order.

No. 5. The duties and functions of members shall be held to include:

(a) To study their Association with a view to obtaining a full understanding of its general purposes and arrangements, and give loyal support to its objects, aims and purposes;

(b) To be actively interested in the Association's affairs and attend as many meetings of the Association as possible, and by discussion and voting to provide a basis for the determination of policies by the directors;

(c) To participate in the formulation of, and to abide by, all the rules, regulations and bylaws governing the Association;

(d) To endeavour to co-operate with and encourage the co-operation of all members;

(e) To care for such property or goods of the Association as may be assigned for use, either personally or in the interests of the Association;

(f) To contribute their time and service if elected or appointed on the Board of Directors or any committee or committees which may be appointed, and to do other reasonable things which may be in the best interests of the Association.

No. 6. At all annual, semi-annual, general, or special meetings of the Association one-half of the membership of the Association shall constitute a quorum until such time as the membership of the Association is greater than twenty, after which time ten members or one-tenth of the total membership of the Association, whichever is the greater, shall constitute a quorum.

Administration

No. 7. The Board of Directors of this Association shall consist of nine members duly elected.

No. 8. The Board of Directors shall direct and supervise the business of the Association as prescribed in the Standard Bylaws governing co-operative associations. They shall, amongst other matters:

(a) Meet regularly, to consult with the manager regarding the operation of the Association, in the interests of deciding generally on the most equitable and efficient methods of rendering services to the members;

(b) Appoint annually from the membership an appraisal committee to evaluate all personal resources which may be turned over to the Association for capital purposes and other financial requirements;

(c) Appoint a general manager annually from the membership;

(d) Appoint a committee from time to time, at the request of the membership, to deal with the matter of revaluation of capital and other financial resources subscribed, and in the event of a member appealing such action, make the necessary provision for arbitration in accordance with the bylaws of the Association;

(e) Provide for a proper system of bookkeeping and accounting records, which may be subject to the approval of the Registrar of Co-operative Associations.

No. 9. The general manager shall manage all operations of the Association in accordance with the policy which may be set out by the Board of Directors, and shall have power to assign farming duties to all members, appoint whatever assistants, or hire whatever outside labour he deems necessary, and shall be responsible for indicating to the treasurer or timekeeper the allowances of time for those contributing services to the farming operations of the Association.

No. 10. The manager, any member or any employee of the Association who may have as a part of his responsibility the handling, management or expenditure of the funds of the Association shall be required to furnish a fidelity bond, or such other security as may be satisfactory to the directors.

No. 11. The fiscal year of this Association shall end on December thirty-first.

No. 12. In cases of need, particularly with reference to the revaluation of capital items, any member may, after having appealed to a meeting of the Association without a satisfaction to himself, seek arbitration by means of a tribunal, which shall be composed of a representative appointed by the member, a representative appointed by the Board of Directors of the Association, together with a non-member, approved by Registrar of Co-operative Associations, in the event that the other two members cannot agree as to who shall be the independent member. The findings of such a tribunal shall be final, and all members shall agree to abide by them.

No. 13. Services performed in the community by other co-operatives may be utilized insofar as possible, and such co-operatives shall be given such assistance deemed possible in the circumstances.

Financing

No. 14. An applicant for membership, after approval of his application by the directors, shall, before he may enjoy the privileges of a member, be required to pay to the Association his membership fee in full.

No. 15. No interest shall be paid on the membership fee.

No. 16. A member may with the approval, or upon the request of the directors, loan to the Association such funds as may be required to finance the purchase of such property, equipment and goods as may be required, and to furnish such other fixed and working capital requirements as may be necessary to achieve the objects of the Association, and such loans shall be repayable to the member at such time and in such manner as the directors may determine and as the business of the Association may warrant.

(a) A member shall be entitled to a statement showing

the amount loaned by him to the Association, and the date upon which the loan was made.

(b) Amounts standing to the credit of a member as a result of contributions to the Association may be credited with interest at a rate not exceeding six per cent per annum, provided always that the total amount paid in interest on loans from members in any year shall not exceed fifty per cent of the earnings of the Association for the current year, after ordinary expenses and valuation reserves, such as depreciation, are deducted therefrom.

(c) A member shall be entitled to an annual statement from the Association, showing the amount payable to him in the membership loan account, and the amount of any interest credited thereon.

(d) A member may be required to agree to give a certain period of notice prior to any withdrawal of his loans to the Association, such agreement to be in writing, and duly signed and recorded at the time the member loans the said funds to the Association.

No. 17. The directors may borrow and secure the payment of money on such terms and conditions as they may determine, and in accordance with the provisions of The Co-operative Associations Act.

Operating methods

No. 18. The Association shall maintain a standard wage basis for all members, and at all times ensure as satisfactory working conditions as possible.

No. 19. The Association shall maintain a standard wage basis for non-member service, which shall be approved by the members from time to time, until the non-member has served the Association continuously over a period of time, to be approved by the directors, when he may make application for membership, or receive the benefits of labour dividends, or both.

No. 20. Certain work, incidental to the success of the Association, but not readily placed on a time basis, shall have allowance made for it, the Association guaranteeing to pay each member a minimum annual wage of two hundred and forty dollars ($240.00), provided the said member is available for service to the Association for at least nine months of the year. In cases of sickness, accident, or other circumstances beyond his control, a member shall receive credit with respect to the minimum of nine months availability for service mentioned in this section. Those members qualifying through recorded time and standard wage provisions for any amount in excess of two hundred and forty dollars ($240.00) either from the Association, or from his own earnings during leave of absence, or from both the aforesaid sources, in excess of this amount, shall not qualify for any assistance within the meaning of this section.

No. 21. All net earnings of members for services rendered to other than the Association shall be paid into the treasury of the Association, and such members shall receive standard wages during the period of time such services were given in the same manner as would have applied had they been working for the Association. A member may, however, apply for leave of absence without pay or benefits from the Association if outside labour services are likely to be in excess of six weeks in any one year, and if leave of absence is granted, the member will then retain any earnings which he may make, rather than pay them over to the Association. A member shall not at any time do work for other than the Association without the consent of the general manager of the Association.

No. 22. A member may, upon application to the Board of Directors, be given time off with full pay to perform various community duties which may, or may not, give such member a net return. This privilege may not be extended for more than one month in any one year, except under special circumstances, approved by the Board of Directors, and no more than two members may be absent on such community service at the same time during the seeding, harvesting or threshing periods of farm operations. Except where special leave of absence is granted under the provisions of Bylaw No. 21, any net earnings from such community service shall be paid in to the treasury of the Association.

No. 23. The degree of efficiency in which services, related to farm operations, have been rendered to the Association shall be determined by the general manager, and his decision shall be binding on the members of the Association with respect to work done. Remuneration shall be paid according to this decision. In the event of a dispute arising, the member may place his complaint before a special arbitration board of three members, approved by the directors, and the decision of this arbitration board shall be final.

No. 24. Earnings received from the rental of the machinery of the Association, or from custom work done by members with the equipment of the Association, shall be paid into the accounts of the Association as a part of its general revenue.

Distribution of Surplus

No. 25. (1) After paying all ordinary expenses, including standard and guaranteed wages, and allowing for proper valuation and expense reserves, chargeable to the year's business, and providing for interest on membership loans, in accordance with the provisions of Bylaw No. 16, the remainder, if any, of the earnings from the yearly operations of the Association shall be apportioned in the following order:

(a) By setting aside not less than ten per cent of the balance of the earnings for a reserve, in accordance with the provisions of The Co-Operative Associations Act, until such time as this reserve shall be equal to at least ten per cent of the total assets.

(b) By setting aside an amount not exceeding three per cent of the balance of the earnings to be used in special circumstances, approved by the directors, in cases of sickness, accident or other unusual hardship affecting any member.

(c) By setting aside an amount not exceeding two per cent of the balance of the earnings to be used in special circumstances, approved by the directors, for the purpose of making loans to members or their children for the continuing of their education in any field which, in the opinion of the directors, they appear to have special qualifications.

(d) By setting aside an amount not exceeding one per cent of the balance of the earnings to be used from time to time for general educational or community purposes.

(2) The remainder of the earnings, if any, after making provision for those items indicated in Bylaw No. 25, Subsection (1), shall be divided among those members and non-members contributing their services to the Association at standard wages, and in proportion to the amount of time contributed by each. In the case of non-members eligible for patronage dividends in accordance with Bylaw No. 19, these may be retained to the non-members' credit for a specific purpose, or paid out immediately, as may be determined by the directors, except that the non-member shall be fully informed of amounts credited to him, and for what purpose these amounts are retained.

No. 26. Subject to the provisions of the other supplemental bylaws of this Association, up to fifty per cent of all dividends due to a member for service or labour rendered may be retained in a special revolving reserve account, for the purpose of providing sufficient funds to carry on the operations of the Association, in accordance with its objects, and after the dividends so retained have accumulated in an amount deemed sufficient for the operations of the Association as aforesaid, the directors shall, at such time and in such manner as they may determine, pay to the member the amounts retained from dividends due to him.

(a) The first payment to a member of dividends retained in accordance with the provisions of this bylaw may be equivalent to the amount considered by the directors as available for payment at the time and as may be warranted by the financial requirements of the Association, and subsequent payments from this reserve may be in amounts determined likewise by the directors at such future periods as they may decide.

(b) As dividends which have been retained by the Association are paid to a member, additional amounts may be retained from current dividends due to him in order that sufficient funds may be maintained to achieve the objects of the Association, provided, however, that dividends so retained shall in turn be paid to the member in accordance with the provisions of this bylaw.

(c) A member shall be entitled to a statement after the end of every fiscal year, showing the amount retained from dividends due to him in accordance with the provisions of this bylaw, together with a statement of any dividends paid to him.

(d) Interest may be payable on dividends retained in a special revolving reserve.

No. 27. In order that capital contributions from members, by way of membership fees, membership loans, and retained dividends, may be more equalized in amount, the directors may require a member who has an investment in capital contributions of less than fifty percent of the largest member investment to allow any balance of dividends accruing to him for payment in any year to be placed in the credit of his membership loan account until such time as his investment equals or exceeds fifty percent of the largest member investment. After such action has been taken, the directors may, with due consideration for the finances of the Association, determine to repay part of the membership loans of the member or members with the largest capital contributions to their credit.

General

No. 28. The directors and members of the Association shall be generally responsible at all times for advancing ideas for improved farm practices, for improved living conditions, for well-considered operational expansion arrangements, for good relationships with other co-operative organizations, and for generally carrying on all the operations of the Association in a manner which will deserve praise from farm and community leaders, as well as from various governments.

No. 29. The directors and members of the Association shall be generally responsible for improvements, considered to be of benefit to their community, as may be suggested by authoritative sources, such as the University of Saskatchewan, the Departments of Agriculture of Saskatchewan and Canada, the Saskatchewan Department of Co-operation and Co-operative Development and various other educational and farm organizations.

Certified correct,

_____

President

_____

Secretary

Bibliography

PRIMARY SOURCES

NATIONAL ARCHIVES OF CANADA, Ottawa, Ontario — The Co-operative Commonwealth Federation and the New Democratic Party, Canada.

ARCHIVES OF ONTARIO, Toronto, Ontario — A.M. Nicholson Papers, and early Bruce County records.

SASKATCHEWAN ARCHIVES BOARD, Regina & Saskatoon, Saskatchewan — A.M. Nicholson Papers.

A.M. Nicholson and Marian Nicholson — personal papers.

Ruth Nicholson Dibbs.

Interviews with: Stanley Knowles, Magnus Eliason, Margaret Telford Thomas, J.T. Bradford, Ellen Knight and Nettie Forsiuk.

Written reminiscences include testimonies from: Allan Blakeney, Donald C. MacDonald, Lloyd R. Shaw, Pat Plank Armstrong, Florence Pratt, Pearl Isabelle-Viner.

BOOKS

ALLEN, Richard. *The Social Passion: Religion and Social Reform in Canada 1914-28*. Toronto, University of Toronto Press, 1971.

BADGLEY, Robin F., and Samuel WOLFE. *Doctors' Strike*. Toronto, Macmillan of Canada, 1967.

BERGER, Carl. *The Writing of Canadian History: Aspects of English-Canadian Historical Writing, 1900-1970*. Toronto, Oxford University Press, 1976.

BRENNAN, J. Wm., ed. *Building the Co-operative Commonwealth: Essays on the Democratic Socialist Tradition in Canada*. Regina, Canadian Plains Research Center, University of Regina, 1984.

ENGLEMANN, F.C. and M.A. SCHWARTZ. *Canadian Political Parties: Origin, Character, Impact.* Scarborough, Ontario, Prentice-Hall of Canada Ltd., 1975.

FERNS, H.S. *Reading from Left to Right: One Man's Political History.* Toronto, University of Toronto Press, 1982.

FOX, William Sherwood. *The Bruce Beckons — The Story of Lake Huron's Great Peninsula.* Toronto, University of Toronto Press, 1952.

GREY OX MEMORIAL PLAQUE COMMITTEE, *Tales from the Grey Ox.* 1981.

HIGGINBOTHAM, C.H. *Off the Record: The CCF in Saskatchewan.* Toronto, McClelland & Stewart Ltd., 1968.

HOLT, Simma. *The Other Mrs. Diefenbaker.* Toronto, Doubleday, 1982.

HORN, Michiel. *The League for Social Reconstruction: Intellectual Origins of the Democratic Left in Canada 1930-1942.* Toronto, University of Toronto Press, 1980.

LEWIS, David. *The Good Fight: Political Memoirs 1909-1958.* Toronto, Macmillan of Canada, 1981.

LIPSET, Seymour. *Agrarian Socialism: The Cooperative Commonwealth Federation in Saskatchewan.* Toronto, Oxford University Press, 1950.

McCLASKEY, Angus. *Angus McClaskey Remembers . . .* Toronto, 1976.

McLEOD, Thomas H. and Ian McLEOD. *Tommy Douglas: The Road to Jerusalem.* Edmonton, Hurtig Publishers Ltd., 1987.

MORTON, Desmond. *A Short History of Canada.* Edmonton, Hurtig Publishers, 1983.

MORTON, W.L. *Manitoba: A History.* Toronto, University of Toronto Press, 1957 (reprinted issue 1979).

REID, Escott. *On Duty — A Canadian at the Making of the United Nations, 1945-1946.* Toronto, McClelland & Stewart, 1983.

ROBERTSON, Norman. *History of the County of Bruce.* Toronto, William Briggs, 1906.

SHACKLETON, Doris French. *Tommy Douglas: A Biography.* Toronto, McClelland & Stewart, 1975.

STINSON, Lloyd. *Political Warriors: Recollections of a Social Democrat.* Winnipeg, Queenston House, 1975.

THOMAS, Lewis H., ed. *The Making of a Socialist: The Recollections of T.C. Douglas.* Edmonton, University of Alberta Press, 1982.

TOLLEFSON, E.A. *Bitter Medicine: The Saskatchewan Medicare Feud*. Saskatoon, Modern Press, 1963.

TROFIMENKOFF, Susan Mann. *Stanley Knowles: The Man From Winnipeg North Centre*. Saskatoon, Western Producer Prairie Books, 1982.

ZAKUTA, Leo. *A Protest Movement Becalmed: A Study of Change in the CCF*. Toronto, University of Toronto Press, 1964.

NEWSPAPERS

Canora Courier   *Edmonton Journal*
Hudson Bay Post   *Lucknow Sentinel*
North-East Review (Sturgis)   *Preeceville Progress*
Saskatchewan Commonwealth/The Commonwealth
Star-Phoenix (Saskatoon)   *The Leader-Post* (Regina)

Notes

The chief source for this book was its subject. A.M. (Sandy) Nicholson had created with the Archives of Ontario a series of autobiographical interviews. These interviews, conducted with Roger E. Nickerson, Archivist (Private Manuscripts Section) were taped between 18 June and 18 September 1979, and they may be found in the Archives of Ontario Audio Visual Collection (A.V. Coll. #10). A transcript of the tapes provided the base for the book. Further personal interviews and correspondence between subject and author made available material previously not available, as well as clarifying the sequence of events and supplying detailed information on specific subjects.

Many people responded to newspaper notices soliciting memories, anecdotes and information about their association with Sandy Nicholson. A brief questionnaire sent to political colleagues and personal friends, as well as subsequent interviews with some of them, resulted in amassing additional pertinent facts.

The Nicholsons' guestbook, deposited in the Archives of Ontario, kept from the day of their marriage in 1928 to the present, provided peepholes into the past in the succinct comments made by prominent people who visited the Nicholson home.

Other main sources include *The Commonwealth*, the Saskatchewan CCF-NDP weekly newspaper, House of Commons *Debates*, and the *Debates and Proceedings of the Legislative Assembly* of Saskatchewan.

Chapter 1

1 *The Sheaf*, 15 October 1925, 1.

2 Ibid., 2.

3 Pat O'Dwyer, *Saskatoon Star-Phoenix*, 17 May 1969.

4 Early documents are signed "Norman Nicolson." The author chose to use "Nicholson" for consistency, following the explanation.

5 Canada, House of Commons, *Debates*, 3 June 1955, vol. 4, 4396 (hereafter *Debates*).

6 Archives of Ontario, A.M. Nicholson Papers. Norman Nicholson was born near Uigishadder, Portree, Isle of Skye, in 1821. He married Ann Cameron, from the same area, who was born in 1824.

7 Norman Robertson, *History of Bruce County* (Toronto: William Briggs, 1906), 38. ". . . described more formally in an Act of Parliament, Vic., Chap. 37, passed May 23rd. 1846 as 'That part of the province lying to the northward of the District of Huron, bounded on the north by Lake Huron and the Georgian Bay, which is not included in either the Districts of Wellington or Simcoe . . .'"

8 The location of Port Albert may be found in H.F. Walling, *Atlas of the Dominion of Canada* (Montreal: George N. Tackabury, 1975), 135.

9 Robertson, *Bruce County*, 11. "On the 19th of April 1847 an Order-in-Council . . . to open up wastelands . . . also a single concession along the rear of the Township of Wawanosh and Ashfield." (This single concession became the first concession in the township of Kinloss, Bruce County.)

10 *Tales from the Grey Ox* (Grey Ox Memorial Plaque Committee, 1981), 143. A row of houses facing onto a roadway was known as a concession.

11 *Debates*, 1 August 1940, vol. 3, 2299.

12 *Debates*, 9 February 1944, vol. 1, 318.

13 Robertson, *Bruce County*, 67-68.

14 Ibid., 68.

15 A.M. Nicholson to B.L. Dyck, 24 November 1983, A.M. Nicholson Papers, M-16, Saskatchewan Archives Board, Saskatoon (hereafter Nicholson Papers). "The School was

built on Lot 11 for that concession. The Nine Mile River ran through the one hundred acres and it had never been good farm land . . . Nephew Donald MacIntyre who is living where we moved in 1903 owns this fifty acres still."

16 *Tales from Grey Ox*, 124.

17 Richard Allen, *The Social Passion: Religion and Social Reform in Canada, 1914-28* (Toronto: University of Toronto Press, 1971), 4.

18 Robertson, *Bruce County*, 474. " . . . until the grist mill at Lucknow was running in 1859, a trip to Walkerton, Kincardine or Dungannon was necessary whenever a few bags of wheat had to be ground."

19 A.M. Nicholson, transcription of interview with author 5 August 1983, 5. Nicholson Papers. "The records are in the Presbyterian Church at Goderich, Ontario, to the effect that Alexander MacDonald and Mary Stewart were married in that church in 1857 on April 29."

20 Benoît Forest, Archives of the Canadian Railroad Historical Association (Canadian Railway Museum, St. Constant, Quebec), to B.L. Dyck, 28 May 1984, Nicholson Papers.

21 Sally McDougall to B.L. Dyck, 22 January 1984, Nicholson Papers.

22 *Lucknow Sentinel*, 28 May 1936. The big Church " . . . was dedicated on May 26, 1912 during the pastorate of Rev. Finlay MacLennan, who left about a year later after a pastorate of 25 years."

23 Ibid.

24 *Tales from Grey Ox*, 155. Hugh MacMillan and his wife Donalda (née MacIntosh) were born in Bruce County. They married after MacMillan's graduation and ordination as a minister and after Donalda's graduation as a nurse. Following their marriage, they went to Formosa (Taiwan) as missionaries, serving for twenty-eight years. In 1957, when the South Kinloss Cemetery observed its centennial, the Reverend Hugh MacMillan, then in Canada on furlough, and the Reverend A.M. Nicholson, took part in the service, paying tribute to the pioneers. Seven years later, MacMillan became moderator of the Presbyterian Church in Canada.

25 Today's equivalents to school grades in those days: Junior 1-4 = today's grades 1-4; Senior 1-4 = today's grades 5-8.

26 "Limit Table," 1898, Bruce County Board of Education Municipal Documents Range 22, Shelf 26, Archives of Ontario.

Chapter 2

1 Graham MacNay to B.L. Dyck, 7 February 1984, Nicholson Papers. MacNay became a teacher and later worked for the federal government. After high school graduation, MacNay and Nicholson did not meet again until 1942 when the Nicholson family shared the Ottawa home of the MacNay family during a housing shortage.

2 *Debates*, 19 November 1953, vol. 1, 190-91.

3 Later changed to Saskatchewan Association for the Mentally Retarded (SAMR).

4 *Debates*, 24 January 1957, vol. 1, 621.

Chapter 3

1 *Saskatchewan History* 37 (Autumn 1984): outside front cover.

2 Gordon Barnhart, "The Prairie Pastor — E.H. Oliver," *Saskatchewan History* 37 (Autumn 1984): 81.

3 *The United Church of Canada Record of Proceedings of First General Council Meeting*, Toronto, 10-18 June 1925, 164-65, United Church of Canada Archives, University of Winnipeg, (hereafter UCCA).

4 *The Canadian Student* 5 (February 1923): 1.

5 Escott Reid, *On Duty — A Canadian at the Making of the United Nations 1945-1946* (Toronto: McClelland and Stewart, 1983), 5.

6 *Encyclopedia Canadiana*, s.v. "Student Christian Movement of Canada."

7 Helen R.H. Nichol, "What Internationalism Did for the Conference," *The Canadian Student* 5 (February 1923): 29.

8 George M. Wrong, "An Impression of the Conference," *The Canadian Student* 5 (February 1923): xvii.

9 His Excellency Lord Byng, Governor-General of Canada, "Character," *The Canadian Student* 5, 1-4.

10 E.H. Oliver, "The New Canadian Situation," *The Canadian Student* 5, 39-48.

11 Richard Roberts, "Religion in National Life," *The Canadian Student* 5, 51-61.

12 Newton W. Rowell, "Canada's International Responsibility," *The Canadian Student* 5, 65-70.

13 Helen R.H. Nichol, "What Internationalism Did for the Conference," *The Canadian Student* 5, 29-32.

14. Ibid.

15 *The Sheaf*, 15 March 1923.

16 Ibid., 12 October 1922.

17 Ibid., 18 October, 1923.

18 *The United Church of Canada Record of Proceedings of First General Council Meeting*, 1925, 164-65, UCCA.

19 *The Sheaf*, 25 October 1923.

20 Ibid.

21 Allen, *The Social Passion*, 16.

22 *The Sheaf*, 1 November 1923.

23 Ibid., 16 October 1924.

24 Ibid., 12 March 1925.

25 Ibid., 8 October 1925.

26 Ibid., 22 October 1925.

27 Andy Russell, *Memoirs of a Mountain Man* (Toronto: Macmillan of Canada, 1984), 27.

28 Jack Beveridge to A.M. Nicholson, 11 March 1984, Nicholson Papers.

29 Presbyterian Church in Canada, *General Assembly Acts and Proceedings, 49th General Assembly, 1923*, 28, UCCA.

30 Craig, McGowan and Mather to B.L. Dyck, n/d, Nicholson Papers.

Chapter 4

1 *The Sheaf*, 4 March 1926.

2 Ibid., 12 October 1926.

3 Ibid., 25 November 1926.

4 Ibid., 20 October 1927.

5 Ibid., 4 March 1926.

6   *Debates*, 15 October 1945, vol. 1, 1086.

7   The Student Christian Movement (SCM) had been given land at Swanwick, Hampshire, England, for use as a conference centre away from the temptations of city life. All overseas students travelled by bus from London, and returned to London after the conferences ended.

8   *Debates*, 19 November 1953, vol. 1, 191.

9   "May Day", *The Commonwealth*, 1 May 1946.

10 *Debates*, 26 March 1945, vol. 1, 234.

11 *The Sheaf*, 13 January 1927.

12 Ibid. The Saskatchewan delegation included Vera Waugh, Edith Sutherland, Mildred Wright, Mollie Musselman, Harold Fennell, George Porteous, Stanley Steer, David Russell, George Manson, Miss E. Brown.

13 Student Christian Movement Minute Book (Manitoba Branch), 5 December 1926, UCCA.

14 *The Sheaf*, 13 January 1927.

15 *Wadena News*, August 1928.

16 Marian Nicholson diary, 16 August 1928, Nicholson Papers.

17 Ibid.

18 *The Canadian Encyclopedia*, 1st ed., s.v. "United Church of Canada."

19 *Supplementary Reports on the Schemes of the Church of Scotland* (Edinburgh: William Blackwood & Sons Ltd., 1929), 78-79, UCCA.

20 *The Commonwealth*, 4 May 1960.

21 First footing is a Scottish New Year's Day custom, whereby the first person to cross the doorstep of a house is believed to influence the residents' fortunes during the succeeding twelve months. A dark-haired "first footer" is believed to bring especially good fortune.

Chapter 5

1   *United Church of Canada, Record of Proceedings, 1932*, 339-43, UCCA.

2   A town in Saskatchewan is a place with a population of five hundred or more residents.

3   Edythe Forsythe to B.L. Dyck, February 1984, Nicholson Papers.

4   *Debates*, 13 December 1945, vol. 1, 163-64.

5   *United Church of Canada Records of Proceedings, 1932*, 341, UCCA.

6   *The United Church Yearbook, 1931*, 480, 633, UCCA.

7   *The New Outlook*, 1 February 1933.

8   Barnhart, "Prairie Pastor," 84.

9   Ibid., 88.

10 Ibid., 90. "By late 1931 . . . through the efforts of the relief committee, the West had received one hundred and sixty-five and one half tons of clothing and a total of one hundred and fifty-nine cars of relief to Saskatchewan, Manitoba, and Alberta. Saskatchewan received most of the relief . . . Each car of relief served approximately two hundred and fifty to three hundred families."

11 *The New Outlook*, 11 October 1923.

12 Barnhart, "Prairie Pastor," 93.

13 *The Canadian Encyclopedia*, 1st ed., s.v. "Forster, John Wycliffe Lowes."

14 *Debates*, 5 June 1940, vol. 1, 550.

15 *The Commonwealth*, 30 June 1954.

16 Carl Berger, *The Writing of Canadian History: Aspects of English-Canadian Historical Writing, 1900-1970* (Toronto: Oxford University Press, 1976), 128-29.

17 *Winnipeg Free Press*, 9 April 1984.

18 *Debates*, 4 May 1947, vol. 3, 2754-58.

19 Saskatchewan, Department of Education, *Annual Report 1933*, 31.

20 Ivy McVicar to B.L. Dyck, undated correspondence, Nicholson Papers.

21 Irene A. Poelzer, "Local Problems of Early Saskatchewan Education," *Saskatchewan History* 22 (Winter 1979): 1.

22 Nettie Forsiuk to B.L. Dyck, 8 November 1983, Nicholson Papers.

23 *The New Outlook*, 1 February 1933.

24 Ibid.

25 Ibid.

26 Ibid.

27 Norman Massey died on 11 November 1932.

28 *Debates*, 9 February 1944, vol. 1, 318.

29 *Hudson Bay Post*, 21 March 1946.

30 Dr. E.H. Oliver to A.M. Nicholson, 12 July 1932, Nicholson Papers.

31 A.M. Nicholson to Norma Nicholson, 17 April 1933, Nicholson Papers.

32 *Saskatoon Star Phoenix*, 17 April 1933.

33 Anna Nicholson to Norma Nicholson, 22 April 1933, Nicholson Papers.

34 *The Commonwealth*, 13 February 1946.

35 Kay MacKinnon to B.L. Dyck, 10 February 1985, Nicholson Papers.

36 *Hudson Bay Post*, 7 March 1946.

37 Berger, *Writing of Canadian History*, 139.

38 Lewis H. Thomas, ed., *The Making of a Socialist: The Recollections of T.C. Douglas* (Edmonton: University of Alberta Press, 1982), 320-21.

39 *Hudson Bay Post*, 28 March 1946.

40 Ibid., 11 April 1946.

41 Ibid., 25 April 1946.

42 *Debates*, 5 June 1940, vol. 1, 550.

43 King Gordon, "Christianity and Socialism," *Saskatchewan CCF Research Review*, vol. 1, no. 10, May 1934, 4-9.

44 Allen, *The Social Passion*, 4.

Chapter 6

1 Stanley Knowles, interview with author, Ottawa, 21 September 1983.

2 Allen, *The Social Passion*, 7.

3 George Hoffman, "The Entry of the United Farmers of Canada, Saskatchewan Section, into Politics: A Reassessment," *Saskatchewan History* 30 (1979): 99.

4 C.H. Higginbotham, *Off the Record: The CCF in Saskatchewan* (Toronto: McClelland & Stewart, Ltd., 1968), 64.

5 Saskatchewan, Legislative Assembly, *Debates and Proceedings,* 14th Leg., 2d. Session, 26 October 1961, vol. 12, 12 (hereafter *Debates and Proceedings*).

6 King Gordon to A.M. Nicholson, 31 May 1933, Nicholson Papers.

7 King Gordon to B.L. Dyck, 16 May 1984, Nicholson Papers.

8 Ibid.

9 David Lewis, *The Good Fight: Political Memoirs, 1909-1958* (Toronto: Macmillan of Canada, 1981), 425.

10 Lloyd Stinson, *Political Warriors: Recollections of a Social Democrat* (Winnipeg: Queenston House, 1975), 92-93.

11 *The Commonwealth,* 2 February 1966.

12 *Directory of Members of Parliament and Federal Elections for the Northwest Territories and Saskatchewan, 1887-1966* (Regina/Saskatoon: Saskatchewan Archives Board, 1967), 34. J.A. MacMillan (Liberal): 5, 926; L. St. G. Stubbs (CCF): 4, 312.

13 Jack Douglas to B.L. Dyck, 30 January 1984, Nicholson Papers.

14 M.J. Colwell Memoirs, 28 November 1963, Nicholson Papers.

15 Allan Blakeney to B.L. Dyck, 29 December 1983, Nicholson Papers.

16 Berger, *Writing of Canadian History,* 79.

17 *Debates,* 21 May 1940, vol. 1, 110-13.

18 *Debates,* 1 August 1940, vol. 3, 2300.

19 Charles Endicott to A.M. Nicholson, 28 November 1934, Nicholson Papers.

20 J.L. Nichol to A.M. Nicholson, 29 November 1934, Nicholson Papers.

21 R.B. Cochrane to A.M. Nicholson, 15 December 1934, Nicholson Papers.

22 *Preeceville Progress,* 28 November 1934.

23 Oscar Sorestad to B.L. Dyck, 16 February 1984, Nicholson Papers.

24 Lewis, *The Good Fight,* 446.

25 Doris French Shackleton, *Tommy Douglas: A Biography* (Toronto: McClelland and Stewart, Ltd., 1975), 71.

26 Berta McClure Campbell to B.L. Dyck, undated correspondence, Nicholson Papers.

27 *Canora Courier,* 3 October 1935.

28 Ibid., 10 October 1935.

29 *The Commonwealth,* 27 April 1949.

30 *Directory of Members of Parliament,* 34. J.A. MacMillan (Liberal); 6, 595; A.M. Nicholson (CCF): 4, 451.

31 *The Commonwealth,* 30 June 1954.

32 Lloyd R. Shaw to B.L. Dyck, 18 May 1984, Nicholson Papers.

Chapter 7

1 In Dr. Hugh MacLean's first foray into politics, in the 1921 federal election, he ran as a Progressive candidate in Regina and came in third. He persuaded M.J. Coldwell to run as a Progressive in Regina in the autumn 1925 election, but Coldwell lost. When the CCF was formed, MacLean was a founding member, and he agreed to run on the party's ticket in Regina in the 1935 election. He again placed third.

2 Lewis, *The Good Fight,* 90-91.

3 D.F. Young to A.M. Nicholson, 10 March 1936, Nicholson Papers.

4 *The Canadian Encyclopedia,* 1st. ed., s.v. "The League for Social Reconstruction."

5 Shona McKay, "The Father of the CBC," *Macleans,* 5 December 1983, 70.

6 Lewis, *The Good Fight,* 197.

7 Ibid., 204.

8 Ibid., 110.

9 *Preeceville Progress,* 4 November 1936.

10 Circular letter, 14 December 1936, Nicholson Papers.

11 Before redistribution in 1936, the Mackenzie constituency included parts of seven provincial ridings: Melfort, Tisdale, Torch River, Wadena, Kelvington, Canora, and Pelly.

12 *The Commonwealth,* 29 June 1949.

13 *The Commonwealth,* 29 June 1949.

14 Ibid.

15 Ibid.

16 Shackleton, *Tommy Douglas*, 100-101.

17 Magnus Eliason, interview with author, 10 February 1984, Nicholson Papers.

18 P.R. Sinclair, "The Saskatchewan CCF and the Communist Party in the 1930s," *Saskatchewan History* 26:6. "Williams responded with the official saw-off policy . . . [he] instructed that co-operation with other progressives was good provided there was no compromise of programme, no sinking of identity in fusion and no joint candidates . . . if the CCF were stronger, it would be your undoubted duty to place your candidate in the field . . . "

19 Shackleton, *Tommy Douglas*, 118.

20 Higginbotham, *Off the Record*, 8.

21 Madge Rogers McCullough recollections, undated, Nicholson Papers.

22 Gladys Byrnes Compagnon recollections, 1984, Nicholson Papers.

23 William Boschman recollections, 16 November 1983, Nicholson Papers.

24 Leo Zakuta, *A Protest Movement Becalmed: A Study of Change in the CCF* (Toronto: University of Toronto Press, 1964), 55.

25 *Canora Courier*, 18 April 1940.

26 P.S. Quan to A.M. Nicholson, 8 September 1940, Nicholson Papers.

Chapter 8

1 Lewis, *The Good Fight*, 216.

2 "Parliamentary Personalities," *Canadian Business*, May 1943.

3 *Debates*, 21 May 1940, vol. 1, 549-55.

4 Ibid., 19 May 1942, vol. 3, 2568.

5 A.M. Nicholson, "Ottawa Letter," *Canora Courier* 16 May 1940.

6 William Boschman to B.L. Dyck, 16 November 1983, Nicholson Papers.

7 *Debates*, 21 June 1940, vol. 1, 1002.

8   Ibid., 14 June 1940, vol. 1, 787.

9   Ibid., 4 July 1940, vol. 1, 1320.

10 Ibid., 3 June 1941, vol. 4, 3461-62.

11 Ibid., 11 February 1943, vol. 1, 348.

12 *Canadian Business*, May 1943.

13 *Debates*, 1 June 1942, vol. 3, 2949.

14 Lewis, *The Good Fight*, 188.

15 *Edmonton Journal*, 29 March 1942.

16 Lewis, *The Good Fight*, 202.

17 Ibid., 200.

18 Lloyd R. Shaw to B.L. Dyck, 18 May 1984, Nicholson Papers.

19 Stinson, *Political Warriors*, 16.

20 J. Atkinson to A.M. Nicholson, 23 July 1943, Nicholson Papers.

21 Margaret Telford Thomas to B.L. Dyck, 11 May 1984, Nicholson Papers.

22 Pat Armstrong to B.L. Dyck, November 1983, Nicholson Papers.

23 *Debates*, 24 March 1943, vol. 2, 1534.

24 Ibid., 12 March 1942, vol. 2, 1260-62.

25 Margaret Telford Thomas to B.L. Dyck, 11 May 1984, Nicholson Papers.

26 Magnus Eliason, interview with author, 10 February 1984, Nicholson Papers.

27 Nettie Forsiuk to B.L. Dyck, 8 November 1983, Nicholson Papers.

28 *Debates*, 13 September 1945, vol. 1, 166-67.

29 Ibid., 27 June 1944, vol. 4, 4285.

30 Ibid., 9 February 1944, vol. 1, 317.

31 Ellen Knight, interview with author, November 1984, Nicholson Papers.

32 *Debates*, 26 March 1945, vol. 1, 231-33. The 1941 census placed the number of Ukrainians at 18,334. Scandinavians came next with 8,000, the English 6,000, Scots 4,000, Irish 3,000, Polish 5,000, and Russians 4,664.

33 Dr. T. Percival Gerson to A.M. Nicholson, 17 January 1946, Nicholson Papers.

34 P.S. Quan biography, 1984, Nicholson Papers.

35 *Debates*, 19 June 1954, vol. 6, 6320.

36 Lewis, *The Good Fight*, 322-25.

37 Ibid., 329.

38 Dr. Hugh MacLean to A.M. Nicholson, 19 April 1948, Nicholson Papers.

39 Alexander Fishman to A.M. Nicholson, 5 May 1948, Nicholson Papers.

40 A.M. Nicholson to Alexander Fishman, 24 May 1948, Nicholson Papers.

41 *Debates*, 19 February 1947, vol. 1, 596-97.

42 *The Commonwealth*, 31 March 1948.

43 A.M. Nicholson to G.W. Cadbury, 15 March 1949, Nicholson Papers.

44 *The Commonwealth*, 16 February 1949.

45 A.M. Nicholson to Dr. Morris Shumiatcher, 15 March 1949, Nicholson Papers.

46 *Sturgis North-East Review*, 7 April 1949.

47 Ibid.

48 *The Commonwealth*, 15 June 1949.

49 Ibid., 4 May 1949.

50 *Saskatoon Star-Phoenix*, 29 June 1949.

51 Donald MacDonald to B.L. Dyck, 28 March 1984, Nicholson Papers.

Chapter 9

1 Shackleton, *Tommy Douglas*, 185.

2 A.M. Nicholson to Alex Turner, 25 March 1945, Nicholson Papers.

3 "Supplemental Bylaws of the Sturgis Farm Co-operative Association Limited," Bylaw No. 22, 4. Nicholson Papers.

4 A.M. Nicholson to Elmer Sjolie, 11 April 1946, Nicholson Papers.

5 *Debates*, 13 December 1945, vol. 3, 3446.

6 Sturgis Farm Co-operative Association Limited, Nicholson Papers.

7 A.M. Nicholson to Olga Fredericksen, 26 March 1946, Nicholson Papers.

8 Ruth Dibbs to B.L. Dyck, 13 November 1984, Nicholson Papers.

9 *Debates*, 21 February 1955, vol. 2, 1347.

10 "CCF Fights for Co-ops," CCF pamphlet 1946.

11 Sturgis Farm Co-operative Association Limited, Nicholson Papers.

12 Ibid.

13 Ruth Dibbs to B.L. Dyck, 13 November 1984, Nicholson Papers.

14 *Sturgis North-East Review*, 31 March 1949.

15 "Supplemental Bylaws of the Sturgis Farm Co-operative," Bylaw No. 20, 4, Nicholson Papers.

16 Ibid., Bylaw No. 21, 4.

17 A.M. Nicholson to Elmer Sjolie, 9 March 1948, Nicholson Papers.

18 A.M. Nicholson to Dr. Hugh MacLean, 28 January 1947, Nicholson Papers.

19 *The Commonwealth*, 8 August 1951.

20 A.M. Nicholson to Elmer Sjolie, 19 February 1947, Nicholson Papers.

21 A.M. Nicholson to Olga Fredericksen, 26 March 1946, Nicholson Papers.

22 *The Commonwealth*, 22 October 1947.

23 Ibid., 7 December 1949.

24 Ibid., 19 July 1950.

25 Lewis, *The Good Fight*, 375-76.

26 *The Commonwealth*, 12 July 1950.

27 *Vancouver Daily Province*, 27 July 1950.

28 Lewis, *The Good Fight*, 416.

29 William Boschman recollections, 16 November 1983, Nicholson Papers.

30 *The Commonwealth,* 9 July 1952.

31 *Sturgis North-East Review*, 29 August 1952.

Chapter 10

1 *The Commonwealth*, 12 November 1952.

2 Ibid., 2 September 1953.

3 *Debates*, 19 November 1953, vol. 1, 189-92

4 *Debates*, 7 June 1954, vol. 5, 5569. The SS *Begonia* was chartered to the Rank Milling Company of London, England, by her owners, the Stag Steamship Company of Newcastle. The agent in Churchill was the Montreal Shipping Company.

5 *Debates*, 19 November 1953, vol. 1, 818-89.

6 Ibid., 27 May 1954, vol. 5, 5152-53.

7 Ibid., 8 December 1953, vol. 1, 721.

8 Norman Massey to B.L. Dyck, 27 November 1983, Nicholson Papers.

9 *Debates*, 19 February 1954, vol. 2, 1666-67.

10 Ibid., 16 March 1954, vol. 3, 3059.

11 Ibid., 19 March 1954, vol. 3, 3170.

12 Ibid., 25 July 1955, vol. 6, 6717.

13 Ibid., 29 March 1954, vol. 4, 3451-52.

14 Ping Quan biography, 1984, Nicholson Papers.

15 *Debates*, 10 June 1954, vol. 6, 5783.

16 *The Commonwealth*, 22 December 1954.

17 *Debates*, 28 January 1955, vol. 1, 655-57.

18 Ibid., 2 April 1954, vol. 4, 3638-40.

19 Ibid., 28 January 1955, vol. 1, 654.

20 Ibid., 11 May 1955, vol. 4, 3675.

21 Ibid., 16 May 1955, vol. 4, 3813-14.

22 *The Commonwealth*, 10 August 1968.

23 Ibid., 19 October 1966.

24 Ibid., 5 May 1955.

25 Lewis, *The Good Fight*, 430.

26 *Debates*, 17 May 1955, vol. 4, 3854.

27 Lewis, *The Good Fight*, 431.

28 Ibid., 433.

29 Ibid.

30 *Debates*, 31 January 1957, vol. 1, 855.

31 Magnus Eliason, interview with author, 10 February 1984, Nicholson Papers.

32 *The Commonwealth*, 8 May 1957.

33 Lewis, *The Good Fight*, 484.

34 *Debates*, 25 October 1957, vol. 1, 423.

35 George Stephen, clerk of the Saskatchewan Legislature was assigned as secretary. Others in the group included: Jean Paul Deschatelets, G.H. Doucette, J.W. Murphy, F.D. Shaw, Irwin William Studer, Senator W.M. Aseltine, and Richard Donahoe (then Attorney General of Nova Scotia).

36 *Regina Leader-Post*, 28 December 1957.

37 Richard Donahoe to A.M. Nicholson, 28 May 1984, Nicholson Papers.

38 A.M. Nicholson diary, 2 December 1957, Nicholson Papers.

39 *Regina Leader-Post*, 28 December 1957.

40 Ibid.

41 A.M. Nicholson diary, 4 December 1957, Nicholson Papers.

42 Ibid., 10 December 1957.

43 *Regina Leader-Post*, 28 December 1957.

44 *The Commonwealth*, 5 March 1958.

45 Lewis, *The Good Fight*, 485.

46 Stinson, *Political Warriors*, 164-65. The CCF helpers from Ontario were Stephen Lewis, John Brewin, Gerry Caplan, and Bill Tepperman.

47 *Canora Courier*, 26 June 1958.

48 *The Commonwealth*, 19 November 1958.

49 Ibid., 1 October 1958.

Chapter 11

1 *The Commonwealth*, 4 May 1960.

2 Ibid.

3 Ibid.

4 Thomas, *The Making of a Socialist*, 360.

5 Ibid., 369-70.

6   *The Commonwealth*, 15 June 1960.

7   *Debates and Proceedings*, 2 April 1965, vol. 2, pt. 3, 1440.

8   *The Dome*, August-September 1960.

9   Thomas, *The Making of a Socialist*, 373.

10 Allan Blakeney to B.L. Dyck, 29 December 1983, Nicholson Papers.

11 A.M. Nicholson, speech to Catholic Hospital Conference, 17 September 1960, Nicholson Papers.

12 A.M. Nicholson, speech to Wascana Kiwanis Club, Regina, 20 October 1960, Nicholson Papers.

13 A.M. Nicholson, speech to Melfort District Pioneer Lodge, 11 January 1961, Nicholson Papers.

14 Dr. Hugh MacLean to A.M. Nicholson, February 1946, Nicholson Papers.

15 Pat Armstrong to B.L. Dyck, 16 November 1983, Nicholson Papers.

16 Florence Pratt to B.L. Dyck, 14 November 1983, Nicholson Papers.

17 *Debates and Proceedings*, 8 March 1961, vol. 20, 3-11.

18 *The Commonwealth*, 6 April 1961.

19 Thomas, *The Making of a Socialist*, 376.

20 Ibid., 374.

21 *The Commonwealth*, 28 February 1962.

22 Higginbotham, *Off the Record*, 108.

23 *The Commonwealth*, 23 March 1966.

24 *Debates and Proceedings*, 15 March 1962, vol. 16, 4-7.

25 James M. Pitsula, "The CCF Government in Saskatchewan and Social Aid, 1944-1964," in *"Building the Co-operative Commonwealth" — Essays on the Democratic Socialist Tradition in Canada*, ed. J. William Brennan (Regina: Canadian Plains Research Center, 1984), 207.

26 Thomas, *The Making of a Socialist*, 371-72.

27 *Debates and Proceedings*, 27 March 1961, vol. 33, 12.

28 A.M. Nicholson, speech to nursing home personnel, Saskatoon, 7 June 1961, Nicholson Papers.

29 *Debates and Proceedings*, 26 October 1961, vol. 12, 17.

30 *Regina Leader-Post*, 17 May 1962.

31 A.M. Nicholson autobiography, Audio-Visual Collection no. 10/168-191, Archives of Ontario.

32 *Regina Leader-Post,* 23 July 1962.

33 *The Commonwealth*, 1 August 1962.

34 Florence Pratt to B.L. Dyck, 14 November 1983, Nicholson Papers.

35 *The Commonwealth*, 28 March 1962.

36 Florence Pratt to B.L. Dyck, 14 November 1983, Nicholson Papers.

37 *The Commonwealth*, 29 May 1963.

38 Ibid., 6 May 1964.

39 Ibid., 23 December 1964.

40 Higginbotham, *Off the Record*, 10.

41 *The Commonwealth*, 2 March 1966. Dr. A.L. Swanson, executive director of the hospital's training system, had already left. Within three months, two of his assistants, J.L. Sommers and A.R. Thorfinnson, had followed him.

42 *The Commonwealth*, 1 February 1967.

43 Ibid., 2 March 1967.

44 *Saskatchewan Executive and Legislative Directory 1905-1970.* Brockelbank/Tisdale, 1938-52; Kelsey, 1952-67. Cooper-Hunt/ Regina City, 1952-64; Regina West, 1964-67. Nollet/Cut Knife, 1944-67.

45 *The Commonwealth*, 29 November 1967.

46 Ibid., 1 February 1967.

Chapter 12

1 *Prairie Messenger,* 13 May 1984.

2 Pearl Isabelle-Viner to B.L. Dyck, 16 November 1983, Nicholson Papers.

3 Saskatchewan Association For Retarded Children (SARC), Summary Report 1967. "Both projects were launched on or before the target date. The Alvin Buckwold Unit began operating July 1, 1967, with the appointment of Dr. Zaleski as director. The Work Training Project was well established before 1967 with Mr. Sigfusson as director. As of September

1, 1967, this project has been fully integrated within the department of education program, and completely financed through the department's regular budget."

4 Pearl Isabelle-Viner to B.L. Dyck, 16 November 1983, Nicholson Papers.

5 Dr. G. Allan Roeher to A.M. Nicholson, 23 December 1966, Nicholson Papers.

6 *Debates and Proceedings,* 24 February 1966, vol. 3, pt. 3, 32.

7 Dr. J.W. Gerrard, head, Department of Pediatrics, University of Saskatchewan, was selected in 1962, along with two associates at the Children's Hospital, Birmingham, England, as a recipient of the John Scott award. The award was given for his participation in the research leading to the development of a healthy diet for PKUs.

8 Dr. J.W. Gerrard to B.L. Dyck, 4 December 1983, Nicholson Papers.

9 *Humboldt Journal,* 26 January 1967.

10 *Debates and Proceedings,* 24 February 1966, vol. 4, 37.

11 Ibid., 37-38.

12 *The Commonwealth,* 15 March 1967.

13 *Debates and Proceedings,* 14 March 1967, vol. 5, pt. 1, 1283.

14 Pearl Isabelle-Viner to B.L. Dyck, 16 November 1983, Nicholson Papers.

15 John Dolan to A.M. Nicholson, 24 April 1981, Nicholson Papers.

16 Saskatchewan Association For Retarded Children, Annual Report 1968.

17 John Owen to B.L. Dyck, 2 April 1984, Nicholson Papers.

18 Ibid., "Thanks to the gift of a house in Lowther Avenue from Margaret McLeod, a long-time advocate for the physically handicapped, the Toronto group which registered provincially as Cheshire Homes Foundation (Canada) Inc., were able to go into business almost immediately."

19 Canadian Universities Service Overseas (CUSO) is an independent non-government organization which recruits skilled individuals to work in under-developed countries. It provides financial support for Third World countries; in addition, it promotes an educational programme in Canada encouraging awareness of Third World problems.

20 Glen Williams, *Not for Export: Towards a Political Economy of Canada's Arrested Industrialization* (Toronto: McClelland and Stewart, 1983), viii.

21 William Boschman to B.L. Dyck, 16 November 1983, Nicholson Papers.

22 *Debates*, 11 July 1955, vol. 6, 6252.

23 Roger E. Nickerson to B.L. Dyck, 28 November 1983, Nicholson Papers.

24 Archives of Ontario, *Keeper of the Record* (Toronto: Archives of Ontario, 1982), 11.

25 Earl Leard to B.L. Dyck, 2 December 1983, Nicholson Papers.

Epilogue

1 A.C. MacAuley to B.L. Dyck, 1984, Nicholson Papers.

2 Charles Gordon, "How Canadians Mistreat Heroes," *Macleans*, 5 December 1983, 17.

3 Wallace Campbell to A.M. Nicholson, 1984, Nicholson Papers.

4 Wes Robbins to B.L. Dyck, 11 January 1985, Nicholson Papers.

5 Stanley Knowles, interview with author, 21 September 1983, Nicholson Papers.

6 The service for Andrew Brewin was held at St. Simon the Apostle Anglican Church, Toronto, 31 October 1983. Brewin was called to the Ontario Bar in 1930; appointed King's Counsel in 1948; member of Parliament for Greenwood (Toronto) 1962-1979.

7 Shona McKay, "The Father of CBC," *Macleans*, 5 December 1983, 70. McKay's obituary stated, "Spry won the John Drainie Award in 1972 for his distinguished contribution to broadcasting and became a Companion of the Order of Canada in 1970."

8 *Winnipeg Free Press*, 14 March 1984.

9 Stanley Knowles to A.M. Nicholson, 15 April 1984, Nicholson Papers.

10 Stanley Knowles to Allan MacEachen, 3 October 1984, Nicholson Papers.

11 Stanley Knowles to B.L. Dyck, 13 June 1984, Nicholson Papers.

12 Richard Gwyn, *The 49th Paradox: Canada in North America* (Toronto: McClelland & Stewart, 1985), 161.

13 The Mom Sheong Foundation is a Chinese-Canadian charitable organization which built and operates a sixty-five bed home for the aged on D'Arcy Street, Toronto.

14 The annual Senior Achievement Awards were inaugurated by the Secretariat of the Ontario provincial government in 1984. The awards were created to permit the Province of Ontario to recognize the outstanding contribution senior citizens have made to communities and the quality of life in Ontario. Ping Quan accepted his award at a ceremony in the Legislative Building, Queen's Park, 20 June 1984.

15 Gordon H. Dean, MPP, to Ping Quan, 8 June 1984, Nicholson Papers.

16 *Winnipeg Free Press,* 4 March 1986.

17 *Canora Courier,* 9 June 1982, A.M. Nicholson had not altered his views in 1986 and, in a conversation with the author, commented that this statement expressed his thoughts adequately.

18 Lloyd Shaw to B.L. Dyck, 18 May 1984, Nicholson Papers.

Index

Brown, Kathy, 190
Buchanan (Saskatchewan), 89
Buckle, Walter, 59
Buckwold, Mayor Sidney, 179,
    195, 198
Bulow Lumber Company, 57
Bunce, "Bunny," 39, 40, 41, 100
Bunn, Willie, 83
Burns, Harold, 13
Burns, Stanley, 13
Burton, Joe, 110, 119
Byng, Lord, Governor-General
    of Canada, 26
Byrnes, Gladys, 111, 112

C

Calgary (Alberta), 202
Cameron, Colin, 168
Cameron, Donald, 203
Campbell, Angus, 73
Campbell, Berta McClure, 91
Campbell, Milton, 80
Canada Elections Act, 163-64
Canada Grain Act, 162
Canada Housing and Mortgage
    Corporation, 142
Canadian Association for
    Retarded Children, 195
Canadian Association for the
    Mentally Retarded, 198
Canadian Broadcasting
    Commission, 75
Canadian Brotherhood of
    Railway Employees, 133
Canadian Business, 121
Canadian Congress of Labour,
    163
Canadian Co-operative
    Implements Ltd., 144
Canadian Favorites, 128
Canadian Federation of Mayors
    and Municipalities, 179

Canadian Labour Congress,
    163, 176
Canadian Medical Association,
    186
Canadian National Railway, 9,
    25, 36, 53, 54, 55, 57, 59, 61,
    62, 64, 83, 84, 160
Canadian Pacific Railway, 40
Canadian Radio League, 75
Canadian Red Cross, 61
Canadian University Services
    Overseas, 201-203
Cannington (Saskatchewan),
    108
Canora (Saskatchewan), 55, 60,
    86, 92, 93, 94, 113, 135, 142,
    177
Canora Courier, 93
Castleden, Hugh, 110, 113, 114,
    116
Castleden, Mrs. Hugh, 110
Catholic Hospital Conference of
    Saskatchewan, 177
Centre for Community Studies,
    Saskatoon, 192
Chambers, Alan, 154
Cheshire, Group Captain
    Leonard, 199, 200
Cheshire Homes
    first international conference,
    200; of Covelong, India, 201;
    of Saskatchewan, 199, 200,
    204
Chinese Immigration Act, 66
Church of Scotland, 47-51
    Deed of Union, 51. *See also*
    Presbyterian church
Churchill (Manitoba), 40, 52,
    54, 55; port of Churchill,
    121, 154, 155-56
Civil Service Commission of
    Canada, 157-58

Cobourg (Ontario), 102, 156
Cobourg Tannery, 102
Cochrane (Ontario), 139
Cochrane, R.B., 60, 72, 88
Coldwell, M.J., 83, 84, 85, 89,
90, 93, 94, 95, 107, 110, 112,
113, 119, 123, 124, 135, 136,
149, 168, 190, 191, 205
Coldwell, Mrs. M.J., 89
Colombo Plan, 167
Commonwealth, The, 92, 94,
95, 137, 151, 161, 169, 173,
174, 189, 191
Commonwealth Parliamentary
Association, 165, 213; 1957
conference, 165-68, 213
Communist party, 109, 130
Connor, Ralph.
See Gordon, C.W.
Conservative party, 59, 109, 130
Cooper-Hunt, Majorie, 192
Co-operative Commonwealth
Federation, 2, 35, 69, 77, 78,
79, 80, 81, 84, 87, 93, 94, 95,
98, 99, 101-14, 116-18, 120,
123-38, 141, 145, 149-51,
153, 154, 158, 160, 162-65,
167-69, 172-76, 178-85, 187,
189, 190-93, 195, 208-15; and
Woodsworth House, 133;
formation of New Party, 174-
76; Saskatchewan CCF and
affiliation with NDP, 176;
Saskatchewan CCF changes
name to NDP, Saskatchewan
Section, 193
Co-operative Commonwealth
Youth Movement, 150
co-operative movement in
Canada, 140-43, 145, 146,
148-49
Co-operative Union of
Saskatchewan, 145

co-operative school-work
training project for educable
mentally retarded, Regina,
195
Copeland, Bruce, 45, 47, 50
Copeland, Margaret, 47, 50
Cornwall (Ontario), 139
Cripps, Sir Stafford, 101
Crittenden, Harold, 195
Crooked River (Saskatchewan),
52, 64, 68, 83
Crystal Lake (Saskatchewan),
94, 105, 154
Cumberland, R.M., 72

D

Dafoe, J.W., 80
Dalton, H.W. (Herb), 99
Dennison, William, 102
Depression, The, 5, 36, 54, 57,
59, 60, 61-63, 66-67, 69, 75,
78, 186; Saskatchewan "work
with wages programme," 62
Dibbs, Ruth Nicholson, 28, 64,
71, 72, 106, 149-50, 155, 184,
185
Diefenbaker, John G., 160, 168,
186
Dix, D.S., 23, 57, 58
Dolan, John, 196, 198
Dominion Electric Company,
54, 76, 90, 92
Donahoe, Richard, 165, 167
Doncrest (Saskatchewan), 58,
65, 70
Doncrest School, 70
Douglas, Irma, 210
Douglas, T.C., 75, 77, 78, 95,
99, 107, 109, 110, 113, 114,
119, 121, 126, 127, 148, 153,
162, 163, 171, 172, 174, 175,
176, 185, 186, 189, 190, 210,
211, 212; death of, 214;

Nicholson, Marian Massey
(wife), 8, 18, 24, 25, 32, 36,
37, 44, 45, 46, 47, 48, 49, 50,
51, 52, 71, 79, 81, 82, 84, 88,
89, 93, 94, 95, 97, 98, 101,
106, 112, 113, 120, 125, 127,
128, 140, 142, 149, 155, 156,
157, 159, 168, 169, 172, 175,
178, 179, 184, 191, 193, 201,
203, 204, 208, 210, 213, 214,
215; and Saskatchewan
Farmer-Labour party, 78;
death of, 208, 214; death of
second child, 72, 100;
interest in drama, 76; interest
in gardening, 76, 152;
pregnancies, 72, 73, 100,
103, 104; role as fund raiser,
189; role on Hudson Bay
Junction relief committee,
63; second university degree,
189, 213
Nicholson, Mary Ann, 3
Nicholson, Norman, 1, 14;
children of, 3; emigration
from Isle of Skye, 2;
marriage, 6; origins, 2;
settlement in Canada, 2-5;
wife's death, 3
Nickerson, Roger E., 205
Nicol, John L., 52, 54, 56, 59,
69, 70, 71, 88
Nicolson, Donald, 2
Nicolson, Norman.
See Nicholson, Norman
Nipawin (Saskatchewan), 36
Nixonville School, 67, 209
Nollet, I.C., 192
Norquay (Saskatchewan), 92

O

O'Dwyer, Pat, 1
Old Tron Kirk, Edinburgh, 50
Oliver, E.H., 22, 26, 59, 60, 64,
72
Olmstead, W.J., 130
Optic Lake (Saskatchewan), 55
Orley (Saskatchewan), 68
Osborne Lake (Saskatchewan),
55
Ottawa (Ontario), 69, 119, 120,
125, 129, 144, 150, 155, 211,
214
Outlook (Saskatchewan), 199
Owen, John, 199, 204

P

Parkinson, J.F., 79
Pasquia Forest (Saskatchewan),
54
Paswegan (Saskatchewan), 91
Paton, Bob, 28, 31, 39, 40
Pearson, Lester B., 161, 182
Peart, Helen, 133
Pelly (Saskatchewan), 81, 94,
104, 106
Penfield, Wilder, 205
Phelps, Joe, 85
Phillips, Jane, 6, 7
Pickersgill, J.W., 159
pipeline debate, 163
Pitsula, James M., 183
Plaunt, Alan, 75
Polar Crescent (Saskatchewan),
33
Political Warriors, 169
Pope, Dorothy, 103
Porcupine Plain
(Saskatchewan), 62, 63, 65,
71, 168
Porcupine Reserve, 54
Port Arthur (Ontario), 164